HARDEN'S

Good Cheap Eats in London 2003

Visit www.hardens.com
- **Register for free updates and newsletters, and to take part in next year's survey**
- **Restaurant searches**
- **News of latest openings**
- **Corporate gift service**
- **Order Harden's guides**

© Harden's Limited 2002

ISBN 1-873721-54-4

British Library Cataloguing-in-Publication data:
a catalogue record for this book is available from
the British Library.

Printed and bound in Finland by
WS Bookwell Ltd

Research Manager: Antonia Russell
Production Manager: Elizabeth Warman
Research assistant: Nicola Semple

Harden's Limited
14 Buckingham Street
London WC2N 6DF

The contents of this book are believed correct
at the time of printing. Nevertheless, the publisher
can accept no responsibility for errors or changes in
or omissions from the details given.

No part of this publication may be reproduced or
transmitted in any form or by any means, electronically
or mechanically, including photocopying, recording or
any information storage or retrieval system, without

CONTENTS

Ratings & prices

	Page
Introduction	8

Recommendations

Best all-round deals – 𝔸★★	9
Best food – ★★	9
Special deals at top restaurants	9
New openings	10
Most interesting ethnic places	10
The most stylish places	11
Best for romance	11
Best breakfast/brunch	11
Top pub grub	12
The best fun places	12

Directory	14

Indexes

Breakfast	104
BYO	104
Children	105
Entertainment	107
Late	108
No-smoking areas	108
Outside tables	109
Pre/Post theatre	111
Private rooms	111

Cuisine indexes	114
Area overviews	124
Maps	136

- 1 – London overview
- 2 – West End overview
- 3 – Mayfair, St James's & West Soho
- 4 – East Soho, Chinatown & Covent Garden
- 5 – Knightsbridge, Chelsea & South Kensington
- 6 – Notting Hill & Bayswater
- 7 – Hammersmith & Chiswick
- 8 – Hampstead, Camden Town & Islington
- 9 – The City
- 10 – South London (& Fulham)
- 11 – East End & Docklands

RATINGS & PRICES

RATINGS

Ratings are based both on our own experiences – we have visited all of the listed establishments at our own expense – and also on the views of the reporters who take part in our annual survey. We have given ratings as follows:

★★ Exceptional
London's top bargains. They offer a quality of cooking which is, given the price, worth travelling for.

★ Very good
Places where the cooking offers above-average value for money.

𝔸 Good atmosphere
Spots with particular "buzz", style or charm.

PRICES

So you can compare the costs of different establishments, we have tried to give a realistic estimate of the cost for a typical meal in each place.

For *restaurants, pubs and wine bars,* we have given an estimate of the cost for one (1) person of two courses with a drink and a cup of coffee.

For *cafés,* the price we show is the approximate cost of a sandwich, a cake and a cup of coffee.

These prices include service (we have included a 10% tip if there is no service charge), VAT and any cover charge.

* Where an asterisk appears next to the price, you can usually keep expenditure to £20 a head or less only at certain times of day (usually lunch), by sticking to a particular menu, or (in a few cases) by eating in a specified area, such as the bar. Eating at other times or from the à la carte menu may be much more expensive – see the text of the entry for details. In the area lists, the ratings for such restaurants appear in brackets, eg (𝔸 ★).

Telephone number – all numbers should be prefixed with '020' if dialling from outside the London area.

Map reference – shown immediately after the telephone number. (Major coffee shop chains are not shown on the maps.)

Website – if applicable, is the first entry in the small print.

Last orders time – the first entry in the small print, after the website (if applicable); Sunday may be up to 90 minutes earlier.

Opening hours – unless otherwise stated, restaurants are open for lunch and dinner seven days a week.

Credit and debit cards – unless otherwise stated, Mastercard, Visa, Amex and Switch are accepted.

Dress – where appropriate, the management's preferences concerning patrons' dress are given.

Smoking – cigarette smoking restrictions are noted. Pipe or cigar smokers should always check ahead.

INTRODUCTION

This is the ninth edition of our guide for anyone who wants to enjoy eating out in London while keeping costs under control. It is less difficult than many people might think to find interesting and satisfying meals at modest cost. And it's not even as if you are restricted to a particular *type* of establishment. The coverage of this guide extends all the way from basic East End canteens to grand, 'big name' restaurants in the heart of fashionable London.

We have decided, once again, to keep the same £20 a head 'cut-off' price as we used for previous editions. For this amount, a qualifying establishment must provide two courses, a drink, coffee and service. (If there is no compulsory service charge, we have allowed for a 10% tip.) Many of the places listed can be visited for light meals or snacks at rather less cost than the 'formula' price we quote.

Diners on a budget, in particular, have to know *where* to go, of course – but it's often almost more important to know *when*. Many of the more interesting experiences are to be had at places where the price is asterisked* – see the previous page for an explanation. These are usually 'proper' restaurants which experience a shortage of custom at lunchtime (or, in some office areas, dinner time). They offer low-price set menus as loss leaders, hoping either to make up the difference through wine sales or to impress customers enough to guarantee a return visit. Whatever the restaurateurs' motives, there are some great bargains to be had – especially for those who do not need too much wine with their meal!

We wish you some excellent lunching and dining. Perhaps you would like to tell us about your successes (or any failures). Every spring, we conduct a detailed survey of the experiences of London restaurant-goers. Those who participate – nearly 7,000 people in 2002 – receive a complimentary copy of the resulting comprehensive guide, *Harden's London Restaurants*.

We invite you, too, to take part in the survey. Just send us your name and address (or register by e-mail with mail@hardens.com), and you will be sent a form the following spring, with a free update about major new restaurants (budget and not) around London and the UK which have opened over the previous few months.

Richard Harden **Peter Harden**

for updates visit www.hardens.com

RECOMMENDATIONS

BEST ALL-ROUND DEALS Ⓐ★★

Arancia (SE16)
Deca (W1)
Frederick's (N1)
The Gate (group)
Havelock Tavern (W14)
Kennington Lane (SE11)
Lundum's (SW7)
Moro (EC1)
Odette's (NW1)
Pizza Metro (SW11)
QC (W1)
J Sheekey (WC2)
Stepping Stone (SW8)
YMing (W1)
Zaika (W8)

BEST FOOD ★★

For £15 & under:

Beirut Express (W2)
Brick Lane Beigel Bake (E1)
Faulkner's (E8)
Geeta (NW6)
Inaho (W2)
Kastoori (SW17)
Lahore Kebab House (E1)
Lisboa Patisserie (W10)
Mandalay (W2)
Mirch Masala (group)
Sabras (NW10)
Sakoni's (HA0)
Sree Krishna (SW17)
Talad Thai (SW15)
Thailand (SE14)
El Vergel (SE1)
Vijay (NW6)

For over £15:

Anglesea Arms (W6)
Basilico (group)
Blah! Blah! Blah! (W12)
Brasserie St Quentin (SW3)
Café Japan (NW11)
Chez Liline (N4)
Chiang Mai (W1)
Chowki (W1)
Incognico (WC2)
Jin Kichi (NW3)
Konditor & Cook (group)
Kulu Kulu (W1)
Mandarin Kitchen (W2)
Moro (EC1)
Parsee (N19)
Rasa (group)
Rôtisserie (group)
Royal China (group)
Sarkhel's (SW18)
Yoshino (W1)

SPECIAL DEALS AT TOP RESTAURANTS

Bank (WC2)
Bank Westminster (SW1)
Blue Elephant (SW6)
Butlers Wharf C-H (SE1)
Brasserie St Quentin (SW3)
Carpaccio's (SW3)
Deca (W1)
L'Estaminet (WC2)
Granita (N1)
Incognico (WC2)
Lou Pescadou (SW5)
Mon Plaisir (WC2)
Odette's (NW1)
Parade (W5)
QC (WC1)
J Sheekey (WC2)
Veeraswamy (W1)
Zaika (W8)
ZeNW3 (NW3)

sign up for the survey at www.hardens.com

RECOMMENDATIONS

NEW OPENINGS

Abu Zaad (W12)
Busaba Eathai (WC1)
Carpaccio's (SW3)
China Dream (NW3)
Chowki (W1)
Dartmouth Arms (NW5)
Deca (W1)
Errays (N1)
Field & Forest (WC2)
Gourmet Burger (NW6, SW15)
Horse (SE1)
Little Bay (EC1)
Mirch Masala (SW17)
Need The Dough! (SW11)
O'Zon (TW1)
Ophim (W1)
Paolo (W1)
Paul (W1)
Petit Auberge (N1)
Pilot (W4)
QC (WC1)
Raks (W1)
Tartuf (SW4)
Thai Noodle Bar (SW10)
Timo (W8)
Tsunami (SW4)
Zamzama (NW1)

MOST INTERESTING ETHNIC PLACES

Abeno (WC1)
Alounak (group)
Babur Brasserie (SE23)
Brilliant (UB2)
Busaba Eathai (group)
Café de Maya (NW3)
Chez Liline (N4)
Chiang Mai (W1)
China Dream (NW3)
Chowki (W1)
Coromandel (SW11)
Fairuz (group)
Gaby's (WC2)
Hakkasan (W1)
Ikkyu (W1)
Inaho (W2)
Jashan (group)
K10 (EC2)
Kandoo (W2)
Kastoori (SW17)
Lahore Kebab House (E1)
Laurent (NW2)
Ma Goa (SW15)
Mandarin Kitchen (W2)
Mela (WC2)
Mirch Masala (group)
Ophim (W1)
Ozer (W1)
Parsee (N19)
Poons, Lisle Street (WC2)
Ranoush (W1)
Rasa (group)
Royal China (group)
Sakoni's (HA0)
Shish (NW2)
Sree Krishna (SW17)
Soho Spice (W1)
Tajine (W1)
Tas (group)
Thai Noodle Bar (SW10)
Tsunami (SW4)
Uli (W11)
Viet-Anh (NW1)
Zaika (W8)
Zaika Bazaar (SW3)

for updates visit www.hardens.com

THE MOST STYLISH PLACES

The Abingdon (W8)
Aperitivo (W1)
Baltic (SW1)
Bank (WC2)
Bank Westminster (SW1)
Benihana (group)
Busaba Eathai (group)
Butlers Wharf C-H (SE1)
Carluccio's Caffè (group)
Carnevale (EC1)
Carpaccio's (SW3)
China Dream (NW3)
Deca (W1)
Eco (SW4)
Fortnum's Fountain (W1)
Granita (N1)
Gung-Ho (NW6)
Hakkasan (W1)
Incognico (WC2)
Kennington Lane (SE1)
Lansdowne (NW1)
Mango Room (NW1)
Nikson's (SW11)
PizzaExpress (group)
Pizzeria Condotti (W1)
QC (WC1)
Raks (W1)
Rocket (W1)
Sarastro (WC2)
Smiths of Smithfield (EC1)
So.uk (SW4)
The Stepping Stone (SW8)
Tate Modern (SE1)
Tom's (W10)
Veeraswamy (W1)
The White House (SW4)
ZeNW3 (NW3)

BEST FOR ROMANCE

Anglo Asian Tandoori (N16)
Arancia (SE16)
Aurora (W1)
Boudin Blanc (W1)
Brass. du Marché (W10)
Frocks (E9)
Gordon's Wine Bar (WC2)
Hakkasan (W1)
Incognico (WC2)
Lundum's (SW7)
Mon Plaisir (WC2)
Odette's (NW1)
Osteria Basilico (W11)
Patio (W12)
Sarastro (WC2)
So.uk (SW4)
Yum Yum (N16)

BEST BREAKFAST/BRUNCH

Aurora (W1)
Balans (group)
Bank (WC2)
Banners (N8)
Brass. du Marché (W10)
Brick Lane Beigel Bake (E1)
Café 206 (W11)
Café Laville (W2)
Café Mozart (N6)
Chamomile (NW3)
Chelsea Bun Diner (group)
Fortnum's Fountain (W1)
Fox & Anchor (EC1)
Frocks (E9)
Gastro (SW4)
Giraffe (group)
Hope & Sir Loin (EC1)
Hudson's (SW15)
Konditor & Cook (group)
Maison Bertaux (W1)
Pâtisserie Valerie (group)
Pizza on the Park (SW1)
Smiths of Smithfield (EC1)
Star Café (W1)
Tapa Room
 (The Providores) (W1)
Tom's (W10)
Troubadour (SW5)
Vingt-Quatre (SW10)

sign up for the survey at www.hardens.com

RECOMMENDATIONS

TOP PUB GRUB

Anglesea Arms (W6)
The Atlas (SW6)
The Builder's Arms (SW3)
The Castle (SW11)
Churchill Arms (W8)
Dartmouth Arms (NW5)
The Eagle (EC1)
George II (SW11)
Havelock Tavern (W14)
Hope & Sir Loin (EC1)
The Ifield (SW10)
The Lord Palmerston (NW5)
Lots Road (SW10)
The Perseverance (WC1)
The Queen's (NW1)
Stonemason's Arms (W6)
The Sun & Doves (SE5)
The White Cross (TW9)
White Horse (SW6)
William IV (NW10)
Windsor Castle (W8)

THE BEST FUN PLACES

Balans (group)
Bar Gansa (NW1)
Bar Italia (W1)
Benihana (group)
Buona Sera (group)
Busaba Eathai (group)
Café Emm (W1)
Cantaloupe (EC2)
don Fernando's (TW9)
don Pepe (NW8)
Eco (group)
Efes Kebab House (group)
Gordon's Wine Bar (WC2)
Gourmet Burger Kitchen (group)
Hakkasan (W1)
Hard Rock Café (W1)
Itsu (group)
Lemonia (NW1)
Little Bay (group)
Mango Room (NW1)
Mediterraneo (W11)
Meson don Felipe (SE1)
Osteria Basilico (W11)
Ophim (W1)
Patio (W12)
La Piragua (N1)
Pizzeria Castello (SE1)
La Porchetta Pizzeria (group)
Pucci Pizza (SW3)
Rebato's (SW8)
Sarastro (WC2)
So.uk (SW4)
Souk (WC2)
The Sun & Doves (SE5)
Tartuf (group)
Tsunami (SW4)
Vingt-Quatre (SW10)
Wagamama (group)
Wong Kei (W1)
Yum Yum (N16)

for updates visit www.hardens.com

DIRECTORY

Abeno WC1   £13*   ★
47 Museum St   7405 3211   2–1C
This friendly Japanese diner, handy for the British Museum, offers a very reasonable 2-course set lunch menu (£6.50). The speciality is okonomi-yaki (a cross between a pancake and an omelette, cooked at your table) — and a typical meal à la carte would be squid and soya bean pancakes (£5.20), followed by a Shinsu mix (a topping of chicken, asparagus and cheese, £9.80). Such prices test our limit, however, especially with house wine at a hefty £13.50 a bottle. / 10 pm; closed Wed L.

The Abingdon W8   £20*
54 Abingdon Rd   7937 3339   5–2A
Although it is only a couple of minutes' walk from Kensington High Street, this intimate former pub is hidden away in a pleasant residential area, and doesn't attract much passing trade. Therefore, the budget diner who seeks out the £13.95 (Mon-Fri) 2-course set lunch is well rewarded — the menu might offer the likes of marinated herring salad followed by Barnsley chops with mustard mash and apple chutney, washed down by house wine at £10.75 a bottle. / 11 pm.

Abu Zaad W12   £10   ★
29 Uxbridge Rd   8749 5107   7–1C
If you're really looking to dine on a budget, this Syrian café/takeaway near Shepherd's Bush Market makes an ideal destination, as most dishes are under a fiver. There's quite a diverse menu, with kebabs a highlight — wash 'em down with Aryan (drinking yoghurt) or Arabic tea or coffee. / 11 pm.

Adams Café W12   £19
77 Askew Rd   8743 0572   7–1B
By day it's a greasy spoon, but by night this popular spot in Shepherd's Bush becomes a funky little bistro, well known for its Tunisian and Moroccan specialities. The 2-course 'menu gourmet' (£13.50), is ideal for the budget diner. You might choose brik au thon (filo pastry filled with egg, tuna and herbs) followed by couscous with lamb. House wine is £8.50 a bottle, or you can always BYO (not so inexpensive, though, with corkage at £3 per person). / 11 pm; D only, closed Sun.

Afghan Kitchen N1   £13   ★
35 Islington Grn   7359 8019   8–3D
For a filling, unusual and top-value pit stop, it is hard to beat this tiny café, overlooking Islington Green (though it's not a place you'd choose for its wealth of creature comforts). There are eight main dishes on offer (four meat and four veggie), which are a fiver apiece (meat dishes, £6), and served in portions to satisfy the hungriest punter. Rice or a large chunk of bread add £2 to the cost, and house wine is £9.50 a bottle. / 11 pm; closed Mon & Sun; no credit cards.

for updates visit www.hardens.com

Aglio e Olio SW10 £19 ★
194 Fulham Rd   7351 0070   5–3B
A surprisingly rare mix – understated chic, welcoming service and reliable Italian cooking – has made this Chelsea diner a particular hit with the trendier (and noisier) end of the younger locals' market. Fresh mussels in ginger (£5.40) might be a good starting point, followed by rigatoni with broad beans, porcini mushrooms and pancetta (£7.20). Or you might skip starters and finish with a tiramisu (£3.50). The house wine is £11.50 a bottle. / 11.30 pm.

Alba EC1 £20* ★
107 Whitecross St   7588 1798   9–1B
Piedmontese cooking is the speciality at this regional Italian near the Barbican, which has long been a popular pre- or post-concert destination. A la carte, it can be quite pricey, so you need to stick to the cheaper pastas and the like to stay within our budget. For example, you could have mushroom and saffron risotto (£10) and finish with tiramisu (£5), washed down with house wine at £12.50 a bottle. / 10.30 pm; closed Sat & Sun.

Alfred WC2 £19* ★
245 Shaftesbury Ave   7240 2566   4–1C
The décor (like a '60s kitchen) is no special attraction, but this Bloomsbury spot has long turned out very acceptable cooking, with a (rare) defiantly British twist. You'll tend to spend a little beyond our budget à la carte, but there is a 2-course set menu (£12), available at all times, which might include the likes of Glamorgan pâté with tomato chutney, followed by crispy pork with red cabbage and mash. The house wine is £12.55 a bottle. / 11 pm; closed Sat L & Sun.

Ali Baba NW1 £15
32 Ivor Pl   7723 5805   2–1A
They haven't wasted any money on the décor of this living room-style BYO café, located at the back of an Egyptian takeaway near Marylebone Station. Prices really are quite low, so if you go in a small party you can sample a good range of the specialities, such as tabbouleh salad (£3) and cabsa (red rice and lamb, £6); BYO (no corkage). / 11.30 pm; no credit cards.

Alma SW18 £18   Ⓐ
499 Old York Rd   8870 2537   10–2B
The bar at this boisterous Wandsworth pub, a popular hang-out for rugby-playing locals, offers the bargain-seeker plenty of scope. Eat in the bar, or head to the rear dining room for a meal such as salmon fishcakes (£4.75), followed by a steak burger with Emmental and chips (£7.95). Drink bitter at £2.25 a pint, or house wine at £10.40 a bottle. / www.thealma.co.uk; 10.30 pm.

sign up for the survey at www.hardens.com

Alounak £16 ★
10 Russell Gdns, W14 7603 1130 7–1D
44 Westbourne Grove, W2 7229 0416 6–1B
If you're looking for some real meat cooking at modest cost, you won't do better than at these welcoming Olympia and Bayswater Iranians, where the BYO policy (with no corkage charge) helps keep costs low. Lamb is the speciality (though there are also chicken options), and most main dishes range from £5-£11.50. Kick off with a selection of meze (£8.90 for two people) and finish with a pastry (around £3).
/ www.alounak.com; 11.30 pm; no Amex.

Anarkali W6 £14
303-305 King St 8748 6911 7–2B
This Hammersmith subcontinental has been a reliable destination for over a quarter of a century now. Starters include kebabs (£3) and puréed prawns (£3.95), and can be followed by either a standard curry or one of the unusual specials which cost around the £7.50 mark. House wine is £10.95 a bottle.
/ midnight.

The Anglesea Arms W6 £20 ★★
35 Wingate Rd 8749 1291 7–1B
The Hammersmith and Shepherd's Bush area seems to have established itself as the spiritual home of the London gastropub, and this is one of the best. It's cosy and stylish, and its cooking is held in high repute. Most starters are around a fiver, and main courses under a tenner – you might have duck foie gras salad (£5.95) followed by sautéed calf's liver (£9.75), but you can never be quite sure, as the menu changes twice a day. The house wine is £10.50 a bottle. / 10.45 pm; no Amex; no booking.

Anglo Asian Tandoori N16 £15
60-62 Stoke Newington Church St 7254 9298 1–1C
Romance and curries don't usually go hand in hand, but this low-lit Stoke Newington subcontinental is the exception which proves the rule. It offers all the traditional dishes at reasonable prices – a main course will set you back about £6.50, and house wine is £8.95 a bottle. On Sundays, the all-you-can-eat buffet lunch (£6.95) is particularly good value.
/ www.angloasian.co.uk; 11.30 pm, Fri & Sat 11.45 pm; no smoking area.

Antipasto & Pasta SW11 £18
511 Battersea Park Rd 7223 9765 10–1C
With starters and main courses at half-price all day on Sun and Mon (and also on Thu evening), this good-quality Battersea Italian is a particularly attractive proposition for the budget diner. Even a full price a meal won't break the bank, however – a typical selection might start with warm chicken liver salad (£6), followed by pasta carbonara (£6.50), washed down by the house wine at £10.50 a bottle. / 11.30 pm; need 4+ to book.

for updates visit www.hardens.com

Antipasto e Pasta SW4   £19*   ★
31 Abbeville Rd   8675 6260   10–2D
This good-quality Italian restaurant in Clapham is rather out of our price-range à la carte, but there are top-value 3-course set menus available at lunch (£8.80, including coffee) and dinner (£11.80, Sun-Thu, 7pm-11pm) from which you might have Caesar salad followed by veal with lemon, and then chocolate mousse. A bottle of the house wine is £10.50. / 11.30 pm.

Aperitivo W1   £18   𝔸
41 Beak St   7287 2057   3–2D
This chic Italian tapas bar in the heart of Soho offers a range of interesting dishes. Share a selection with a friend – you might choose polenta with pancetta and Gorgonzola (£4.95), prawns wrapped in bacon (£6.75), walnut salad (£4.95) and some fries (£2.95), washed down with the house wine, at £12.50 a bottle. Traditional desserts, maybe tiramisu or pannacotta (around £4), are also available. / 11 pm; closed Sun.

Arancia SE16   £18   𝔸★
52 Southwark Park Rd   7394 1751   11–2A
The success of this cosy Bermondsey Italian rests on a down-to-earth approach and quality seasonal cooking which can be sampled within our budget at any time – starters are around £4, and most main courses are £9. For top value, however, seek it out for the set lunch (two courses, £7.50; three courses £10.50), from which you could fill up on, say, pumpkin gnocchi, followed by fishcakes with green bean salad, with apple strudel for dessert. The house wine is £8.40 a bottle.
/ www.arancia-london.co.uk; 11 pm; closed Mon L & Tue L; no Amex.

Arkansas Café E1   £14   ★
107b Commercial St   7377 6999   9–1D
"Bubba", the chef-patron, presides over the grill at this Spitalfields Market fixture, where basic but tasty and filling fare is served to stockbrokers and shoppers alike. Most main courses – the wide, meaty range includes the likes of Barbary duck and Irish steak platters – cost around £9, and puddings, such as pecan pie (if you still have room), are £2.50. Drink the house wine at £8.95 a bottle, or swig American beers (from £2.50 a bottle). / L only, closed Sat; no Amex; no smoking.

Aroma II W1   £20   ★
118-120 Shaftesbury Ave   7437 0377   4–3A
On the fringe of Chinatown, this oriental restaurant has gained quite a name for its unusual dishes. Unfortunately, the more exotic choices will take you rather beyond our budget, but you might try vegetarian spring rolls (£3) followed by chicken with cashew nuts (£6), washed down with a bottle of house wine at £9.50 a bottle. / www.aromarestaurant.co.uk; 10 pm.

sign up for the survey at www.hardens.com

L'Artiste Musclé W1 £20   A
1 Shepherd Mkt   7493 6150   3–4B
For sheer Gallic authenticity, it's difficult to beat this bistro, on a cramped corner of Mayfair's characterful Shepherd Market. Though there are no set menu deals, the tasty fare is modestly priced – from around £4.50 for a starter of farmhouse pâté, to about £9.50 for a main course like boeuf bourguignonne. The house wine is £10.50 a bottle. / 11.30 pm.

Ask! Pizza £16   A
160-162 Victoria St, SW1   7630 8228   2–4B
121-125 Park St, W1   7495 7760   2–2A
48 Grafton Way, W1   7388 8108   2–1B
300 King's Rd, SW3   7349 9123   5–3C
345 Fulham Palace Rd, SW6   7371 0392   10–1B
23-24 Gloucester Arc, SW7   7835 0840   5–2B
145 Notting Hill Gate, W11   7792 9942   6–2B
41-43 Spring St, W2   7706 0707   6–1C
Whiteley's, 151 Queensway, W2   7792 1977   6–1C
219-221 Chiswick High Rd, W4   8742 1323   7–2A
222 Kensington High St, W8   7937 5540   5–1A
52 Upper St, N1   7226 8728   8–3D
197 Baker St, NW1   7486 6027   2–1A
30 Hawley Cr, NW1   7267 7755   8–2B
216 Haverstock Hill, NW3   7433 3896   8–2A
34 Shad Thames, SE1   7403 4545   9–4D
Station Rd, SW13   8878 9300   10–1A
103 St John St, EC1   7253 0323   9–1A
Cooler décor than PizzaExpress – the obvious competitor – is one advantage that this fast-growing pizza-and-pasta chain enjoys over its larger rival. Starters all cost less than £4, but most folk just go for pasta (about £7) or pizza (£5-£7.50), washed down with house wine at £10.70 a bottle. The party policy offers a neat budget-busting opportunity – pre-book (with £5 deposit per person) for a £13.95 three-courses-plus-coffee deal. / www.askcentral.co.uk; 11.30 pm; some branches only – no booking after 7.30 pm.

The Atlas SW6 £19   A
16 Seagrave Rd   7385 9129   5–3A
From the outside, this Fulham backstreet spot (near Earl's Court 2) looks rather like a sad old boozer, but its good-quality Mediterranean dishes in fact make it one of the best gastropubs in these parts. To start, you could share a plate of antipasti (£6) with a friend, followed by a fillet of roast salmon (£9.50). The house wine is £10 a bottle, or a pint of bitter will set you back £2.40. / 11 pm; no Amex; no booking.

for updates visit www.hardens.com

Aurora W1 £20* Ⓐ
49 Lexington St   7494 0514   3–2D
This sweet Soho bistro is a popular romantic destination, thanks to the intimate atmosphere, low evening lighting and tiny rear courtyard. The menu includes the likes of miso soup with shiitake mushrooms (£3.95), and Mediterranean vegetable, blue cheese and pumpkin gratin (£10.50), so you could be at risk of spending beyond our price-limit. Not so for Saturday brunch, of course, or for the coffee and cakes, which are a forte. / 10.30 pm; closed Sun; no Amex.

Azou W6 £20
375 King St   8563 7266   7–2B
North African cuisine is quite trendy nowadays, but no news of this has yet reached Hammersmith, where this unpretentious, family-run operation offers a short menu of specialities from Morocco, Algeria and Tunisia. Starters include mechouia (a kind of ratatouille) and chakchouka (ditto, but with merguez sausages) both at £3.90. Main courses generally involve a choice between couscous and tajines (stews), most of which cost around £9.50, the same as a bottle of the house wine. / 11 pm; no Amex.

Babur Brasserie SE23 £19   ★
119 Brockley Rise   8291 2400   1–4D
Cooking far beyond the realms of your average curry house has created a deserved reputation for this Forest Hill Indian. The Sunday lunch buffet (£8.95) is the only set menu offered, but the food is generally reasonably priced. A typical meal might comprise spiced crab (£5.50) followed by raan gulnar (lamb shank, £7.95), washed down with house wine at £8.95 a bottle. / www.babur-brasserie.com; 11 pm; closed Fri L; no smoking area.

Balans £19
60 Old Compton St, W1   7439 2183   4–3A
239 Old Brompton Rd, SW5   7244 8838   5–3A
187 Kensington High St, W8   7376 0115   5–1A
These breezy, gay-friendly diners make quite laid-back destinations, whether you're gay or straight. Breakfasts, including the Full Monty (£6.50) and eggs Benedict with smoked salmon (£7.50), are a highlight, and are served until the wee hours. Otherwise, a typical meal might be thyme and tomato tart (£4.35) followed by Cumberland sausage and mash (£7.95), washed down by house wine at £10.50 a bottle. / www.balans.co.uk; 1 am – W1 Mon-Sat 5 am, Sun 1 am; W1 no booking – SW5 Sat & Sun no booking.

sign up for the survey at www.hardens.com

Baltic SE1 £18* 🅐
74 Blackfriars Rd   7928 1111   9–4A
This impressively-converted former carriage-making factory has made quite a contribution to the gentrification of Borough. The top-value choice – ideal after a morning in Tate Modern – is the 2-course set lunch (£11.50), which might be borscht followed by roast belly of pork, washed down by house wine at £10.50 a bottle (or a Polish beer at £2.75 a bottle). You'd have to choose pretty carefully à la carte to stay within our price limit. / www.balticrestaurant.co.uk; 11 pm; closed Sat L.

Bangkok SW7 £17 ★
9 Bute St   7584 8529   5–2B
It's smartened up a bit in recent years, but nothing much changes at the UK's longest-established Thai restaurant, which has been serving consistently good grub for some 30 years. Old favourites like satay (£5.50) and green Thai curry (£7.30) are faithfully interpreted at prices that are reasonable for South Kensington, although the house wine isn't exactly a bargain at £14 a bottle. / 10.45 pm; closed Sun; no Amex or Switch.

Bank Aldwych WC2 £20* 🅐★
1 Kingsway   7379 9797   2–2D
This vast Aldwych spot is probably the best of the 'mega-brasseries' which briefly dominated London's dining scene a few years ago. It's quite pricey à la carte, but there's nearly always a budget option available – the all-day breakfast or brunch will set you back around a tenner, and at lunch, pre- and post-theatre (5.30pm-7.30pm, 10pm-11.30pm) there's a 3-course set menu (£12.50), from which you might choose halloumi & roast vegetable salad followed by grilled lamb with tzatsiki, with cherry & almond tart to finish. The house wine is £12.90 a bottle. / www.bankrestaurants.com; 11 pm.

Bank Westminster SW1 £20* 🅐★
45 Buckingham Gate   7379 9797   2–4B
This large and would-be trendy restaurant seems rather oddly situated in the grey, corporate no-man's-land near St James's Park tube. A la carte, it's clearly out of our price bracket, so it's all the more worth availing yourself of the £12.50 lunch, pre- and post-theatre menus (5.30pm-7pm and 10pm-11.30pm), which might offer you the likes of gazpacho followed by seared salmon with puntalette pasta. The house wine is £12.90 a bottle. / www.bankrestaurants.com; 11 pm; closed Sat L & Sun.

for updates visit www.hardens.com

Bankside SE1 £19
32 Southwark Bridge Rd   7633 0011   9–4B
If you're looking for somewhere reasonably priced to eat in the vicinity of Tate Modern, this bland but comfortable basement is one of the few tolerable choices. All starters (such as mint-cured salmon) are £4, and all mains are either £7 (which might be Cumberland sausage with mash and onion gravy) or £9 (perhaps duck breast with green beans and raspberry jus). The house wine is £10.50 a bottle. / 10.30 pm; closed Sat D & Sun D; no smoking area.

Banners N8 £19
21 Park Rd   8348 2930   1–1C
It's as a mellow weekend hang-out – especially for those with kids in tow – that this funky Crouch End bar/diner is best known, and brunch (£6.25) is its natural forte (although the 2-course set weekday lunch (£5.95) is a pretty special feature, too). A la carte, starters (perhaps Thai fishcakes or calamari) are around £4.50 and main courses (such as Jamaican jerk chicken or grilled swordfish) around £9. The house wine is £10.75 a bottle. / 11.30 pm, Fri & Sat midnight; no Amex.

Bar Capitale £18 ★
The Concourse, 1 Poultry, EC2   7248 3117   9–2C
Bucklersbury Hs, 14 Walbrook, EC4   7236 2030   9–3C
The City is sparsely provided with places for a speedy but satisfying lunch. The number of Italian customers, however, hints at the good quality of the simple fare – mainly pizza and pasta (around £8) – on offer at these fast and friendly spots near Bank. The house wine is £11.50 a bottle.
/ www.mithrasbars.co.uk; 10pm; closed Sat & Sun; no smoking area; EC4 no booking at L.

Bar Gansa NW1 £15   Ⓐ
2 Inverness St   7267 8909   8–3B
This buzzing Camden Town tapas bar has been serving up good and inexpensive snacks such as meatballs, tortillas and calamari (all around the £3-£4 mark) to trendy north London twentysomethings for some years now, but it never seems to lose its buzz. More substantial dishes are available at around £7.50, and house wine is £10 a bottle. / midnight; no Amex.

Bar Italia W1 £ 8   Ⓐ
22 Frith St   7437 4520   4–2A
A long-established cult venue for Soho trendies, this very Italian coffee bar, which is open 23 hours a day, is the quintessential post-clubbing hang-out. The food, of course, is not the main attraction, but runs to the likes of sandwiches and pizza (around the £3-£8 mark). No alcohol – wash down your snack with an espresso or cappuccino (£1.50), or fresh juices (from £3). / open 24 hours Mon-Sat, Sun 4 am; no booking.

sign up for the survey at www.hardens.com

Bar Japan SW5 £15* ★
251 Old Brompton Rd   7370 2323   5–3A
It's not an exciting place to look at, but this Earl's Court café is a consistently popular choice for a quick and interesting bite. Sushi is the best bet – a small mixed set for £5.50 would make a good snack – or you might have a more filling selection such as a bento box for about twice that sum. House wine is £10 a bottle, or drink green tea for £1. / 10.30 pm; no Amex.

Barracuda N16 £19   Ⓐ
125 Stoke Newington Church St   7275 0400   1–1C
For simple, laid-back charm – especially on a sunny day, in the overgrown rear garden – this Stoke Newington restaurant is a top destination. Free jazz nights (Fri & Sat) are a further attraction. The menu offers a mixture of dishes of miscellaneous inspiration, such as fishcakes (£4.50), and gingered pork with egg-fried rice (£10.50). The house wine is £9.50 a bottle. / 11 pm; open Sun L in summer only; no Amex.

Basilico £18 ★★
690 Fulham Rd, SW6   0800 028 3531   10–1B
175 Lavender Hill, SW11   0800 389 9770   10–2C
178 Upper Richmond Rd, SW15   0800 096 8202   10–2B
Take-outs are what these pukka pizzerias are really all about, but devotees are willing enough to fight for elbow room to 'eat in', even though the branches are quite cramped. The pizzas come in two sizes, 13" (£8.75-£12) and 18" (£12-£15.75), and may be accompanied by a Caesar salad (£2.95) or followed by tiramisu (£3.75), and washed down with house wine at £7.90 a bottle. / www.basilico.co.uk; 11pm; no Amex; no booking.

Bedlington Café W4 £15
24 Fauconberg Rd   8994 1965   7–2A
This Chiswick greasy spoon won quite a reputation in the (now rather distant) past for the quality of its fiery Thai fare. Its glory days are now well behind it, but it still offers reasonably-priced grub, albeit from a fairly standard menu nowadays – starters are £3.75, curries around £4.20 and vegetable dishes are £4.20; BYO (corkage 60p) – there's an off-licence nearby.
/ 10 pm; closed Sun L; no credit cards; no smoking.

Beirut Express W2 £15 ★★
112-114 Edgware Rd   7724 2700   6–1D
Lovers of Middle Eastern cooking can enjoy excellent fare in smart café surroundings at this authentic Bayswater Lebanese. Prices are very reasonable (especially if you stick to the meze dishes – about £3.75). Alcohol is not served, but you could have a fruit juice (including melon, mango and carrot, £1.65) or a banana milkshake (£1.90). / www.maroush.com; 1.45 am; no credit cards.

for updates visit www.hardens.com

Ben's Thai W9 £16
93 Warrington Cr   7266 3134   8–4A
The first-floor dining-room of a palatial Victorian pub (The Warrington Hotel) in Maida Vale is an unlikely setting for one of the more characterful Thai eateries in town. It's very successful, and booking is essential. Starters, such as spring rolls, are £3.25, there's a good selection of main courses for £5.35-£8, and the house wine is £9.20 a bottle. Tipping is discouraged.
/ 10 pm; D only; no Amex or Switch.

Bengal Clipper SE1 £17* ★
Shad Thames   7357 9001   9–4D
This smart subcontinental near Tower Bridge offers some impressive deals for the budget diner, with a 2-course set lunch or dinner for £10 (and a 2-course Sunday lunch for £7.75). A la carte, with starters around £4.50 and main courses around £9.95, you could easily spend over our budget. The cover charge of £1.50 includes poppadoms and chutneys, and house wine is £11.50 a bottle. / www.bengalrestaurants.co.uk; 11.30 pm.

Benihana £18* A★
37 Sackville St, W1   7494 2525   3–3D
77 King's Rd, SW3   7376 7799   5–3D
100 Avenue Rd, NW3   7586 9508   8–2A
This swanky American chain of teppan-yaki bars – where your food is prepared and griddled by a knife-juggling chef before your very eyes – is generally well beyond our budget, but there's a range of 5-course set lunches (from £8.75) that make rather luxurious shopping breaks. Easy on the booze, though – house wine is £15 a bottle. / www.benihana.co.uk; 10.30 pm, Fri & Sat 11 pm; smoking restricted during cooking.

Bersagliera SW3 £17
372 King's Rd   7352 5993   5–3B
It has had a bit of a refurbishment in recent times, but the attractions of this World's End trattoria/pizzeria are pretty much as they always were – it offers tasty pizza and pasta dishes (mainly around £6.20-£8.80) in a friendly but noisy environment. The house wine is £7.80 a bottle. / 11.30 pm; no Amex.

Bibo SW13 £19 A★
190 Castelnau   8748 3437   7–2C
If you didn't know of its existence, it would be easy to zoom past this Italian newcomer on the busy stretch of road south of Hammersmith Bridge. Previously a short-lived Italian (Lemon Thyme) it's now been taken over by the owner of nearby Sonny's, and is a worthy cousin to that great all-rounder. The welcome is warm, the setting is simple but stylish, and the cooking is very good value. The most economical options are the range of pizzas (from £6.50), but there's also quite a wide selection of other dishes, such as char-grilled squid with borlotti beans (from £9.50), with house wine at £9.95 a bottle.
/ 10.30 pm, Sat & Sun 10 pm.

sign up for the survey at www.hardens.com

Bistro 1 £13 𝔸
50 James St, W1   7486 9185   3–1A
75 Beak St, W1   7287 1840   3–2D
33 Southampton St, WC2   7379 7585   4–3D
There are remarkably few bistros in London which work on the principle so common in France – offering simple and cheap but tasty dishes, in friendly but cramped surroundings (on which little has apparently been spent). So it's no surprise that this small chain is flourishing mightily. A daily-changing menu offers five choices at each of two courses for the bargain price of £5.90 (£7.90 at dinner). The food is described as 'Mediterranean', and might include hearty casseroles, sausages and mash, pasta dishes or mixed meze. House wine is £9.90 a bottle. / 11.30 pm.

Blah! Blah! Blah! W12 £19 ★★
78 Goldhawk Rd   8746 1337   7–1C
This Shepherd's Bush bistro is unusually stylish and lively for a veggie, and has earned itself quite a chic following. It's not particularly cheap, but good-quality nosh keeps the punters coming back. A typical meal might be yam and aubergine tostada (£3.95) followed by saffron pasta with pumpkin (£9.50). The place is not licensed, so remember to BYO (£1.25 corkage). / 11 pm; closed Sun L; no credit cards.

Blue Elephant SW6 £18*   𝔸★
3-6 Fulham Broadway   7385 6595   5–4A
London's best Thai restaurant of long standing, this Fulham establishment, decorated in OTT jungle style, offers a top-value, loss-leading set lunch for £10. Choose any two courses from a choice of four (starter, soup, main and dessert) – you might have chicken satay with tom yam soup, or lamb curry followed by ice cream (maybe black pepper or ginger flavoured), washed down with house wine at £12.50 a bottle. / www.blueelephant.com; 11.30 pm; closed Sat L.

Blue Jade SW1 £19
44 Hugh St   7828 0321   2–4B
This comfortable Thai restaurant in a Pimlico back street serves good-quality cooking at competitive prices. There's a 2-course set lunch for £10.50, but – with starters costing around £4-£6 and most curries about £5-£9 – you can eat within our budget at any time. House wine is £10.95 a bottle. / 11 pm; closed Sat L & Sun.

Blue Lagoon W14 £14*
284 Kensington High St 7603 1231 7–1D
*The extensive menu of this spacious but slightly tackily
furnished oriental includes all the familiar Thai staples. It's
a touch out of our price-range à la carte, but a couple of
set-price meals, including a vegetarian dinner (£13.95) and
a 3-course set lunch (£7.95, available all week) bring it within
it. A typical meal might comprise satay or fishcakes to start,
yellow curry or Pad Thai to follow, and lychees to finish. The
house wine is £9.99 a bottle.* / www.blue-lagoon.co.uk; 11 pm;
no smoking area.

Blues W1 £17* A★
42 Dean St 7494 1966 4–2A
*On a Saturday night until 7.30pm, and all night Mon, Tue and
Sun, small parties (less than four) can enjoy a 3-course meal at
this trendy (and loud) Soho joint for a mere £10 a head. The
menu might include the likes of chicken liver salad, followed by
smoked haddock fishcakes, with warm carrot cake for pudding.
Outside these hours, you'd easily stray outside our budget. The
house wine is £11.25 a bottle.* / www.bluesbistro.com; 11.30 pm,
Thu-Sat midnight; closed Sat L & Sun L.

Boiled Egg & Soldiers SW11 £10
63 Northcote Rd 7223 4894 10–2C
*During weekdays, this celebrated café at the heart of
Wandsworth's 'Nappy Valley" is the official gathering-point
for the local nannies and their charges. At weekends, however,
it's celebrated for the recuperation possibilities offered by its
popular fry-ups – the full English works will set you back £4.95.*
/ L & afternoon tea only; only Switch; no booking.

La Bouchée SW7 £12* A
56 Old Brompton Rd 7589 1929 5–2B
*Improving standards are making this ever-popular,
younger-scene South Kensington bistro again worth seeking out,
especially before 7pm, when there's a £5.95 set menu – you
might choose mixed salad followed by salmon with spinach and
citrus sauce, washed down by house wine at £9.95 a bottle.
Dining here à la carte will take you outside our price-limit.*
/ 11 pm; no Amex.

Boudin Blanc W1 £17* A★
5 Trebeck St 7499 3292 3–4B
*If you have not visited this cosy Gallic restaurant in Shepherd
Market for some time, you may still have in mind a destination
offering budget possibilities at any time. Since its expansion
a couple of years ago, however, it has increased its aspiration
level quite significantly and it now only offers inexpensive dining
if you stick to the 3-course set menu (available until 7pm) – for
£10.95 you might choose soup or tomato salad followed by
salmon, with cheesecake for dessert. The house wine is £10.95
a bottle.* / 11 pm.

sign up for the survey at www.hardens.com

Boulevard WC2 £17*
40 Wellington St   7240 2992   4–3D
A variety of set menus make this unpretentious Covent Garden bistro a useful central stand-by, at any time of day. At lunch (all week) and pre-theatre, two courses cost £9.95 (three courses, £12.50), while a 2-course dinner is only slightly more, at £11.90. You might have baked Brie followed by chicken stuffed with goats cheese and sun-dried tomatoes. A la carte prices may stretch our budget. House wine is £9.50 a bottle.
/ www.boulevardbrasserie.com; midnight; no smoking area.

The Brackenbury W6 £18*
129-131 Brackenbury Rd   8748 0107   7–1C
This popular Hammersmith spot keeps the punters coming back with simple but tasty modern British grub at reasonable prices. Choices from the 2-course set lunch menu (£10.50) might include celeriac and apple soup followed by pan-fried halibut with leeks. Add a pudding for just £5 more, and drink the house wine at £12 a bottle. / 10.45 pm; closed Sat L & Sun D.

Bradley's NW3 £17*   ★
25 Winchester Rd   7722 3457   8–2A
Excellent seafood is a menu highlight at this friendly local restaurant in St John's Wood. No great surprise then that it's rather out of our price range in the evening, but there is a good value 2-course set lunch – your £10 might buy you the likes of crispy duck and watercress salad followed with salmon fishcakes with sorrel sauce, washed down with house wine at £11.50 a bottle. / 11 pm; closed Sat L.

Brady's SW18 £16   ★
513 Old York Rd   8877 9599   10–2B
Brady's is one of a very small number of restaurants that still give us reason to be proud of that Great British Dish, fish 'n' chips, and has earned itself a devoted local following in doing so. You could start with potted shrimps (£2.95), followed by a large order of haddock & chips (£6.50), all washed down with house wine at £8.75 a bottle. You could even squeeze some apple crumble (£1.95) in to our budget! / 10.30 pm; D only, closed Sun; no credit cards; no booking.

Brahms SW1 £15
147 Lupus St   7233 9828   5–3D
For top value at this budget Pimlico bistro, opt for the 2-course weekday set lunch, for the amazing price of just £5. However, even à la carte – with starters and desserts around £2.50 and main courses around £5-£7 – it's almost impossible to stray outside our budget. You might go for marinated sardines (£2.50) followed by chicken supreme (£5.50). The house wine is £9.50 a bottle. / 10.45 pm; no Amex.

for updates visit www.hardens.com

Brass. du Marché aux Puces W10 £20* 🅐
349 Portobello Rd   8968 5828   6–1A
This fashionable North Kensington bistro may sound thoroughly French, but its menu is in fact quite eclectic. Best weekday value – and the only real choice if you want to stay within our budget – is the 2-course set lunch menu at £11.95. Scottish sirloin with red wine jus followed by crème brûlée are the sort of dishes you can expect. At weekends, you might go for a full English breakfast (£8.50). The house wine is £10.95 a bottle.
/ 11 pm; closed Sun D; no smoking area.

Brasserie St Quentin SW3 £19* ★★
243 Brompton Rd   7589 8005   5–2C
It's as grand a brasserie as you'll find in London, but in recent years this Knightsbridge establishment languished in the ownership of a large chain. Now again in private hands, it's offering classic Gallic fare at reasonable prices. 'Reasonable' is a relative term, of course, and in this part of town that means the budget diner will have to stick to the 2-course set menu (£12.50), which is available all week from lunch until 7pm – black potato salad with chicken livers followed by braised beef is the sort of fare you can expect. Vin de la maison is £12.50 a bottle. / www.brasseriestquentin.co.uk; 10.30 pm.

La Brasserie Townhouse WC1 £16* ★
24 Coptic St   7636 2731   2–1C
Despite its handy location near the British Museum, this side street townhouse restaurant never seems to get quite the following it deserves. Bad luck for the management, but good luck for the budget-conscious luncher, who should seek out the £9.95 3-course set menu – which might comprise sweet potato & ginger soup followed by chicken stuffed with mushrooms, and then chocolate mousse – washed down with house wine at £10 a bottle. Dinner would fall a little outside our budget.
/ www.townhousebrasserie.co.uk; 11 pm; closed Sun L; no smoking area.

Bread & Roses SW4 £17 🅐
68 Clapham Manor Street   7498 1779   10–1D
This Clapham boozer – with its nice decked garden – makes an especially pleasant sunny-day destination. The fare on offer is the likes of chicken satay salad (around £4) followed, perhaps, by tagliatelle with wild mushrooms (£7). At weekends, it tends to be more adventurous, and on Sunday 'Family Days', there's something of an African theme. Desserts – simple stuff such as pancakes with pears – are £3.50, and a bottle of the house wine is £9.75. / www.workersbeer.co.uk; 9.30 pm; no Amex; no smoking area; no booking.

sign up for the survey at www.hardens.com

Brick Lane Beigel Bake E1   £ 3   ★★
159 Brick Ln   7729 0616   1–2D
This 24-hour take-away beigel bakery is a true East End institution, attracting a crowd whatever the time of day (or night) and for good reason. With a wide selection of bargain filled beigels on offer for less than £1, it's no wonder the queue is a permanent feature. No alcohol. / *open 24 hours; no credit cards; no smoking; no booking.*

Brilliant UB2   £ 18   ★
72-76 Western Rd   8574 1928   1–3A
This famous suburban Indian is on the trail of many ardent curry lovers, but as fame has increased so have the prices. However, with starters costing £2-£8 and main courses £8 there's still scope for the budget diner. If the menu doesn't turn you on, there's always the Friday and Saturday night entertainment – karaoke in both English and 'Indian'! House wine to wash down your curry is £9 a bottle, or drink Cobra (£3.50 for a large bottle). / *www.brilliantrestaurant.com; 11 pm; closed Mon, Sat L & Sun L.*

La Brocca NW6   £ 18   Ⓐ
273 West End Ln   7433 1989   1–1B
This West Hampstead Italian isn't much to look at, but it's a popular local destination, and thanks to the quality of its pizza and pasta dishes (mainly in the £7-£9 range), the cosy basement restaurant is always buzzing. House wine is £9 a bottle. / *11 pm; booking: max 8.*

Bu San N7   £ 15   ★
43 Holloway Rd   7607 8264   8–2D
Just round the corner from Highbury & Islington tube, this inauspicious-looking Korean serves up some surprisingly good, well-spiced fare. Veggies are well catered for, with starters including deep-fried aubergine (£2.60), spiced cucumber (£2) and fried marrow (£2.30), which could be followed by a more carnivorous main course such as sizzling marinated ribs (£6.90). If you are in the area for lunch, there's a selection of 2-course menus for £4-£7, inclusive of rice and tea. House wine is £9.45 a bottle. / *11 pm, Fri & Sat 11.30 pm; closed Sat L & Sun L; no Amex.*

The Builder's Arms SW3   £ 20   Ⓐ
13 Britten St   7349 9040   5–2C
If you're looking for one of those modernised pubs serving good food (or gastropubs as they're often called nowadays), this Chelsea boozer has one of the handiest destinations in inner south west London. Dishes include the likes of soup of the day (£4.25) followed by Italian sausages with olive oil mash (£9.95), which you could wash down with house wine at £10.50 a bottle, or Heineken at £2.40 a pint. / *9.30 pm; no Amex; no booking.*

for updates visit www.hardens.com

Buona Sera £17 A

289a King's Rd, SW3   7352 8827   5–3C
22 Northcote Rd, SW11   7228 9925   10–2C

This ever-buzzing Italian mini-chain is a long-running success thanks to the reliable quality of its long, fairly traditional menu – there are all the usual pizza and pasta dishes (around £5-£7), or you could opt for the likes of aubergines stuffed with Mozzarella (£4.60), followed by lamb with lentils (£8.50). House wine is a modest £9.80 a bottle. / midnight; SW3 closed Mon; no Amex.

Busaba Eathai £17 A★

106-110 Wardour St, W1   7255 8686   3–2D
22 Store St, WC1   2–1C

As the regular queues attest, if you're looking for glamour on a budget, you won't do much better than these stylish low-lit noodle canteens in Soho and, opening as we go to press, Bloomsbury. Prawn stir-fried noodles (£5.90) followed by chicken in coconut soup (£6.10) might be a typical meal, washed down by house wine at £10.50 a bottle, or Thai beers at £3.30. / 11 pm, Fri & Sat 11.30 pm; no smoking; no booking.

Butlers Wharf Chop-house SE1 £18* A★

36e Shad Thames   7403 3403   9–4D

This traditional British component of Sir Terence Conran's enormous restaurant complex near Tower Bridge is hardly a budget establishment in any normal sense – the cheapest wine is £14 a bottle! Happily, however, there's a bar where one can enjoy two courses for only £9 and three for £11 (available Mon-Fri 12noon-3pm, and Mon-Sat 6pm-11pm). There are three choices for each course – your selection might be sweetcorn chowder followed by roast pork with apples and black pudding, and Bakewell tart to finish. / www.conran.com; 10.45 pm; closed Sun D.

Café 206 W11 £18 A

206 Westbourne Grove   7221 1535   6–1B

This isn't a seriously foodie destination, but if you're looking for a light bite while hanging out with the Notting Hill set, this popular café is an excellent location. It's perhaps at its best for breakfast (full English, £7), but later in the day you might have the likes of pasta (£7) or chicken with rosemary (£9.50), followed by a cake (£2.75), washed down with house wine at £11.95 a bottle. / 4 pm; L only.

sign up for the survey at www.hardens.com

Café 209 SW6 £13 A
209 Munster Rd   7385 3625   10–1B
If you're looking for a decent dinner with a bit of a laugh thrown in, you won't do much better than this BYO Chinese/Thai café in deepest Fulham, presided over by the ever-present chef-patronne Joy. Chicken satay (£3.25) followed by pad Thai (£4.55) is the sort of fare which ensures there a great crush nightly, and economy is aided by the fact that this is strictly a BYO spot (corkage £1), although there is a minimum charge of £8. / 10.45 pm; D only, closed Sun; no credit cards.

Café de Maya NW3 £13
38 Primrose Hill Rd   7209 0672   8–3B
It's worth venturing a few steps off the main restaurant drag in Primrose Hill to discover this cheap and cheerful Malaysian, where the long menu includes interesting fish dishes such as snapper with chilli alongside staples such as red Thai chicken curry (all £5-£7), and the house wine is only £7 a bottle. While there's ample choice within our price range, many regulars opt for the laksa noodle soups (around £7), which constitute a meal in themselves. / 11 pm; D only; no Amex; no smoking area.

Café du Jardin WC2 £16* A★
28 Wellington St   7836 8769   4–3D
This modern British restaurant would be a boon to any area, but in tourist-trap Covent Garden its set menu is a positive beacon of value. This offers two courses, plus coffee, for £9.95 (three courses, £13.50), and is available at lunch and pre- and post-theatre (5.30pm-7.30pm; 10pm-midnight; all day Sun), The menu typically includes a soup, terrine or pasta, followed by grilled meat or fish, with apple crumble or chocolate mousse to finish. House wine is £9.75 a bottle. / midnight.

Café Emm W1 £15
17 Frith St   7437 0723   4–2A
The range of reasonably-priced meals – including a 'Lunchtime Snack' menu of toasted giant baps or jacket potatoes with a variety of fillings (£3.99) – makes this rather student Soho destination hugely popular. The 'Special' dishes (£5.95) include the likes of sausage and mash, burgers and lentil rissoles, while the grander 'Brasserie' items (£7.95) include jerk chicken, blackened salmon and rump steak. The house wine is £9.90 a bottle. / www.cafeemm.com; 10.30 pm, Fri & Sat 11.30 pm; closed Sat L & Sun L; no Amex; no booking at D.

Café Indiya E1 £14 ★
30 Alie St   7481 8288   9–3D
If you're looking for relief from the grey environs of the City's eastern fringes, it's well worth seeking out this colourful Indian, where a warm welcome is assured. Prices are not demanding – you might have king prawn poori (£4.45) followed by a chicken curry (£4.95), washed down with house wine at £7.95 a bottle. / 11.45 pm; closed Sun; no smoking area.

for updates visit www.hardens.com

Café Japan NW11 £18* ★★
626 Finchley Rd   8455 6854   1–1B
This Japanese diner, near Golders Green station, offers very good value, particularly at lunchtimes, when one can feast on, for example, a sashimi set for £6.90. Prices are steeper in the evenings, but it's still possible to have a full meal, such as a sushi set (£13.90, or less at lunch), within budget, accompanied by the house wine (£8.50 a bottle), sake (£2.80) or a Japanese beer (Kirin, £2.90). / 10.30 pm; closed Mon & Tue L; no Amex; no smoking area.

Café Laville W2 £19   Ⓐ
453 Edgware Rd   7706 2620   8–4A
Let's be honest, dining out is never just about food, and sometimes it isn't even mainly about food. That's certainly the case at this diner whose whole point is a setting of positively Venetian charm, above the canal at Little Venice. Breakfast (on a sunny day) is the best time to go – the full works will set you back about £6.95 – or you could fit a light lunch or dinner comfortably within our price limit. The house wine is £13.50 a bottle. / www.cafelaville.co.uk; 10 pm; no Amex; no smoking area.

Café Mozart N6 £15   Ⓐ
17 Swains Ln   8348 1384   8–1B
This Highgate coffee-house-cum-bistro really comes into its own on sunny afternoons, when trampers from Hampstead Heath can relax at the outside tables. Otherwise, breakfast is served from 9am and, as the day progresses, the menu assumes a more East European accent, with such specialities as schnitzel Holstein (£7.75) alongside the soups (£3.25) and pasta dishes (from £5-£6.50). The house wine is £8.95 a bottle. / 10 pm; no Amex; no smoking; no booking at L.

Café Portugal SW8 £18   Ⓐ
5a-6a Victoria Hs, South Lambeth Rd   7587 1962   10–1D
This family-run Portuguese café near Vauxhall serves coffee, pastries and tapas-style snacks all day, and more substantial, authentic home cooking at night. Prices are fair, with caldo verde (cabbage soup) at £2.50 and the rich, meaty stews and salt cod dishes (for which this place is locally renowned) costing around £10-£12. The regional wine list kicks off at a modest £8.20 a bottle. / www.outworld.ision.co.uk/cafe; 11 pm; no Amex; no smoking area.

sign up for the survey at www.hardens.com

Caffè Nero £ 8
Branches throughout London
The most overtly 'Italian' players in London's ever-more contested coffee shop market are quite cool places to hang out (but can get too 'authentically' smoky). Really good coffee (from £1.35), plus a variety of cakes and pastries (from 90p) are the mainstays, but even their more substantial snacks (including bagels, pasta dishes and sandwiches, £1.50-£4) are of better quality than many of the 'American' chains. / 8 pm-11 pm – City branches earlier; most City branches closed all or part of weekend; no credit cards; no booking.

Calzone £ 17
335 Fulham Rd, SW10   7352 9797   5–3B
2a Kensington Park Rd, W11   7243 2003   6–2B
35 Upper St, N1   7359 9191   8–3D
66 Heath St, NW3   7794 6775   8–1A
This small chain of smart pizzerias was once one of the best budget bets in town. It's been through a very sticky patch over the past few years, but it's nice to see it's on the up again – calzone (folded-over pizza, £4.45-£8) is, naturally, the house speciality, or you could have salads or pasta dishes (around the £7 mark). The house wine is £10.95 a bottle. / midnight.

Cantaloupe EC2 £16*   A
35-42 Charlotte Rd   7613 4411   9–1D
This large bar is credited by many people as the advance party which led the trendification of Shoreditch. Suits are rather more in evidence nowadays than they once were, but this remains a pleasant place for a glass of vino – there's a fair selection from £11.50 a bottle – accompanied by a selection of tasty tapas (£2.50-£5.50). The rear restaurant is less atmospheric. / www.cantaloupe.co.uk; 11.30 pm; bar menu only Sat L & Sun.

Cantina del Ponte SE1 £18*   A
36c Shad Thames   7403 5403   9–4D
Standards at this Conran group riversider are generally rather poor, but on a sunny day its position – with a view of Tower Bridge and a good number of outside tables – makes it worth a visit for the £10, 2-course set menu. This deal is available all day, and your choice might be a tricolore salad, followed by roast organic salmon, washed down with house wine at £13.95 a bottle. / www.conran.com; 10.45 pm.

Cantina Italia N1 £20*
19 Canonbury Ln   7226 9791   8–2D
This Islington eatery lives down to its name, unceremoniously serving hearty portions of pasta and pizza for around £7. Starters, like marinated swordfish (£7.90), can be relatively adventurous, but they're also rather pricey, so go for a comforting dessert, such as tiramisu (£3.50), instead. The house wine is £11.50 a bottle. / 11 pm, Fri & Sat 11.30 pm; D only; no Amex; no smoking area.

for updates visit www.hardens.com

Cantinetta Venegazzú SW11 £13* ★
31-32 Battersea Sq   7978 5395   5–4C
On a sunny weekday lunchtime, head for the 2-course set lunch (£6.90) on offer at this Venetian restaurant in Battersea – it will be a simple affair, such as a mixed salad followed by spaghetti with mussels, but pretty well done, and there is attractive seating outside. A bottle of the house wine is £11.90, and à la carte prices are such that you'd have to scrimp to stay within our price-limit. / 11 pm.

Carluccio's Caffè £17
3-5 Barrett St, W1   7224 1122   3–1A
8 Market Pl, W1   7636 2228   3–1C
2 Nash Court, E14   7719 1749   11–1C
12 West Smithfield, EC1   7329 5904   9–2A
Avuncular TV chef Antonio Carluccio's chain of traditional Italian caffès goes from strength to strength. It offers delights such as Sicilian deep-fried rice balls filled with Mozzarella (£3.95) and calzone (£4.95), as well as a few more pricey dishes. House wines start at £9.95. Pop in for a quick coffee or a full meal – be warned that the 'no booking' policy means lunchtime queuing, but as all branches double-up as Italian delis you can shop while you wait. / www.carluccios.com; 11.30 pm; no booking weekday L.

Carnevale EC1 £18* ★
135 Whitecross St   7250 3452   9–1B
This chic little veggie deli, near the Barbican, serves stupendous sandwiches (from £2.25) but also a full menu of enterprising dishes (which could rather stretch our budget). Of most interest, therefore, is the set lunch menu (£11.50), which offers three courses (or two, plus a glass of wine), from which you might choose curly cress & tabbouleh salad followed by panzerotti (deep-fried pastries) filled with asparagus and plum tomatoes, with apple & date bread pudding to finish off. The house wine is £9.95 a bottle. / www.carnevalerestaurant.co.uk; 10.30 pm; closed Sat L & Sun; no Amex.

Carpaccio's SW3 £19* Ⓐ★
4 Sydney St   7352 3433   5–2C
Ziani and Como Lario are two of the stalwarts of the Chelsea Italian restaurant scene, and their recently-opened sibling looks set similarly to become something of an institution. It's out of our range in the evenings, but at lunchtimes – which are very jolly affairs – you might enjoy the likes of pancakes filled with prawns and cheese fondue (£8) followed by pannacotta with fruits of the forest (£4), washed down with a bottle of the house wine at a reasonable (for the area) £9. / 11.15 pm; closed Sun.

sign up for the survey at www.hardens.com

The Castle SW11 £18 ★
115 Battersea High St   7228 8181   10–1C
It's rather lost among the tower blocks of Battersea, but this revamped old boozer occupies quite a characterful building, benefits from an unusually pleasant garden and offers consistently satisfactory cooking. Your choice might perhaps be Cobb salad (£4.25) followed by lamb kebabs (£8.50). The house wine is £11.85 a bottle, or drink bitter at £2.20 a pint. / www.thecastle.co.uk; 9.45 pm; no Amex.

Chamomile NW3 £13
45 England's Ln   7586 4580   8–2B
Huge all-day breakfasts (£5.95) and home-made pastries (£1.20) are particular strengths of this Belsize Park café, which is a great place to meet up with friends or to hang out with the weekend papers. There's also a wide selection of vegetarian fare available – most dishes are around £5-£7. Wine is £2.95 for a miniature bottle, or drink Becks at £2.50 a bottle. / 7 pm; L & early evening only; no Amex; no smoking area; no booking.

The Chapel NW1 £20
48 Chapel St   7402 9220   6–1D
The daily-changing blackboard menu at this lively gastropub near Edgware Road tube tends to the exotic, and you'll have to stick to the simpler items – perhaps roast chicken with blue cheese and apple (£10.50) followed by banoffi pie (£3.50) – to stay within our price-range. The house wine is £9.90 a bottle. / 9.50 pm.

Chelsea Bun Diner £16
9a Lamont Rd, SW10   7352 3635   5–3B
70 Battersea Bridge Rd, SW11   7738 9009   5–4C
The Chelsea original is really the only branch of this mini-chain worth bothering with. It comes into its own as an ultimate hangover venue – for £7.95 you might have the 'New York brunch' (pancakes, French toast, eggs and hash browns), or a more modest egg, bacon and toast for £1.90 (available Mon-Fri, 7am-noon), both served with tea or coffee. At other times, such staple dishes as lasagne (£6.05) provide suitable fodder for a quick bite. House wine is £8.90 a bottle. / SW10 10.45 pm – SW11 L only; no Amex.

Chez Liline N4 £19* ★★
101 Stroud Green Rd   7263 6550   8–1D
Don't judge by appearances – this endearingly-scruffy Mauritian fish emporium offers some of the most interesting and best-value cooking in town. An à la carte dinner is slightly outside our budget – and, if you were looking for a place to blow our budget, this place would be an ideal candidate – but at lunchtime you can keep comfortably within it. Two courses from a 'market menu' cost £12, washed down with house wine at £10.25 a bottle. / 10.30 pm; closed Mon L & Sun L.

for updates visit www.hardens.com

Chez Lindsay TW10 £18* A★
11 Hill Rise   8948 7473   1–4A
Breton crêpes and ciders – and good seafood – are highlights of the fare at this authentic café/bistro near Richmond Bridge. Although it is just about feasible to eat à la carte within our budget, the 2-course lunch menu (£5.99) offers special value. Choices might include tomato salad followed by a buckwheat pancake with two fillings of your choice. The house wine is £10.95 a bottle, and cider is £6.75 (for a large bottle). / 11 pm; no Amex.

Chiang Mai W1 £16* ★★
48 Frith St   7437 7444   4–2A
The 2-course set lunch (£9.90) is the prime attraction for budget diners at this unprepossessing, but highly-regarded, Thai in the heart of Soho – you'd otherwise be likely to burst our budget. Six choices for each course offer the likes of deep-fried spare ribs or spring rolls followed by stir-fried aubergine with chillies. The house wine is £10.90 a bottle, but Singha beer (£2.90) is a more popular choice. / 11 pm; closed Sun L; no smoking area.

China City WC2 £17
25a Lisle St   7734 3388   4–3A
It may have a tucked-away location, but this central oriental is on quite a scale, even by Chinatown standards (and it's also more friendly than the local norm). Don't expect the gastronomy to scale any great heights, but if you're looking for competent realisation of the standard dishes – set menus start at £11 a head – this is a pretty satisfactory destination all round. The house wine is £8 a bottle. / 11.45 pm; no smoking area.

China Dream NW3 £16* A★
68 Heath St   7794 6666   8–1A
This jolly oriental – convivially located in a stylishly-converted boozer – has become a popular Hampstead destination for informal celebrations. It's a little beyond our budget à la carte, but you could visit for dim sum (daily, with dishes costing £1.45-£2.25 each). The house wine is £11 a bottle. / 10.30 pm, Thu-Sat 11.30 pm.

Chiswick Restaurant W4 £15* ★
131-133 Chiswick High Rd   8994 6887   7–2A
A la carte, this local restaurant par excellence is priced beyond our limit. The set lunch and pre-theatre menus (until 8pm), however, allow the budget-conscious diner an opportunity to try, say, baked sardine and parsley salad followed by deep-fried skate with pea purée for a bargain £9.50, washed down with house wine at £11.50 a bottle. / www.thechiswick.co.uk; 11 pm; closed Sat L & Sun D; no smoking area.

sign up for the survey at www.hardens.com

Chowki W1   £17   ★★
2-3 Denman St   7439 1330   3–2D
Mela (see also) has developed quite a reputation as one of the best-value of the West End Indians (and there are few enough of those worthy of a recommendation). This comfortable and quite atmospheric new sibling near Piccadilly Circus is, if anything, even more promising. The top deals are the £9.95, 3-course set menus, always available, each offering the cuisine of a different region. The house wine is £9.95 a bottle.
/ www.chowki.com; 11.30 pm; no smoking area.

Chuen Cheng Ku W1   £17
17 Wardour St   7437 1398   4–3A
This gaudy behemoth serves up the familiar Cantonese repertoire, and a 'classic' Chinatown experience to boot. Dim sum (from £1.95 a dish, until 6pm), served from trolleys dashing between tables, is the highlight, washed down with house wine at £9.80 a bottle. In the evening, the place is no more than a stand-by. / 11.45 pm; no smoking area.

Churchill Arms W8   £12   A★
119 Kensington Church St   7792 1246   6–2B
This popular Thai restaurant, at the back of a Kensington pub, is famed for its one-plate dishes (all priced at £5.50, including rice), so it's best to book if you want to secure a seat in the conservatory dining-annexe. The 20 choices include stir-fried pork with prawns and chilli, or stir-fried beef and peppers with oyster sauce. The house wine is £10.50 a bottle. / 9.30 pm; closed Sun D; no booking at L.

Chutneys NW1   £14   ★
124 Drummond St   7388 0604   8–4C
This vegetarian restaurant in the Little India near Euston station is best known for its lunchtime buffet (£5.45, also served all day on Sunday). Even à la carte, though, you'd be hard pushed to breach our budget, as most dishes are under a fiver, and the house wine is a mere £6.95 a bottle. / 11 pm; no Amex or Switch; no smoking at L; need 4+ to book.

Cinnamon Cay SW11   £17*   A★
87 Lavender Hill   7801 0932   10–1C
It looks a bit like your regular Battersea local restaurant, but this establishment is more ambitious than it might at first sight appear, and its fusion cooking has won it quite a following. A la carte you'd spend beyond our limit (if not by a great deal), but at lunch and dinner there's a 2-course set menu (Mon-Sat) for £10 – you might have pan-fried squid with balsamic oranges followed by honey-marinated duck in a Thai broth, washed down by house wine at £10.95 a bottle.
/ www.cinnamoncay.co.uk; 11 pm; closed Sun.

for updates visit www.hardens.com   36

Le Colombier SW3 £19* A★
145 Dovehouse St   7351 1155   5–2C
Hidden away on a Chelsea corner – and benefiting from one of the nicest terraces of any restaurant in town – this classic Gallic bistro offers all the dishes you'd expect. It's beyond our price-limit à la carte, but makes a splendid sunny-day lunching destination, when two courses will set you back £13, washed down with house wine at £12.90 a bottle. / 11 pm.

Coopers Arms SW3 £17 A
87 Flood St   7376 3120   5–3C
This civilised Young's pub in Chelsea serves pretty decent grub at prices that are reasonable for the area. Starters might include asparagus soup (£3.95), perhaps followed by pork chops with chive and bacon mash (£7.95). Puddings cost £3.50, and there's a fair selection of wines, from £11.75 a bottle, or a pint of bitter is £2.25. / www.drinkatthecoopers.co.uk; 9.30 pm; closed Sun D; no booking, Sun.

Coromandel SW11 £19 ★
2 Battersea Rise   7738 0038   10–2C
Fans of south Indian cooking should certainly seek out this (over-)bright restaurant at the end of the Battersea's restaurant strip, as the cooking it offers is well above-average. You'll need to exercise some care to stay within our price limit, but it's perfectly possible with starters such as deep-fried dahl dumplings (£3.45) followed by Kerala chicken (£6.95), washed down by the house wine at £12.50 a bottle. / 11.30 pm; no smoking area.

Costa's Fish Restaurant W8 £12 ★
18 Hillgate St   7727 4310   6–2B
This long-established chippy, just off Notting Hill Gate, is often eclipsed by its larger and more famous neighbour, Geale's – which is a shame, as any odious comparisons made nowadays would tend to point in favour of the smaller establishment. Cod, haddock, lemon sole and plaice – all served with chips, salad or mushy peas – are around £6.50. You can wash all this down with house wine at £7.50 a bottle. / 10 pm; closed Mon & Sun; no credit cards.

The Cow (Dining Room) W2 £16*
89 Westbourne Park Rd   7221 0021   6–1B
If you want to hang out in Notting Hill at reasonably modest cost, this packed and fashionable boozer – owned by Tom Conran, son of Sir Terence – is just the place. The restaurant upstairs is out of our price-bracket, but in the downstairs "Oirish" boozer you could have six rock oysters and a pint of the Black Stuff for £9, or warm porcini mushroom tart for £6.75. / 11 pm; D only Mon-Fri, L only Sat & Sun; no Amex.

sign up for the survey at www.hardens.com

Coyote Café W4 £19
2 Fauconberg Rd   8742 8545   7–2A
London is desperately short on good southern American hang-outs, and this creditable stab at the formula crops up where you least expect it – in the depths of Chiswick. It's an informal bar/café where the cheaper dishes tend to be in classic Tex/Mex style – you might kick off with nachos (£3.95) or hot chicken wings (£4.50) over a bottle of Sol (£2.50), and then, if you felt like eating more substantially, move on to fajitas (£7.95-£11.50). / www.coyotecafe.co.uk; 10.30 pm; Mon-Thu D only, Fri-Sun open L & D.

Daphne NW1 £14
83 Bayham St   7267 7322   8–3C
Certainly not to be confused with the Chelsea ladies-who-lunch spot, this long-running Camden Town Greek offers good-value and filling nosh. It's especially nice in summer, when you should try to bag a table on the attractive roof terrace. There's a 2-course lunch menu (£6.25) – from which you might have marinated anchovies or halloumi followed by moussaka – but dining à la carte also fits easily within our budget. The house wine is £9 a bottle. / 11.30 pm; closed Sun; no Amex.

Dartmouth Arms NW5 £15
35 York Rise   7485 3267   8–1B
Truly reasonable prices put this Dartmouth Park boozer well within the range of the budget diner at any time. You could even go for three courses within our price limit, say, wild boar pâté (£3.25) followed by pork & herb sausages and mash (£6.95), with rhubarb crumble (£2.50) for pudding. Wash it down with a pint of Carlsberg (£2.50), or if you prefer, the house vino (£11 a bottle). / 10 pm; no Amex.

Deca W1 £20* A★★
23 Conduit St   7493 7070   3–2C
Budget dining experiences just don't come better than at the Ladenis family's grand new restaurant, in the heart of Mayfair. So slip on your Savile Row suit – or go a touch more informal, if you prefer – to avail yourself of the £12.50, 3-course set lunch menu, which might comprise a smoked salmon starter, then saddle of lamb, followed by prune & armagnac ice cream. Stray from this narrow path, though, and you'll blow our budget big time – as you'd expect with house wine at £14.50 a bottle. / 11 pm; closed Sun.

La Delizia SW3 £14
63-65 Chelsea Manor St   7376 4111   5–3C
The only remaining remnant of this small former chain of pizzerias can still induce the occasional pang of nostalgia for the days when its crisp, modernistic styling seemed, well, modern. The place still does good pizzas (around £8) and other dishes such as asparagus risotto (£6.95), and it's very reasonably priced by Chelsea standards. A bottle of the house wine will set you back £8.95. / midnight; no Amex.

for updates visit www.hardens.com

Le Deuxième WC2   £17*   A★
65a Long Acre   7379 0033   4–2D
With an ideal location for the Royal Opera House, this bright modern Gallic restaurant – the second outlet from the people who run the Café du Jardin (see also) – has already eclipsed its parent. It's out of our price-range à la carte, but there's a 2-course lunchtime and pre/post-theatre (5pm-7pm and 10pm-midnight) menu – from which your selection might be penne with tomato and black olives followed by char-grilled minute steak with onion gravy, with coffee to finish – for £9.95. The house wine is £11.50 a bottle. / midnight.

Ditto SW18   £14*   A★
55-57 East Hill   8877 0110   10–2B
This cosy and relaxed Wandsworth-fringe spot has established quite a local following. A la carte prices are rather beyond our budget, but the 2-course set lunch (£10, including a glass of wine) offers a good opportunity to try dishes like twice-cooked lamb shank, honey-glazed duck with date sauce or pan-fried tuna niçoise, followed perhaps by sticky toffee pudding, and washed down with house wine at £10.95 a bottle.
/ www.doditto.co.uk; 11 pm; closed Sat L & Sun D; no Amex.

Diwana Bhel-Poori House NW1   £12   ★
121-123 Drummond St   7387 5556   8–4C
For top value, visit this long-established veggie Indian near Euston at lunchtime, when there's a £5.45 buffet menu – to see what's on offer, check out the bowls in the window. Even à la carte, you would be hard-pushed to spend anything approaching our price-limit – for an evening visit, though, the rather sparse '60s surroundings may not be everyone's cup of tea. BYO (no corkage). / www.diwanarestaurant.com; 11.10 pm; no smoking area; need 5+ to book.

don Fernando's TW9   £17   A
27f The Quadrant   8948 6447   1–4A
Tapas are designed for sharing, and this large and lively place by Richmond station is definitely best experienced by groups, who could fill up on the tapas (all under a fiver), or enjoy one of the paellas (£7.50-£12.75 per person), washed down with the house Rioja at £10.25 a bottle. / www.donfernando.co.uk; 11 pm; no booking.

Don Pepe NW8   £18
99 Frampton St   7262 3834   8–4A
London's most venerable Spanish restaurant, near Lord's, remains a reliable choice for consistent (if not especially inspired) cooking. This is most economically sampled from the 3-course set dinner (£13.95), but it's much more fun to have tapas (around £5) in the bar, especially when there's live music (most nights). The all-Hispanic wine list kicks off at £8.95 a bottle. / midnight; closed Sun.

sign up for the survey at www.hardens.com

The Eagle EC1 £15 A★
159 Farringdon Rd   7837 1353   9–1A
The original London gastropub is still a great place to eat down Clerkenwell way – if you can stand the crush. Zesty cooking with an Iberian accent is dispensed in such heroic portions that one dish will usually suffice. Roast stuffed aubergine (£8) and marinated steak sandwich (£8.50) are representative of a menu that might also include paella (£10). A strong wine list starts at £10.50 a bottle. / 10.30 pm; closed Sun D; only Switch; no booking.

Eco £18 ★
162 Clapham High St, SW4   7978 1108   10–2D
4 Market Row, Brixton Mkt, SW9   7738 3021   10–2D
The tiny (and unlicensed) Brixton Market branch of this small chain, now refurbished to match its sibling, remains many South Londoners' favourite pizzeria – the Clapham original has become too loud and possibly too popular for its own good. Still, the pizzas (all around £7) are pretty good and you can't argue with success (not unless you're prepared to shout at the top of your voice, that is). The house wine is £11 a bottle.
/ SW4 11 pm, Sat 11.30 pm – SW9 L only; SW9 closed Wed & Sun; SW9 no booking.

Efes Kebab House £17
1) 80 Gt Titchfield St, W1   7636 1953   2–1B
2) 175-177 Gt Portland St, W1   7436 0600   2–1B
These Turkish restaurants have been twin beacons of value, up Marylebone way, since the early '70s, and they continue to satisfy all comers with an impressive range of 22 kebabs (£6.95-£9.25), plus undemanding starters like houmous and taramasalata (£3.95), washed down with house wine at £11.90 a bottle. The Great Portland Street branch stays open until 3am at the weekends, with belly dancers adding to the atmosphere.
/ 11.30 pm – Gt Portland St Fri & Sat 3 am; Gt Titchfield St closed Sun.

Errays N1 £19
305 Upper St   7359 7487   8–3D
This new concept from the people behind the successful Ask! pizza 'n' pasta stops aims one stage up the restaurant food chain – it's a surprisingly successful attempt to offer fusion fare on the (relatively) cheap, in a stylish setting. And prices are such that you can dine here within our price-limit at any time – some care is needed, but with the likes of pumpkin ravioli (£4.25) followed by king prawn & chilli linguine (£7.95), it's perfectly possible. The house wine is £11 a bottle,
/ www.askcentral.co.uk; 11 pm.

for updates visit www.hardens.com

L'Estaminet WC2 £19* A★
14 Garrick St   7379 1432   4–3C
This long-established Gallic establishment in Covent Garden continues to re-establish its reputation. It's well out of our price range à la carte, but it's worth knowing about as a pre-theatre destination – the 3-course menu, which might comprise of duck salad, followed by grilled fish, with a dessert of fruit salad, will set you back £12.99 (£14.50 on Saturdays), and the house wine is £11.50 a bottle. / 11 pm; closed Sun.

Fairuz £20
3 Blandford St, W1   7486 8108   2–1A
25 Westbourne Grove, W2   7243 8444   6–1C
These Lebanese restaurants in Marylebone and Westbourne Grove are good all-rounders, and if you're looking for somewhere you can eat at any time within our price limit (just about), well worth bearing in mind. Starters such as houmous or olive salad are £3.95-£5, and meaty mains, such as chicken kebabs, are around £10.95 – or go veggie for fractionally less. A bottle of Lebanese wine is £12.95. / W1 11 pm – W2 midnight.

Il Falconiere SW7 £17*
84 Old Brompton Rd   7589 2401   5–2B
The 3-course set lunch (£10) ensures that you'll stay well within budget at this well-worn and reassuringly old-school trattoria in South Kensington – at other times you'd spend rather over our price-limit. Starters of grilled sardines or rocket and Parmesan salad and mains of pasta, veal, or grilled chicken are typical. Desserts are, of course, from a trolley, and the house wine is £11.50 a bottle. / 11.45 pm; closed Sun.

Faulkner's E8 £15 ★★
424-426 Kingsland Rd   7254 6152   1–2D
Despite its impossible location (get a cab driver to take you there), this East End chippy is justly renowned for dishing up some of the best fish and chips in the capital. It's not especially cheap, with prices ranging up to £12.50 for Dover sole or prime halibut, but the quality is extremely high. You might start with smoked salmon (£3.95), and you absolutely must finish with the sticky toffee pudding (£2.50). House wine is £7.95 a bottle. / 10 pm; no Amex; no smoking area.

Ffiona's W8 £19* A
51 Kensington Church St   7937 4152   5–1A
'Homely' is not a style particularly in favour with Kensington's restaurants, but Ffiona Reid-Owen's English bistro has built quite a following by offering just such an approach. Three courses will set you back only £12.99 (before 8.30pm). At other times, stay within budget by sticking to something simple like pork sausages with bubble 'n' squeak (£10.95) and a good old-fashioned pud, such as sticky toffee (£4.50). The house wine is £11 a bottle. / 11 pm; closed Mon, Tue-Sat D only, Sun open L & D.

sign up for the survey at www.hardens.com

Field & Forest WC2 £13*
22 Short's Gdns   7240 5777   4–2C
This smartly turned-out new Canadian canteen is just the sort of place you'd hope to come across if you were looking for a lunch venue among the trendy fashion shops of north Covent Garden. In the months following the launch, they were offering a simple 2-course menu for only £10, including a glass of wine – you might have the likes of chicken & merguez sausage with couscous followed by strawberry & brownie mess. A la carte, grills kick off around the £9 mark, so you'd just about be able to dine within our price-limit. / 12.30 am; no Amex; no smoking area.

Fileric SW7 £ 7   ★
57 Old Brompton Rd   7584 2967   5–2C
French pâtisseries don't come much more authentic than this tiny Gallic-run place, not far from the South Kensington Lycée. Delights include éclairs (£2) and millefeuilles (£2.50), and savoury snacks such as quiches (£3.50). The excellent coffees start at £1.10. / 8 pm.

**Film Café
National Film Theatre SE1** £ 15
Waterloo Rd   7928 5362   2–3D
If you're visiting the 'Eye' – or anywhere on the South Bank – there's still not a brilliant selection of local dining possibilities. One of the best snack options is this lively café, and it's especially good with kids. In summer, the outside seating is very popular. A wide range of simple dishes is offered, including quiches, pizza slices, stews and a few veggie alternatives, fairly priced from around £5 for salads and £6.50 for more substantial dishes. House wine is £10.70 a bottle. / 9 pm; no smoking area.

Fish in a Tie SW11 £ 13   Ⓐ
105 Falcon Rd   7924 1913   10–1C
Be sure to book ahead if you want a table at this small budget bistro, whose very modest pricing makes it an ever-popular Battersea destination. The food – dominated, as you might guess, by fish and seafood – is good, and so is the service. Seafood cocktail with avocado dressing (£3.25) could be followed by swordfish with pesto (£6.95), and set menus bring prices even lower. The house wine is £8.75 a bottle. / 11.45 pm; no Amex.

Food for Thought WC2 £ 11   ★
31 Neal St   7836 0239   4–2C
This cramped veggie basement in Covent Garden offers no frills – just wholesome, meat-free grub at generous prices. Lunch might be the likes of carrot soup (£2.70), followed by seared broccoli with black bean sauce (£3.90). The place is unlicensed, and you can BYO with no corkage charge. / 8.15 pm; closed Sun D; no credit cards; no smoking; no booking.

for updates visit www.hardens.com

Il Forno W1 £18
63-64 Frith St   7734 4545   4–2A
Good food at reasonable prices is a foolproof formula for success anywhere, and this unpretentious modern trattoria in Soho has established a regular following. Starters, such as aubergine with Mozzarella, are priced around £5. Main courses include pastas (from £6.50) and pizzas (bresaola, £8.50). Classic Italian desserts include tiramisu (£3.75), and house wines start from £12.50 a bottle. / www.ilforno-restaurant.co.uk; 10.30 pm, Fri & Sat 11 pm; closed Mon L & Sun.

Fortnum's Fountain W1 £19*   A
181 Piccadilly   7734 8040   3–3D
Her Majesty's grocers might seem an odd budget suggestion, but the grand ground-floor buttery (with a separate entry from Jermyn Street) is a useful place to spoil yourself for breakfast (full works around £12) or for lunch – when you might have Welsh rarebit (£8.95) followed by apple pie (£4.95). Wines start at £13 a bottle. / www.fortnumandmason.co.uk; 7.45 pm; closed Sun; no smoking area; no booking at L.

The Four Seasons W2 £15   ★
84 Queensway   7229 4320   6–1C
Although you never read about it in the tourist guides, Bayswater is in fact the best part of town to head if you're looking for a quality Chinese meal. This particular place has all the brusque charms that generally characterise such experiences, but the food is consistently very good, and reasonably priced. Roast duck (£6.50) is a highlight, and the house wine £7.50 a bottle. / 11.15 pm.

Fox & Anchor EC1 £17
115 Charterhouse St   7253 5075   9–1B
The Great – better make that Legendary – British Breakfast (£7.50) is served at this Smithfield boozer from 7am, when, thanks to the Weird English Licensing Laws, you can wash it down with a pint of beer, or the house wine at £9.85 a bottle. Later in the day, a range of meaty grills and pies is available. / breakfast (Mon-Fri) & L only; bar open in evening; closed Sat & Sun.

Frantoio SW10 £18*   A★
397 King's Rd   7352 4146   5–3B
It's had something of a slow start, but this World's End trattoria – which has now been in business for a couple of years – is beginning to establish quite a local following. It's well outside our price-range à la carte, but offers a 2-course set lunch menu (£11), from which your selection might be veal and rocket salad followed by grilled lamb steak, washed down with house wine at £11 a bottle. / 10.30 pm.

sign up for the survey at www.hardens.com

Frederick's N1 £20* A★★
106 Camden Pas   7359 2888   8–3D
You'd easily spend twice our budget dining at this smart and perennially popular Islington institution, whose special feature is its large and airy rear conservatory. The Gallic cooking is quite good too, and (just) affordable if you visit for the lunchtime and pre-7pm menu, when two courses – perhaps garlic field mushrooms followed by roast red mullet with oriental cabbage – will set you back just £12.50 (including coffee). The house wine is £10.95 a bottle. / www.fredericks.co.uk; 11.30 pm; closed Sun; no smoking area.

Frocks E9 £16* A
95 Lauriston Rd   8986 3161   1–2D
Weekends – when hearty breakfasts (around a fiver) are served all day, from 11am-4pm – see smart East Enders congregating at this cosy English bistro. Those who find themselves around Victoria Park on a weekday can take advantage of the set lunch menu, which offers two courses for only £9.50. The cooking – simple grilled meat and fish – is sound, and the vegetarian options are imaginative. House wine is £9.75 a bottle. / 11 pm; closed Mon & Sun D; no booking for Sun brunch.

Fryer's Delight WC1 £ 7
19 Theobald's Rd   7405 4114   2–1D
Central London is woefully short of decent chippies, so this no-nonsense Bloomsbury outfit is worth seeking out. Deep-fried cod, fully accessorised with chips, bread and butter and tartare sauce and a cup of tea, will set you back little more than a fiver. No alcohol, but you're welcome to BYO (no corkage). / 10 pm; closed Sun; no credit cards.

Fujiyama SW9 £ 11 A
7 Vining St   7737 2369   10–2D
This buzzy new noodle bar offers an ideal pit stop for those checking out the delights of Brixton. Main dishes – an example would be a big bowl of pork ramen (miso soup with noodles, topped with slices of grilled pork) – cost £5-£10.50, and the house wine is £8 a bottle. / www.newfujiyama.com; 10.45 pm; no Amex; no smoking area.

Furnace N1 £ 17 ★
1 Rufus St   7613 0598   9–1D
For our money, this is the best inexpensive place to eat if you want to hang out with the Hoxton trendies. Just off the Square, it's a buzzing, brick-lined establishment, where pizzas are around £8.50, or you can opt for other simple Italian fare such as the pasta of the day (£6.95). A bottle of house wine costs £9.55. / 11 pm; closed Sat L & Sun; no Amex.

for updates visit www.hardens.com

Fusion EC2 £11
13 Devonshire Row   7375 1202   9–2D
Perhaps it will grow up to be a big chain one day, but for the moment this tucked-away oriental spot by Liverpool Street is a stand-alone that's distinguished by its very welcoming and personal service. Dishes include salads (£1.40-£4.15 eat in) and sushi (from £1.75). No alcohol – drink organic juices (£1.50) instead. / www.fusionpacific.com; L only, closed Sat & Sun; no Amex; no smoking; no booking.

Futures EC3 £8 ★
8 Botolph Alley   7621 9508   9–3C
Regular queues advertise the continuing charms of this smart vegetarian take-away, hidden in lanes near the Monument, as a destination for City lunching. Soups (£2.85), salads (from £1.30) and bakes (£4) are typical of the midday fare. Good, if not inexpensive, breakfast items are also available.
/ www1e.btwebworld.com/futures1; breakfast & L only, closed Sat & Sun; no credit cards; no smoking; no booking.

Gaby's WC2 £17
30 Charing Cross Rd   7836 4233   4–3B
For a Mediterranean or Middle Eastern snack in the heart of the West End, this long-established Formica-chic café is well worth checking out. For £6.90 you could fill up on the 2-course set meal, which might include falafel followed by Moroccan-style aubergines. A la carte prices are just as reasonable – the very popular salt beef sandwich is £4.50, and house wine £8.50 a bottle. / www.gabys.net; 11.15 pm; no credit cards.

Galicia W10 £18
323 Portobello Rd   8969 3539   6–1A
The trendification of Portobello has – mercifully – passed this long-established Spanish joint by. Its set lunch is only £7.50 for three courses (50p more on Sundays), and might comprise soup, roast lamb with all the trimmings and a selection from the sweet trolley, with coffee thrown in. Otherwise, there's a selection of tapas (plus a pricier dinner menu). The cooking's not bad, and neither is the house wine – especially at only £8 a bottle. / 11.30 pm; closed Mon.

Gallipoli £18 Ⓐ
102 Upper St, N1   7359 0630   8–3D
120 Upper St, N1   7226 8099   8–3D
This friendly duo of Turkish bistros have become a buzzing linchpin of Islington life. You could dine here à la carte within our budget, but the best value is to be had from the fixed-price menu, which offers any vegetarian meze, plus a main course from the menu (such as chicken with tomatoes and green peppers), plus dessert (perhaps baklava or rice pudding), plus coffee, for £13.50. The house wine is £8.95 a bottle. / 11 pm, Fri & Sat 11.30 pm; no Amex.

sign up for the survey at www.hardens.com

Gastro SW4 £19* 𝔸
67 Venn St   7627 0222   10–2D
*This authentically-French bistro, opposite Clapham Picture
House, is very strong in the 'character' department, and is
a popular local destination all day long. Breakfast is served
from 8am, and coffee and cakes (from £1.75) are available all
afternoon. The evening menu might offer fish soup with rouille
(£4.85) followed by pan-fried tiger prawns with Ricard (£9.60),
so you'd have to choose pretty carefully if you wanted to dine
here within our price-limit. The house wine is £9.95 a bottle.*
/ midnight; no credit cards; mainly non-smoking.

The Gate £20   𝔸★★
51 Queen Caroline St, W6   8748 6932   7–2C
72 Belsize Ln, NW3   7435 7733   8–2A
*Although it now has a (useful enough) Belsize Park offshoot,
it's the original branch of London's best vegetarian restaurant –
off a church courtyard near Hammersmith Broadway – which
is of special interest. Starters, such as plantain fritters with
coconut and coriander chutney, are under a fiver, while main
courses, such as Gruyère and butternut filo pie, are around £9.
House wine is £10.25 a bottle.* / www.gateveg.co.uk; 10.45 pm; W6
closed Sun – NW3 closed Sun D; smoking restrictions at NW3; W6 booking:
max 10.

Geeta NW6 £10   ★★
57-59 Willesden Ln   7624 1713   1–1B
*Little changes at this unprepossessing caff in Kilburn, which
turns out consistently good regional Indian cooking at modest
prices. Most starters cost less than £2, curries are around £6
(or less for the many veggie options), and the rather good
puddings cost about £1.40. House wine is a modest £6.50
a bottle.* / 10.30 pm, Fri & Sat 11.30 pm; no Switch.

George II SW11 £20   ★
339 Battersea Park Rd   7622 2112   10–1C
*This Battersea gastropub looks a fairly 'Identikit' sort of place,
but it offers pretty good food, and you can accommodate
a meal here comfortably within our price limit. Starters are the
likes of leek & Gruyère tart (£3.95), followed by main courses
that might include teriyaki chicken (£8.50). House wine is
£10.80 a bottle.* / 10 pm; no Amex; no booking.

for updates visit www.hardens.com

Giraffe £ 20 Ⓐ
6-8 Blandford St, W1   7935 2333   2–1A
29-31 Essex Rd, N1   7359 5999   8–3D
46 Rosslyn Hill, NW3   7435 0343   8–2A
27 Battersea Rise, SW11   7223 0933   10–2C
This growing all-day mini-chain is developing quite a following, especially for breakfast or brunch – it won more start-the-day nominations in our survey this year than anywhere else. You can, however, eat here just about within our price limit at any time of day, and they are excellent places to take children. Dinner, from the global menu, might be the likes of meze with golden naan bread (£5.50) followed by tequila and lime grilled chicken (£9.95), washed down with house wine at £10.50 a bottle. / 11 pm; no smoking.

Golborne House W10 £ 20 Ⓐ
36 Golborne Rd   8960 6260   6–1A
This once-grotty boozer has established itself as a gastropub-destination of some note among North Kensington Bohemians (and it can get quite crowded). An evolving menu offers the likes of bruschetta of marinated peppers and buffalo ricotta (£5.75) followed by grilled lamb with Greek salad (£9.50). These sort of prices are towards the top end of our budget, so it's a mercy that the house wine comes at a reasonable £9.90 a bottle. / www.golbornehouse.co.uk; 10 pm; no Amex.

Golden Dragon W1 £ 17
28-29 Gerrard St   7734 2763   4–3A
Dragons glare at you from every corner of this Chinatown spot, where a series of set meals (starting at £12.50 a head) are the cheapest and most straightforward budget options (although most main dishes à la carte are little more than £6). The hectic atmosphere makes the place ideal for large parties, buoyed by the house wine at £9 a bottle. / 11.15 pm, Fri & Sat 11.45 pm.

Good Earth SW3 £17* ★
233 Brompton Rd   7584 3658   5–2C
This smart and comfortable Chinese in Knightsbridge is generally way outside our budget, but it's worth knowing about both the set-price lunch, which offers two courses for £9.95, and the one-plate Japanese specials – ramen noodles with salmon, for example – which cost around £8. The house wine, however, is £13 a bottle, so you'd better stick to tea! / 10.45 pm.

sign up for the survey at www.hardens.com

Gopal's of Soho W1   £17   ★
12 Bateman St   7434 1621   4–2A
Traditionally, it has been unusual for Indian restaurants to be 'chef-led', but the eponymous Gopal has a strong track record. His Soho restaurant enjoys a solid reputation and boasts some unusual dishes – such as fish and coconut curry with rare spices (£6.50), or Kashmiri-style chicken in a creamy fruity sauce (£6.75). Prices are good for central London, and even the kulfi (£2.50) is home-made. The house wine is £9.50 a bottle.
/ 11.15 pm.

Gordon's Wine Bar WC2   £15   𝔸
47 Villiers St   7930 1408   4–4D
This endearingly scruffy wine bar, a few paces from Embankment tube, remains tremendously popular, and its wonderfully gloomy cellar setting boast bags of old-fashioned charm. Wines, from £10.95 a bottle, are arguably rather better value than the food, but a satisfying home-made hot dish – quiches are good, or you might go for a piece cut from a large, hot pie – will set you back £8-£9. Or go for a plate of good cheese, with bread and pickles (£7). / 10 pm; no Amex; no booking.

Gourmet Burger Kitchen   £12   ★
331 West End Ln, NW6   7794 5455   1–1B
44 Northcote Rd, SW11   7228 3309   10–2C
333 Putney Bridge Rd, SW15   8789 1199   10–2B
Burgers every possible way – including 'Jamaican' (with mango and ginger) and 'Kiwiburger' (with pineapple, beetroot and cheese), all around £5-£7 – have made this growing chain of diners the capital's key destination for burger-lovers. A side order of fat chips with dips will set you back an extra £2, and house wine is £10.50 a bottle. / 11 pm; no smoking (except at outside tables); no booking.

Gourmet Pizza Company   £18
7-9 Swallow St, W1   7734 5182   3–3D
56 Upper Ground, SE1   7928 3188   9–3A
18 Mackenzie Walk, E14   7345 9192   11–1C
Pizzas more interesting than the norm – perhaps Chinese duck (£8.95) or grilled aubergine and goats cheese – make these basic pizzerias (now part of the PizzaExpress empire) a popular destination. The Gabriel's Wharf branch is particularly worth seeking out for its fine views of the City and St Paul's – expect to queue on a warm evening. The house wine is £11.95 a bottle. / www.gourmetpizzacompany.co.uk; 11 pm; W1 & E14, no smoking area; E14 & SE1, need 8+ to book.

for updates visit www.hardens.com

Granita N1 £14* ★
127 Upper St   7226 3222   8–3D
After its recent change of ownership, we had one of our best budget lunches of the year at this Islington restaurant. It used to be a famously 'modern British' place — now the menu just seems rather odd, perhaps indicating constructive tensions between ownership (Turkish) and chef (French). Who cares? For £7, your 2-course selection might be avocado & prawn salad followed by chicken with oyster mushrooms — with everything really well done, and presented at a very high level. With house wine at £11.50 a bottle dining here within our budget is not really possible. / www.granita.co.uk; 11 pm; no Amex.

Great Nepalese NW1 £16
48 Eversholt St   7388 6737   8–3C
Despite its inauspicious location, beside Euston station, this well-run Nepalese restaurant has long been popular for its unusual menu, which offers plenty of opportunity to experiment within our price range. The simplest choice is the 2-course set lunch (£6.50), but if you'd prefer to choose à la carte, the staff will be pleased to advise. The house wine is £8.50 a bottle. / 11.30 pm.

Grenadier SW1 £10* A
18 Wilton Row   7235 3074   5–1D
There's no way a meal in the tiny rear dining room of this mega-cute pub — in a charming cobbled Belgravia mews — could be accommodated within our budget. The place makes a characterful choice for a bar snack, though — you might have a burger, a club sandwich or salmon fishcakes (all £6.75). Cognoscenti, however, plump for sausages (£1 each) washed down with a Bloody Mary (£4.50), for both of which the place is of some renown. / 9 pm.

Gung-Ho NW6 £18 A★
328-332 West End Ln   7794 1444   1–1B
This stylish West Hampstead Chinese generally offers a friendly welcome and interesting, healthy fare. Temptations are such that it would be easy to overspend, so choose carefully to stick within our budget — you might have smoked chicken (£4.20), perhaps, followed by chilli prawns (£7.40), with toffee apple or banana (£2.80) to finish. The house wine is £9.80 a bottle. Note that Sunday lunchers get 20% off their bills. / 11.30 pm; no Amex.

sign up for the survey at www.hardens.com

Hakkasan W1 £20* 𝔸 ★
8 Hanway Pl   7927 7000   4–1A
An improbable amount of money has been lavished on the décor of this basement oriental, just off the Tottenham Court Road, but it has helped make it one of the hits of the moment with London's Bright Young Things. There are no prizes for guessing that it's well out of our price range in the evenings, then. However, the lunchtime dim sum menu (£3-£6.50 per plate) enables you to check the place out at (relatively) modest cost. Unfortunately, a bottle of the house wine will still set you back a remarkable £18, so maybe go for a bottle of Jebisu beer instead (£4.75). / 11 pm; no smoking area.

Harbour City W1 £16
46 Gerrard St   7439 7859   4–3B
A notably interesting selection of dim sum (served 11am-3pm), at around £1.80-£2.40 a dish, is the primary attraction of this otherwise unexceptional restaurant in the heart of Chinatown. In the evenings, a conventional Cantonese menu is served. The house wine is £8.50 a bottle. / 11.30 pm.

Hard Rock Café W1 £19 𝔸
150 Old Park Ln   7629 0382   3–4B
It's not just the memorabilia or the loud rock music that keeps 'em queuing outside the world's most famous theme diner. The burgers (£7.75-£9.25) and other American fare – including a veggie burger (£7.25), vast sandwiches, smoked ribs and suchlike – seem to keep the punters happy, too. The house wine is £9.95 a bottle, or there's a wide range of cocktails, shakes and beers. / www.hardrock.com; midnight, Fri & Sat 1 am; no smoking area; no booking.

The Havelock Tavern W14 £20* 𝔸 ★★
57 Masbro Rd   7603 5374   7–1C
Caution is needed to stay within budget at this Shepherd's Bush gastropub, but the food really is very good indeed. Arrive early. The most economical course is to skip starters (around £6.50), and have, say, salad of duck confit and duck breast (£8.50) followed by the likes of meringue with white chocolate ice cream and strawberries (£4). The house wine is £9.50 a bottle. / 10 pm; no credit cards; no booking.

Heartstone NW1 £19 ★
106 Parkway   7485 7744   8–3B
Healthy to the core – there are even therapy rooms downstairs – this bright Camden spot has gained quite a following for its good-quality fare, mainly using organic ingredients. A meal might consist of houmous with kalamata olives and crudités (£4.50) followed by chorizo and red pepper panini (£9). No alcohol, but you can BYO (£2.50 per person corkage), or sip freshly-squeezed juices instead (£3.50). Note the early closing time. / 9 pm; closed Mon; no Amex; no smoking.

for updates visit www.hardens.com

Hellenik W1 £18* A★
30 Thayer St   7935 1257   2–1A
If you were looking for a film set for London in the '60s, you really couldn't do much better than this wonderfully unchanged Greek institution in Marylebone, where charming service is a particular strength. You'll need to choose reasonably carefully to stay within our price limit – you might have houmous (£3.75) followed by moussaka with salad (£8.95) – but it is perfectly possible. The house wine is £9.95 a bottle. / 10.30 pm; closed Sun.

Hope & Sir Loin EC1 £20
94 Cowcross St   7253 8525   9–1B
The 'licensed breakfasts', served 7am-9.30am (£10) in the upstairs dining room of this Victorian pub near the Smithfield meat market, are so popular that it's advisable to book. At lunchtimes (noon-2pm), traditional pub grub such as steak & kidney pie (£9) and sticky toffee pudding (£3.50) can be washed down with house wine at £12.50 a bottle. / breakfast & L only, closed Sat & Sun.

Horse SE1 £15
124 Westminster Bridge Rd   7928 6277   2–3D
In the thin area near Lambeth North tube, this fairly basic new gastropub has been a welcome arrival. There's nothing very remarkable about the cooking, but dishes such as a burger with all the trimmings (£6.75) are competently realised. The house wine is £10 a bottle. / 10.30 pm; closed Sat L & Sun; no Amex; need 6+ to book.

Hudson's SW15 £19 A
113 Lower Richmond Rd   8785 4522   10–1A
This jolly Putney bistro is a consistent success-story. That's partially due to the reasonable prices – Portuguese chicken wings (£3.95) to start, and shepherd's pie (£9.95) would be typical. Breakfasts from around the world are also something of a novelty feature all week (10am-noon), as is the 'happy hour' (4pm-7pm, Mon-Sat) – when house wine (normally £9.95 a bottle) and many menu items come at reduced prices. / 10.30 pm.

The Ifield SW10 £20 A
59 Ifield Rd   7351 4900   5–3A
As we go to press, a Belsize Park sibling is being added to this Earl's Court gastropub, which has become a popular, but still laid-back destination. Starters cost around £5 (for, say, eggs Benedict), and the substantial main courses – including fish & chips or bangers & mash – are around a tenner. Puddings, around £3, also tend to be of the comfort-food variety. The house wine is £10 a bottle. / 11 pm; Mon-Thu D only, Fri-Sun open L & D.

sign up for the survey at www.hardens.com

Ikkyu W1 £18 ★
67a Tottenham Court Rd   7636 9280   2–1C
Great sushi and other tasty traditional Japanese dishes are the hallmarks of this top-value restaurant near Goodge Street tube. You could have a large platter of sushi to share for about £12, or perhaps seafood noodles (£4.60) washed down with a glass of sake (£3) or a bottle of house wine (£11). / 10 pm; closed Sat & Sun L; no Switch; no smoking area.

Inaho W2 £15* ★★
4 Hereford Rd   7221 8495   6–1B
Japanese food may be becoming more available and affordable in London, but this tiny Bayswater café is still worth seeking out for brilliant dishes at reasonable prices. The set lunch (£10) is the top-value choice – it might include beef teriyaki, plus an appetiser, miso soup, rice and fruit. At other times, the teriyaki alone would cost £10.50 and a selection of assorted sushi is £14. The house wine is £8.50 a bottle. / 11 pm; closed Sat L & Sun; no Amex or Switch.

Incognico WC2 £20* ★★
117 Shaftesbury Ave   7836 8866   4–2B
The Ladenis family's Gallic brasserie has established itself as one of the more reliable destinations in Theatreland. It's generally outside our price range, but not at lunch or pre-theatre (5pm-7.30pm), when there's a 3-course menu for £12.50. Be warned, though – with house wine at £14 a bottle (£4 a glass), it does slightly stretch our budget. / midnight; closed Sun.

India Club WC2 £12
143 Strand   7836 0650   2–2D
Off the beaten track – up two flights of stairs in a nondescript hotel near Aldwych – this curious, Formica-clad institution has been going for some 50 years. It serves inexpensive curries at around a fiver a plate, with a good selection of vegetarian dishes and dhosas (fried pancakes, £3.60). You can bring your own wine (no corkage), or fetch a drink from the hotel bar. / 10.50 pm; closed Sun; no credit cards; need 6+ to book.

Indian Ocean SW17 £15
216 Trinity Rd   8672 7740   10–2C
It's nothing remarkable to look at, but this comfortable-enough Wandsworth subcontinental has long been a culinarily consistent performer. Curries are around the £6.25 mark, and the house wine £7.25 a bottle. / 11.30 pm; no smoking area.

for updates visit www.hardens.com

Italian Kitchen WC1 £15*
43 New Oxford St   7836 1011   2–1C
This unpretentious Italian, not far from the British Museum, used to be one of the best budget destinations in town. It's gone badly off the boil in recent times, but the 2-course set menu (4pm-7pm) – perhaps minestrone soup followed by spaghetti bolognaise for £7.95 – still makes it a handy early-evening destination. The house wine is £12.95 a bottle. / 10.45 pm.

Itsu £17   A★
103 Wardour St, W1   7479 4794   3–2D
118 Draycott Ave, SW3   7584 5522   5–2C
These glossy Soho and Chelsea conveyor-sushi operations are as much about style as about substance, but they still make fun and elegant places for a light meal. You pay per plate (£1.50-£3.45) – which might contain anything from a conventional sushi dish to something rather more 'evolved' (and including puddings which are positively European). The house wine is £10.15 a bottle. / www.itsu.co.uk; 11 pm; smoking in the bar only; no booking.

Jashan £12   ★
1-2 Coronet Pde, Ealing Rd, HA0   8900 9800   1–1A
19 Turnpike Ln, N8   8340 9880   1–1C
If you haven't booked, expect to queue at these no-frills (but very professionally-run) cafés in Turnpike Lane and Wembley (veggie only). The menus offer an enormous choice, but all of good quality – at the former branch you might have the likes of sweetcorn & paneer pakoras (£3.75) followed by tandoori lamb (£5.75) and rice (£2.25). No alcohol. / www.jashanrestaurants.com; 10.45 pm; N8 closed Mon.

Jenny Lo's Tea House SW1 £14   ★
14 Eccleston St   7259 0399   2–4B
Noodles, noodles and more noodles (£5.50-£7.95) are the proposition at this small and welcoming parlour not far from Victoria Station, run by Jenny Lo, the daughter of Britain's most prolific Chinese cookery writer. Wash them down with house wine at £10.50 a bottle or with one of a range of therapeutic teas. / 10 pm; closed Sun; no credit cards; no booking.

Jin Kichi NW3 £20   ★★
73 Heath St   7794 6158   8–1A
There may not be much room for manoeuvre at this tiny Hampstead Japanese, but it's an authentic place with an excellent variety of dishes and extremely efficient staff. Starters are around £3.50 and main courses (perhaps prawn tempura) around £9.90, or you could opt for a 7-piece sushi set (£12.70). The house wine is £13.80 a bottle. / 11 pm; closed Mon, Tue-Fri D only, Sat & Sun open L & D.

sign up for the survey at www.hardens.com

Joy King Lau W1   £15
3 Leicester St   7437 1132   4–3A
The ambience is nothing special, but this large Chinatown establishment is distinguished by very good cooking and (unusually for the area) a friendly welcome. Lunchtime is a good time to visit, for the notable dim sum (£1.90-£3.60), but the à la carte menu — on which most main dishes are about the £6 mark — is also well realised. House wine is £9 a bottle, or drink tea (50p). / 11.30 pm; no Switch.

K10 EC2   £18   ★
20 Copthall Ave   7562 8510   9–2C
Polite, efficient service and a menu of creative dishes have made this conveyor-belt sushi restaurant — in a futuristic basement near Liverpool Street — a big hit with City types. It's best to arrive early, as the queues can be impressive. Most dishes are relatively modestly priced (£1.50-£3.50), but go easy on the house wine, as it's £12.50 a bottle. / www.k10.net; 10 pm; closed Sat & Sun; no smoking; no booking.

Kandoo W2   £14   ★
458 Edgware Rd   7724 2428   8–4A
This Bayswater Lebanese — on a grim stretch of the Edgware Road — offers competent cooking and welcoming service. Your menu choice might be chicken kebabs (£6.95) followed by Persian ice cream (£2.70). Bills are kept well under control by the fact that this is strictly a BYO place (no corkage). / 11.30 pm; no Amex.

Kastoori SW17   £13   ★★
188 Upper Tooting Rd   8767 7027   10–2C
Quality Indian food has made this long-established restaurant, run by a Gujerati family, a notable place of pilgrimage for vegetarians. Bhajis (£2.25), samosas (£1.95), curries (£4.50) and dhosas (£3.75-£4.75), as well as 'family specialities', are all prepared with devotion and expertise. There's an unusually wide-ranging wine list, starting at £7.95 a bottle. / 10.30 pm; closed Mon L & Tue L; no Amex or Switch.

Kennington Lane SE11   £18*   Ⓐ★★
205-209 Kennington Ln   7793 8313   1–3C
This chic brasserie has become the destination of choice for smart Kennington locals. A la carte, it's rather out of our price bracket, but the 2-course set lunch menu (£11.50; also available 6.30pm-7.30pm) allows you to try the inventive cooking for about half the cost of dining à la carte. A selection of sautéed lamb's kidneys with chorizo followed by salmon wrapped in Parma ham would be typical, washed down with house wine at £10.95 a bottle. / www.kenningtonlanerestaurant.com; 10.30 pm; closed Sat L.

for updates visit www.hardens.com

Khan's W2 £10
13-15 Westbourne Grove   7727 5420   6–1C
It must be some measure of the attractions of the cooking that this vast Bayswater subcontinental – often likened to an Indian railway station – seems to have survived its transition to being a 'dry' zone. Decent curries for around £3.70 seem to be at the root of its appeal. / 11.45 pm; no smoking area.

Khan's of Kensington SW7 £17 ★
3 Harrington Rd   7581 2900   5–2B
This more-than-serviceable South Kensington subcontinental offers a standard tandoori menu, plus a sprinkling of more unusual dishes, such as stuffed lotus leaves (£2.55). Main courses – often realised with a lighter touch than the norm – generally cost around £6.95, vegetable side dishes are £3.10 and kulfi is £2.95. The house wine is £9.95 a bottle. / 11.15 pm, Fri & Sat 11.45 pm; no smoking area.

Khyber Pass SW7 £14
21 Bute St   7589 7311   5–2B
The management has apparently changed in recent times, but this (arguably excessively) unpretentious South Kensington Indian seems little changed. For top value, share a 'Khyber Pass Special' (spring chicken in a mildly-spiced sauce, £12.50 for two), but even à la carte you can comfortably stay within our budget. The house wine is £9.25 a bottle. / 11.15 pm; need 4+ to book.

Konditor & Cook £16 ★★
10 Stoney St, SE1   7407 5101   9–4C
66 The Cut, SE1   7620 2700   9–4A
Famous for its large selection of delicious handmade cakes and pastries, these South Bank cafés are certainly not places for those on a diet! Breakfast is available from 8.30am-11.30am, and includes everything from muffins to a full traditional English breakfast. Lunch might include soup with a herb and cheese scone (£3.75), followed by chicken and avocado with bacon club sandwich (£6.95), washed down with house wine at £11.75 a bottle. Note that the tiny Borough Market branch only has seating on sunny days. / The Cut 8 pm – Stoney St 6.30pm; breakfast, L & early evening only; closed Sun; no Amex.

Krungtap SW10 £13
227 Old Brompton Rd   7259 2314   5–2A
It's by no means the 'destination' it once was, but this unpretentious Thai café maintains a regular following from Earl's Court locals, as it still offers good basic curries at reasonable cost (generally around £4.50). The house wine is £8 a bottle. / 10.30 pm.

sign up for the survey at www.hardens.com

Kulu Kulu W1   £17   ★★
76 Brewer St   7734 7316   3–2D
More authentic than most of its competitors, this conveyor-belt sushi bar, located in a Soho street now full of Japanese eateries, has a proper chef who turns out superior snacks on colour-coded plates – grey for £1.20 (salmon or octopus sushi), white for £1.80 (tuna sushi or California rolls), green for £2.40 (eel or scallop sushi) and blue for £3 (tempura). Miso soup (£1.20) and noodles (£2.40) can also be ordered from the kitchen. The house wine is £12 a bottle, but green tea is free. / 10 pm; closed Sun; no Amex; no smoking; no booking.

Lahore Kebab House E1   £13   ★★
2 Umberston St   7488 2551   11–1A
For sheer food value – this is emphatically not a décor experience – it's difficult to beat this famous Pakistani East Ender, especially as it's BYO-only (no corkage). Start with spicy kebabs (75p) and roti (50p), or tikka (£2.50) before moving on to lamb balti (£6) or the superb lamb chops (£6). Finish with kheer (a sort of rice pudding with cardamom, £2). Hold the front page – as we go to press, news reaches us of impending international expansion, to New York City! / midnight; no credit cards.

Lansdowne NW1   £20*   𝔸
90 Gloucester Ave   7483 0409   8–3B
This Primrose Hill spot was one of London's first gastropubs, and it remains riotously popular. Eat in the bar, from the blackboard menu, and you'll be well fed with robust soups (roast tomato and garlic, £4.50) and pâtés, followed by main courses such as pasta, char-grilled meat or fish (about £9-£13). With house wine at £11.50 a bottle, you'll need to exercise some care to keep within our budget. / 10 pm; closed Mon L; no Amex; book only for upstairs.

La Lanterna SE1   £20*
6-8 Mill St   7252 2420   11–2A
A useful stand-by, just south of Tower Bridge, this friendly pizzeria boasts a menu of classic Italian dishes. It's not exactly bargain-basement – many starters cost over a fiver – so stick to bruschetta (£3.95) and the good-quality pizzas and pastas (mostly around £9), washed down with house wine at £11.50 a bottle. / 11 pm; closed Sat L.

Latymers W6   £14   ★
157 Hammersmith Rd   8741 2507   7–2C
The purlieus of the Hammersmith roundabout are hardly awash with foodie possibilities, making the Thai dining room of this not-especially-inviting pub all the more notable. Top value is to be had at lunch, when all the one-plate dishes, such as pad Thai or red duck curry, are under a fiver. In the evening, there are also starters, such as hot and sour chicken soup (£3). The house wine is £10.50 a bottle. / 10 pm; closed Sun; no smoking; no booking at L.

for updates visit www.hardens.com

Laurent NW2   £16   ★
428 Finchley Rd   7794 3603   1–1B
Laurent no longer presides at this famous Cricklewood couscous house, but his departure has made surprisingly little impact on the menu or the standard of its realisation. Brik à l'oeuf (deep-fried pastry containing a soft-centred egg, £2.70) remains the sole starter, and there are five varieties of couscous (from £9) on offer as the main course. For dessert, you might have crème caramel (£3). The wine list includes a number of North African options, with house wine at £10 a bottle. / 11 pm; closed weekday L.

Lemonia NW1   £19   Ⓐ
89 Regent's Park Rd   7586 7454   8–3B
You'll definitely need to book if you want to dine – not difficult, within our budget – at this ever-popular, family-run taverna in Primrose Hill. You can probably just turn up on spec for lunch, though, which is a particularly good time for the bargain-hunter, whether you go for the 2-course menu (£6.75) or even the 3-course 'special' (£7.95). There's a range of Greek wines – house vino comes by the litre (£12). / 11.30 pm; closed Sat L & Sun D; no Amex.

Lisboa Patisserie W10   £4   ★★
57 Golborne Rd   8968 5242   6–1A
This Portuguese coffee house in North Kensington retains its cult status. Pasteis de natas (custard tarts to you and me, 55p) are the speciality which helps draw the crowds, washed down by a coffee for not very much more. / 8 pm; no Amex; no booking.

Little Bay   £12   Ⓐ
228 Belsize Rd, NW6   7372 4699   1–2B
171 Farringdon Rd, EC1   7278 1234   9–1A
Even choosing a 3-course meal à la carte, you'd have some difficulty spending up to our price-limit at these buzzing budget bistros (in Kilburn, and now, Farringdon). You might start with moules marinière (£1.55) followed by a lamb steak (£4.05), finishing with cheesecake (£1.25) – note that these prices all inflate somewhat after 7.15pm, although still fall easily within our budget. Lunch and early-evening set menus are even more economical (£6.95 or less), and house wine is £9.75 a bottle.
/ midnight; NW6 no credit cards – EC1 no Amex; NW6 no smoking area; NW6 need 4+ to book.

LMNT E8   £18   Ⓐ
316 Queensbridge Rd   7249 6727   1–2D
It's not only because Dalston is hardly over-blessed with quality eating-places that this former boozer has made quite a stir. It is in fact mainly due to the startling operatic-Egyptian décor, though the food – including the likes of grilled mackerel (£2.95) and rib-eye steak (£7.95) – is perfectly well done. The house wine is £10.90 a bottle. / www.lmnt.co.uk; 11 pm; no Amex.

sign up for the survey at www.hardens.com

Lomo SW10 £17   Ⓐ
222-224 Fulham Rd   7349 8848   5–3B
One of the most perennially satisfactory places to hang out on Chelsea's 'Beach', this unpretentious, modern tapas bar offers tasty snacks at reasonable prices. Most dishes on the menu, which is supplemented by a blackboard list of daily specials, are around the £4-£7 mark. The house vino is £10.50, and there's also an exemplary selection of sherries. / www.lomo.co.uk; 11.30 pm; closed weekday L; no booking after 8.30 pm.

The Lord Palmerston NW5 £18
33 Dartmouth Park Hill   7485 1578   8–1B
Reasonable prices – roast guinea fowl with red cabbage will set you back £10.75 and caramelised butternut squash with mushroom risotto £8.50 – are among the attractions which maintain the crush at this gastropub near Archway. Starters, maybe soup or pasta, are under a fiver, and puds, such as blueberry crème brûlée, are £3.50. The house wine is £9.50 a bottle. / 10 pm; no Amex; no booking.

Lots Road SW10 £19   Ⓐ
114 Lots Rd   7352 6645   5–4B
Plain and simple gastropub fare – burgers, salads and the like, with dishes no more than a tenner – are the stock in trade of this airy, elegant and comfortable gastropub, on the way in to Chelsea Harbour. The house wine is £11 a bottle. / 10 pm.

Lou Pescadou SW5 £18*   ★
241 Old Brompton Rd   7370 1057   5–3A
The 3-course set lunch (£9.90, £13.50 at weekends) at this long-established, and very French, Earl's Court fish restaurant has always been a beacon of value. You might start with asparagus soup, followed by moules marinière, and finish with chocolate mousse. A la carte, a meal here would be well beyond our budget. The house wine is £11.20 a bottle. / midnight.

Lundum's SW7 £19*   Ⓐ★★
119 Old Brompton Rd   7373 7774   5–2B
This pretty, family-run Danish restaurant in South Kensington has attracted a devoted following, and it's the sort of place which would be ideal for a (slightly old-fashioned) encounter of a romantic nature. It's out of our price-bracket in the evening, but makes an ideal venue for a relaxed lunch, when the 2-course menu (£12.50) – your selection might be smoked halibut with horseradish mousse, followed by salmon with cucumber confit – can be washed down with house wine at £11.50 a bottle. / 10.30 pm; closed Sun D.

for updates visit www.hardens.com

Ma Goa SW15 £19 ★
244 Upper Richmond Rd   8780 1767   10–2B
This family-run Goan bistro in Putney has long been a reliable destination for lovers of subcontinental fare. Top value is to be had from the 2-course set menu (always available, £9) which one might choose shrimps with tomato followed by Goan pork vindaloo. It also offers interesting specialities à la carte, including sausages with cinnamon and cloves (£4) and chicken cooked in 'amot-tik' (Goan hot & sour sauce, £7.75), though you'd need to exercise some care to stay within our price-limit. The house wine is £9.50 a bottle. / www.magoa.co.uk; 11 pm; closed Mon, Tue–Sat D only, Sun open L & D.

Made in Italy SW3 £20 A★
249 King's Rd   7352 1880   5–3C
Pizza and pasta dishes (around £9.50) are the specialities at this jolly and quite authentic – that's to say smoky and overcrowded – Chelsea spot, which is decorated in rustic style. The house wine is £11 a bottle. / 11.30 pm; closed weekday L; no credit cards.

Madhu's Brilliant UB1 £16 ★
39 South Rd   8574 1897   1–3A
The Punjabi-influenced menu at this Southall Indian spans the range from specialities such as boozi bafu (rich lamb stew, £6) to the more prosaic chicken tikka masala (£7). House wine is £8 a bottle, and there's also a good range of imported beers.
/ 11.30 pm; closed Tue, Sat L & Sun L.

Maghreb N1 £18 ★
189 Upper St   7226 2305   8–2D
Especially if you're looking for a group venue in Islington, it's well worth checking out this comfortable Moroccan bistro, where you can dine à la carte quite comfortably within our price-limit. Starters are the likes of merguez (spicy lamb) sausages (£4.50) and your main course might be aromatic duck tajine with apricots (£9). A bottle of the house wine is £10.95. / www.maghrebrestaurant.co.uk; 11.30 pm; D only.

Maison Bertaux W1 £5 A★
28 Greek St   7437 6007   4–2A
Gallic charm and idiosyncratic service still make Soho's oldest pâtisserie (est.1871) a destination of some note. It's a delightful place to breakfast on coffee (£1.50) and croissants (from £1), or to while away the afternoon scoffing mouth-watering cream cakes (£1.90-£3). / 8.30 pm; no credit cards; no smoking area.

sign up for the survey at www.hardens.com

Malabar W8 £17 A★

27 Uxbridge St   7727 8800   6–2B

More stylish than your average neighbourhood tandoori, this civilised subcontinental, tucked away behind Notting Hill Gate, has long been a local favourite. Starters, such as devilled kaleja (griddled chicken livers) and deep-fried prawn samosas cost less than a fiver, while a main course could combine nimbu gosht (lamb curry with lemon, £6.50) with peshwari naan (£2.40), washed down with house wine at £9.25 a bottle.
/ www.malabar-restaurant.co.uk; 11.15 pm; no Amex.

Malabar Junction WC1 £20* ★

107 Gt Russell St   7580 5230   2–1C

It looks pretty ordinary from the outside, so it can be a surprise to discover the soothing interior of this Bloomsbury Indian (which comes complete with a conservatory). The mainly Keralan menu includes ample choice for vegetarians (spinach vadi, £3.50) and lots of fish (king prawn curry, £9.50). Helpful staff provide encouragement for those who want to try something a little different, but, with house wine at £10 a bottle, you'll need to take some care to keep within our price-limit. / 11.30 pm; no smoking area.

Mandalay W2 £12 ★★

444 Edgware Rd   7258 3696   8–4A

Sample the cuisine of Burma at this friendly, family-run café, around the corner from Lord's – at lunch, a selection of dishes (with coffee) will set you back a mere £5.90. At other times, a typical meal might be shrimp & bean sprout fritters (£3.90), followed by chicken with lemongrass (£5.50) and coconut rice (£2.10). For pudding, don't miss the fragrant sweet coconut jelly (£1.50). Polish it all off with house wine at a reasonable £7.90 a bottle. / 10.30 pm; closed Sun; no smoking.

Mandarin Kitchen W2 £17* ★★

14-16 Queensway   7727 9012   6–2C

This place is reputed to sell more lobsters than anywhere else in London, but sadly the house speciality of this Bayswater Chinese – one of the capital's top oriental seafood specialists – falls outside our budget. There is a 2-course set dinner (£10.90), however, or you can sample more modest dishes such as clams in black bean sauce (£5.90) or squid in ginger sauce (£7.90), washed down with house wine at £10.50 a bottle. / 11.15 pm.

for updates visit www.hardens.com

Mango Room NW1   £ 20   A★
10 Kentish Town Rd   7482 5065   8–3B
This vibrantly-decorated Anglo-Caribbean restaurant in Camden Town, which is at the top end of our price-range, remains an extremely popular destination. For a true taste of the place, start with crab & potato balls (£4.50) and move on to the infamous Camden curried goat (£9), or traditional jerk chicken with rice & peas (£9.50) washed down with Red Stripe (£3), or house wine at £11.50 a bottle. / 10.45 pm; closed Mon L; no Amex.

Manna NW3   £19*   ★
4 Erskine Rd   7722 8028   8–3B
A weekend brunch (12.30pm-3pm) is among the options available at this venerable Primrose Hill vegetarian, but the place also makes a useful venue for weekday lunch (when prices are low) or dinner (when you will have to choose carefully to stay within our budget, as few main courses cost less than £10). Lunchtime options may include the likes of smoked Mozzarella and basil risotto cakes (£5.50), followed by the pasta of the day (£8.25). The house wine is £10.50 a bottle. / www.manna-veg.com; 10.45 pm; closed weekday L; no Amex; no smoking.

Manorom WC2   £ 18
16 Maiden Ln   7240 4139   4–3D
The 2-course set menus (£10.95 at lunch, £13.95 at dinner) at this small, cosy Thai – just a couple of minutes' walk from generally overpriced Covent Garden – are especially worth knowing about. Otherwise the fairly standard menu includes the likes of fishcakes (£4.50) or chicken with ginger (£6.25), with ice cream (£3.50) to follow. The house wine is £10.50 a bottle. / 11 pm; closed Sat L & Sun; no booking, Thu-Sat.

Marine Ices NW3   £ 15
8 Haverstock Hill   7482 9003   8–2B
It's as a family destination that this long-established Chalk Farm pizza and pasta stop (most dishes are around £6) is of most interest – especially as this is London's most popular destination for ice cream. For dessert, you might go the whole hog, with a deliciously decadent sundae (around £6), or display super-human restraint and just have a single scoop of sorbet (£1.35). The house wine is £7.80 a bottle. / 11 pm; no Amex; no smoking area.

Masala Zone W1   £ 14
9 Marshall St   7287 9966   3–2D
An ideal destination to recover from shopping in nearby Carnaby Street, this welcoming restaurant serves Indian street food in a comfortably modern canteen environment. For maximum budget-control go for a one-tray meal – perhaps a lamb thali (£9) – washed down with house wine at £9.75 a bottle, or an Indian beer at £3.10. / www.realindianfood.com; 11.30 pm; no Amex; no smoking; no booking.

sign up for the survey at www.hardens.com

Mawar W2 £12 ★
175a Edgware Rd   7262 1663   6–1D
It's not what you'd call a glamorous place, but this basement canteen on the unlovely Edgware Road makes up for its setting by offering authentic Malaysian cooking at rock-bottom prices. And if it's a light snack you're after, for a fiver you can choose any three dishes from a range of 15. BYO – no corkage. / 10 pm; no Amex; no smoking area.

Mediterraneo W11 £18* 𝔸★
37 Kensington Park Rd   7792 3131   6–1A
This mock-rustic Italian – sibling to the ever-popular Osteria Basilico nearby – has established itself as one of the most popular locations on Notting Hill's trendy restaurant strip. Unsurprisingly, it's a little outside our budget in the evening, but the 2-course weekday-only set lunch (£11.50) is within it, offering the likes of soup, salad or carpaccio followed by pan-fried salmon or pasta. The house wine is £11.50 a bottle. / 11.30 pm; booking: max 8.

Mela WC2 £16 ★
152-156 Shaftesbury Ave   7836 8635   4–2B
'Country-style cooking' – that's Indian country-style cooking – has made a big name for this busy restaurant near Cambridge Circus. You can just about dine within our budget, but the real focus of interest for the budget diner is the lunchtime 'paratha' concept – select a bread or pancake with a choice of hot fillings to create a snack, such as chicken tikka naan (£4.50). The pre-theatre 3-course menu (5pm-7.30pm daily) is also of note – it's £10.95, the same as a bottle of the house wine.
/ www.melarestaurant.co.uk; midnight; no smoking area.

Melati W1 £16
21 Great Windmill St   7437 2745   3–2D
It's not much to look at, but this cramped Indonesian canteen in Soho has long been a beacon of interesting cooking at reasonable prices in the heart of the West End – making it an ideal place for a pre-theatre bite. Most starters and veggie mains are under a fiver, while meaty main dishes (such as beef satay) cost a pound or two more. The house wine is £9.45 a bottle. / 11.30 pm, Fri & Sat 12.30 am.

Mesclun N16 £14* ★
24 Stoke Newington Church St   7249 5029   1–1C
The past year has been a slightly up-and-down one for this Stoke Newington restaurant, which had made quite a reputation for its innovative contemporary cooking. It's still a good-value choice though, as long as you stick to the set menu, always available, which offers two courses for £7.50 (£10 for 3) – moules marinière, roast bream, and sticky toffee pudding are a typical selection. The house wine is £11 a bottle.
/ www.mesclun.co.uk; 11 pm; no Amex.

for updates visit www.hardens.com

Meson don Felipe SE1 £14 Ⓐ
53 The Cut   7928 3237   9–4A
This lively and authentically Spanish institution – one of London's best-known tapas bars – is handy for both the Old and Young Vics. It features an infamous flamenco guitarist, who performs nightly, so it may be wise to go with noisy friends to drown him out! A large jug of sangria (£11.50) is recommended to wash down the good tapas, which cost £2-£5 each, or drink house Rioja at £10.50 a bottle. / 11 pm; closed Sun; no Amex; no booking after 8 pm.

Le Metro SW3 £19*
28 Basil St   7589 6286   5–1D
Discreetly tucked-away by Harrods, this bistro in the basement of a smart, small hotel is a useful destination at any time of day. It serves breakfasts until 11.30am (from £3.50, for egg and toast). Its main attractions, however, are a long list of wines by the glass (with house wine starting at £10.95 a bottle) and a short menu of light meals – perhaps fish and chips (£9.50) or a cheese soufflé (£6.50). / www.capitalgrp.co.uk; 9.45 pm; closed Sun L & D, but open for breakfast; no smoking area.

Mildred's W1 £17 ★
45 Lexington St   7494 1634   3–2D
This popular veggie café recently moved across Soho to the more spacious (and harder-to-find) premises occupied by the former Lexington. Cannellini bean falafel with chilli sauce and tahini (£3.90), followed by Thai green vegetable curry with basmati rice (£6.50) are typical dishes, or try the 'burger' of the day (£5.80). Wash it all down with organic house wine at £10 a bottle. / 11 pm; closed Sun D; only Switch; no smoking; no booking.

Mirch Masala £10 ★★
1416 London Road, SW16   8679 1828   10–2C
213 Upper Tooting Rd, SW17   8672 7500   10–2D
If you're looking for top-quality Indian food at rock-bottom prices, you won't do much better than these plain but welcoming canteens in Norbury and, more recently, Tooting. For top value get there between noon and 4pm for the buffet (£5.99), which offers three starters and five main courses, as well as rice and naan bread. BYO – no corkage charge. / midnight; SW17 no credit cards.

Mohsen W14 £15 ★
152 Warwick Rd   7602 9888   7–1D
Given its uninspiring location (close to the Olympia Homebase), its cramped conditions and the fact that it serves neither dessert nor coffee, this Persian canteen remains remarkably popular. BYO, or drink tea to accompany generous portions of tasty fare, such as char-grilled aubergine (£3) and kebabs – at £9, the latter may seem rather expensive, but they are, in fact, thoroughly worth it. / 11.30 pm; no credit cards; no booking.

sign up for the survey at www.hardens.com

Mon Plaisir WC2 £14* A★
19-21 Monmouth St   7836 7243   4–2B
The pre-theatre menu (table must be vacated by 8pm) at this wonderfully old-fashioned Gallic bistro has long offered some of the very best value in the West End. Your 2-course menu (£13.95) might include the likes of pork rillettes followed by a minute steak, and includes a glass of wine, coffee and service. Do note that prices at other times are well outside our limit. / www.monplaisir.co.uk; 11.15 pm; closed Sat L & Sun.

Moro EC1 £18* A★★
34-36 Exmouth Mkt   7833 8336   9–1A
A trendy venue that actually – unlike so many others – manages to maintain its standards, this Moorish venture in Clerkenwell offers very accomplished and consistent cooking. It's no great surprise that it's outside our price-range in the dining room, but the bar offers affordable tapas dishes (from £3). A selection might include the likes of roasted almonds with paprika, houmous and quails eggs, which you could wash down with house wine at £10.50 a bottle. / 10.30 pm; closed Sat L & Sun.

Moshi Moshi £16
2nd Floor, Cabot Place East, E14   7512 9911   11–1C
Unit 24, Liverpool St Station, EC2   7247 3227   9–2D
7-8 Limeburner Ln, EC4   7248 1808   9–2A
The notion of pay-per-plate sushi (£1.50-£3.50) travelling around a bar on a conveyor belt seemed novel when this pioneer operation started up in Liverpool Street station. It now has three City outlets (and numerous imitators) – it may not be as 'unique' as it was, but it remains very popular. Especially at lunch, hungry suits cluster like traders in a bull market (remember those?). Set meals, including miso soup and rice, cost £4-£17, with house wine at £11.50 a bottle, or beer for £2.90. / www.moshimoshi.co.uk; 9.30 pm; closed Sat & Sun; no Amex; EC2 & E14 no smoking – EC4 no smoking area; EC2 & E14 no booking.

Mr Kong WC2 £14 ★
21 Lisle St   7437 7341   4–3A
This Chinatown basement fixture is a cut above its local rivals, and the chef/patron produces some interesting specialities such as deep-fried stuffed beancurd skin (£7.50) alongside more standard Cantonese dishes – for example, prawn toast (£5.80) and sweet & sour chicken (£5.90). The house wine is £8.70 a bottle. / 2.45 am.

Nautilus NW6 £15 ★
27-29 Fortune Green Rd   7435 2532   1–1B
A major refurb has now swept away the former '60s style of this West Hampstead veteran chippy. As ever though, all the fish is coated in matzo-meal rather than batter before frying. Start with smoked salmon (£3) before tackling a plate of cod and chips (£8.50), washed down with house wine at £8.50 a bottle. / 10 pm; closed Sun; no Amex; no booking.

for updates visit www.hardens.com

Nayaab SW6 £17
309 New King's Rd 7731 6993 10–1B
The proud boast of this Parsons Green Indian – which had a major refurbishment in August 2002 – is that its menu includes dishes that are unavailable elsewhere, such as nihari (slow-cooked lamb, £7.95) and twelve kadi murg (chicken in a unique sauce, £7.95). More conventional dishes are mostly under £6, with an impressive range of biryanis from just a pound more, and the house wine is £9.95 a bottle. / midnight; D only.

Need The Dough! SW11 £18
281 Lavender Hill 7924 8021 10–2C
Can Six Continents – the outfit formerly known as Bass – run a decent restaurant? Those who have noted the ever-declining standards at the famous Brown's chain since they took it over may think not, but this bright Battersea pizza and pasta stop (most dishes around £7) gives some cause for hope. It's a light and airy place with a nice outside area (which bizarre local licensing rules won't allow them to use in the evening!). On the evidence of our visit, the best meal is to be had from a selection of fresh and tasty antipasti (three for £5) and some freshly-baked focaccia (£1.95), washed down with a bottle of the house vino for £9.75. / 11 pm; no smoking area.

New Mayflower W1 £18 ★
68-70 Shaftesbury Ave 7734 9207 4–3A
Tinted windows hide a clean and unfussy interior at this top Cantonese restaurant, on the edge of Chinatown, which features a few unusual dishes including fillet steak Chinese-style (£8.30). There is a 3-course set menu for £12, but the main menu offers ample choice within our price range, especially as house wine is only £8.50 a bottle. / 3.45 am; D only.

New World W1 £16
1 Gerrard Pl 7734 0677 4–3A
It's the lunchtime dim sum (from £1.80 per dish) – served from trolleys – which is the culinary highlight of this large and chaotic Chinatown landmark. Its gaudy red and gold façade may appear to more striking effect in the evening, but dinner is a much less exciting affair, though the long menu offers ample choice within our budget. House wine is £9.95 a bottle. / 11.45 pm; no smoking area; no booking, Sun L.

sign up for the survey at www.hardens.com

Niksons SW11 £19* A★
172-174 Northcote Rd   7228 2285   10–2C
This Battersea bar/restaurant looks pretty ordinary from the outside, but it has an unusually atmospheric rear dining room. It's out of our price bracket in the evening, but there's a 2-course set lunch menu (£12.50, not Sun), from which you might have the likes of venison carpaccio with fig chutney, followed by chicken ballotine with olive oil mash. Alternatively, the bar (a more ordinary space) serves substantial snacks, such as steak burger & chips (£8.50). The house wine is £12 a bottle. / 10.30 pm; closed Mon L.

Noor Jahan SW5 £20
2a Bina Gdns   7373 6522   5–2B
The Earl's Court/South Kensington border was quite a scruffy place 30 years ago – or at least much less smart than it is today. This 'local' Indian has smartened itself up a bit with the passing of the years, but it's still just a good basic subcontinental at heart, and very popular – chicken tikka masala (£7.50, with pilau rice at £2.50) is a popular dish. Wash it down with house wine at £9.95 a bottle. / 11 pm.

North Sea Fish WC1 £18   ★
7-8 Leigh St   7387 5892   8–4C
The dining room of this long-established Bloomsbury chippy has something of the ambience of a seaside tea-room. It's a pretty comfortable place, though, and the fish and chips (generally around £8.50) are pretty good too – early evenings are especially busy, so it's well worth booking ahead. The house wine is £9.95 a bottle. / 10.30 pm; closed Sun.

Noto EC2 £17   ★
2-3 Bassishaw Highwalk   7256 9433   9–2B
Filling fare without pretensions is the theme at this transport-café-style Japanese establishment in the Barbican (now without its EC4 sibling), which offers a good range of sushi (£1.50-£3.20 per piece), noodles and curries (both around £7-£9). The house wine is £9.90 a bottle. / www.noto.co.uk; 9.45 pm; closed Sat & Sun; no Amex.

O'Zon TW1 £19
33-35 London Rd, Twickenham   8891 3611   1–4A
If you're looking for a decent place to eat in the heart of downtown Twickenham, this new Chinese restaurant (on the former site of one of the dismal Yellow River Cafés) is worth seeking out. On Sundays (or by prior telephone agreement at other times), an all-you-can-eat menu is available for £13.80 – not very different from the amount you'd probably spend à la carte. The house wine is £9.80 a bottle. / 11 pm.

for updates visit www.hardens.com

Odette's NW1   £20*   A★★
130 Regent's Park Rd   7586 5486   8–3B
This pretty and romantic Primrose Hill restaurant has long been one of the best in north London, so it's no great surprise that it's well out of our price-bracket in the evening. At lunchtime, though, you can enjoy a 3-course menu for a modest £12.50 – you might choose sea scallop risotto followed by roast lamb, with chocolate mousse to finish. The house wine is reasonably priced, at £11.95 a bottle. / 11 pm; closed Sat L & Sun.

Old Parr's Head W14   £14
120 Blythe Rd   7371 4561   7–1C
A tiny rear courtyard adds to the charm of this cosy Olympia boozer, which is of most note as a good destination for an inexpensive Thai meal. Mixed starters (£4) might be followed by red chicken curry (£5.95), and accompanied by a bottle of house wine (£10). / 10 pm; no Amex.

Ophim W1   £19*   ★
139 Wardour St   7434 9899   3–2D
This richly-decorated new Soho Indian offers a treat for the budget diner – the buffet on the ground floor, where £13.50 (£7.50 at lunch) literally buys you everything on the menu! All the dishes are delivered to your table, and re-filled when empty – the menu might include tomato & lemon soup, aubergine tandoori and tilapia fish curry. Only desserts (£3) and drinks (Cobra, £3) cost extra. In the basement, there's a (more expensive) fine-dining restaurant and bar. / www.ophim.com; 11 pm, Fri & Sat 11.30 pm; closed Sun; no smoking area.

Oriental City Food Court NW9   £12   ★
399 Edgware Rd   8200 6888   1–1A
'Colindale' and 'exotic' may seem to be two words without any great natural affinity, but this (dare one say) dull north London suburb houses one of the most interesting foodie destinations in town – the food court of a large shopping centre catering for the capital's Asian community. Oriental street food experience doesn't come much more authentic than this – not in Europe, anyway – and it's difficult to spend much more than a tenner. / 9.30 pm; no credit cards; no smoking area; no booking.

Osteria Basilico W11   £20*   A★
29 Kensington Park Rd   7727 9957   6–1A
This 'Tuscan farmhouse-style' joint is perennially packed with young Notting Hill trendies, and it's best to arrive early if you want a table. Prices are right at the top end of our budget, so you'll need to stick to the pasta dishes (around £7), after, perhaps, the soup of the day (£4.30). House wine is £9.50 a bottle. / 11 pm; no booking, Sat L.

sign up for the survey at www.hardens.com

Ozer W1 £17* A★
4-5 Langham Pl   7323 0505   3–1C
This stylish restaurant, just a few paces north of Oxford Circus, is especially notable as a good destination for a break-from-shopping lunch, and if you stick to the set menus, it's always within our budget. A full meze selection (£11.50 per person) makes for a convivial light meal, and there are sometimes quite proteinaceous 2-course set menus available for as little as £5. The house wine is £12.50 a bottle. / midnight.

Palatino W4 £16* ★
6 Turnham Green Ter   8994 0086   7–2A
This recently-refurbished Turnham Green Italian is towards the top end of your standard local restaurants. The top-value 2-course set lunch at £8.95 is a key attraction, from which you might choose bruschetta followed by grilled lamb. A la carte, you'd have to base your meal around pizza or pasta (£8.50-£9) to stay within budget. The house wine is £10.55 a bottle.
/ 11 pm; no smoking area.

Pan-Asian Canteen SW1 £17 ★
153 Knightsbridge   7589 6627   5–1D
A bit of a hidden gem, in the heart of Knightsbridge, this modernistic first-floor dining room of a grand traditional pub offers good Thai dishes – most priced around the £6 mark – at low-level communal tables. The house wine is £11 a bottle.
/ 10.30 pm; no smoking area.

Paolo W1 £19
16 Percy St   7637 9900   2–1C
This recently-established Italian restaurant on the fringe of Fitzrovia offers competent cooking at reasonable prices. For our money, its light and bright setting is more suited to lunch than to dinner, but you can stay within our budget at any time if you go for one of the pasta options (around £8.50), accompanied by house wine at £10.50 a bottle. / www.dapaolorestaurants.com; 11.15 pm; closed Sun.

The Papaya Tree W8 £18 ★
209 Kensington High St   7937 2260   7–1D
A family-run Thai restaurant, hidden away in a basement beneath the hustle and bustle of Kensington High Street. It offers better value than anything else you'll find in the vicinity. Dining a la carte, you might choose chicken satay (£4.95) and follow it with green Thai curry (£6.95), or at lunch the one-plate specials cost little more than a fiver. House wine is £11.95 a bottle. / 11 pm; no smoking area.

for updates visit www.hardens.com

Parade W5 £19* A★
18-19 The Mall   8810 0202   1–3A
*This spacious and plainly-decorated Ealing dining room –
a sibling to Barnes's long-popular Sonny's – offers interesting
contemporary cooking. Dinner is well outside our budget,
but lunch – when the likes of gazpacho followed by pork with
mustard and chive sauce will set you back all of £12 – is not.
The house wine is £10.50 a bottle.* / 10.30 pm; closed Sun D.

The Parsee N19 £ 20 ★★
34 Highgate Hill   7272 9091   8–1C
*Highgate has for too long been something of a vacuum when it
comes to quality restaurants. This year-old subcontinental –
which specialises in the Parsee cuisine of India – offers unusual
dishes such as 'akoori' (masala scrambled eggs, £3.95) or
dhansak (lentil & lamb curry with brown rice, £10.95), all
patiently explained by notably solicitous service. Though
reasonably priced, this is emphatically not a budget Indian,
as demonstrated by house wine at £12.90 a bottle.*
/ www.theparsee.com; 10.45 pm; D only, closed Sun; no smoking area.

Patio W12 £19*
5 Goldhawk Rd   8743 5194   7–1C
*Thanks to its festive atmosphere and the fact that its
good-value 3-course menu (£11.90) is always available, this
Mittel-European Shepherd's Bush institution is ideal for parties
(and pretty good for romance, too). Your meal might comprise
Polish chicken consommé, beef stroganoff and a home-made
pudding, perhaps apple charlotte. The menu includes a free
shot of vodka, but extra party lubrication comes in the form of
house wine at £9.50 a bottle.* / 11.30 pm; closed Sat L & Sun L.

Pâtisserie Valerie £ 9
105 Marylebone High St, W1   7935 6240   2–1A
44 Old Compton St, W1   7437 3466   4–2A
8 Russell St, WC2   7240 0064   4–3D
215 Brompton Rd, SW3   7823 9971   5–2C
*The array of tempting goodies in the window make this
impressive chain of pâtisseries hard to resist. They are not just
for the sweet-of-tooth, though – there's plenty in the savoury
line, such as sandwiches (£2-£5), large salads (£7.95),
mini-quiches (£2.75), and so on. The menu and style varies
somewhat from branch to branch – our favourites are the
Soho original and the big and bustly outlet near Harrods.*
/ www.patisserie-valerie.co.uk; 7 pm-11 pm, Sun 6 pm (Soho 7 pm);
no smoking area; no booking.

sign up for the survey at www.hardens.com

Paul £11 Ⓐ★
115 Marylebone High St, W1   7224 5615   2–1A
29-30 Bedford St, WC2   7836 3304   4–3C
Covent Garden and Marylebone have recently joined company with almost all French cities of any note in having branches of that country's major bakery/café chain. They aren't the place for a blow-out, but if you're looking for a light lunch – perhaps a quiche (£4.50) followed by one of the tempting pastries, maybe a tarte au citron (£2.50) – you'd be hard pushed to do better. No alcohol. / 8pm; no smoking; no booking.

Pellicano SW3 £19* ★
19-21 Elystan St   7589 3718   5–2C
In its backstreet location near Brompton Cross, this pleasant trattoria is something of a locals' secret, and it's beginning to gather quite a following. You couldn't dine here within our price limit, but the 2-course set lunch (£12.50) offers the likes of bresaola with lemon followed by veal in Marsala sauce, washed down by house wine at £13 a bottle. / 11 pm.

The Pepper Tree SW4 £12 Ⓐ
19 Clapham Common S'side   7622 1758   10–2D
This canteen-style Clapham Thai is one of south London's most perennially popular places to eat (and you may well have to queue). Well-priced, quality grub is part of the attraction – mushroom tom yam (£2.25) and chicken noodles (£4.75), for example – but quick service is another plus, contributing to the very happy atmosphere. House wine is £8.50 a bottle. / 11 pm, Mon & Sun 10.30 pm; no Amex; no smoking area; no booking at D.

The Perseverance WC1 £20
63 Lamb's Conduit St   7405 8278   2–1D
There's a rather 'proper' atmosphere – by boozer standards, at least – at this year-old Bloomsbury gastropub. You'd have to choose reasonably carefully to stay within our price limit, but it's possible if you go for the likes of smoked salmon with quails eggs (£5.50) and gnocchi with blue cheese, walnuts and broccoli (£10.75), washed down with house wine at £10.50 a bottle. You'd be hard pushed to find a better lazy Sunday lunch venue – the roast of the day is served from midday till 6pm. / 9 pm; closed Sat L & Sun D.

Petit Auberge N1 £17
283 Upper St   7359 1046   8–2D
This is emphatically not a foodie choice, but if you're looking for a 'something for all the family' destination in Islington, this bistro makes a pleasant, if not inspired, destination. It offers a long menu of simple Gallic-inspired dishes – snails (£4.50) and rabbit casserole (£8.95), for example – at quite reasonable prices. There is also a 2-course set lunch menu for just £5.50 – perhaps courgette soup followed by lamb stew. The house wine is £9.50 a bottle. / 11 pm; no Amex.

for updates visit www.hardens.com

Phoenicia W8 £17* ★

11-13 Abingdon Rd   7937 0120   5–1A

You couldn't dine here within our budget, but it's the 2- and 3-course set lunch menus (£9.95 and £11.95) which are top tips for budget diners at this long-established, family-run Kensington Lebanese. Typical dishes include a choice of kebabs, grilled aubergines and so on, washed down with house wine at £12.90 a bottle. / 11.45 pm; no smoking area.

Phoenix Bar & Grill SW15 £20* A★

Pentlow St   8780 3131   10–1A

This bright and airy Putney restaurant has a reputation for consistently delivering contemporary cooking of an unusually high standard. To stay within budget you'll have to dine at lunchtime (not Sun), or early evening (order before 7.45pm, Sun-Thu), when a 2-course set menu (£13.50) is available. Roast tomatoes with Mozzarella, followed by grilled salmon and caperberry salad, might be your choice, washed down with house wine at £10.95 a bottle. / 11 pm; no smoking area.

The Pilot W4 £18

56 Wellesley Rd   8994 0828   7–2A

Nice places to eat are not especially thick on the ground in the environs of Gunnersbury tube, so it's well worth bearing in mind this newly-trendified boozer (which benefits from a pleasant garden). The food has no great aspirations, but realisation of dishes such as Spanish charcuterie (£5,50) and liver & bacon with root vegetable mash (£8.50) is very competent. The house wine is £10 a bottle. / 10 pm.

La Piragua N1 £14

176 Upper St   7354 2843   8–2D

A lively Latino spot in Islington, which makes a great destination for a party. It's popular for its interesting Colombian cuisine, and what are reputed to be the biggest Argentinean steaks in town — all at great prices (with starters from about £2.55, and main courses from £6.95). House wine — from an all-South American list — is £9 a bottle. / midnight; no Amex.

Pizza Metro SW11 £18 A★★

64 Battersea Rise   7228 3812   10–2C

A constant crush of Italian expats hints at the extremely high standards of this cramped Battersea Italian, where top-quality pizza — sold by the metre (£23-£33, for about six people) — is the special draw. Antipasti (around £5 each) are good too, and a carafe of house wine costs £9.95. Booking is essential. / 11 pm; closed Mon, Tue-Fri D only, Sat & Sun open L & D.

sign up for the survey at www.hardens.com

Pizza on the Park SW1 £18 Ⓐ
11 Knightsbridge   7235 5273   5–1D
A grand and airy setting is a particular strength of this long-established pizzeria, whose location makes for special popularity before or after a walk in Hyde Park. The place is a PizzaExpress in disguise, and so offers all the chain's usual pizzas (£7-£10.75), as well as more substantial dishes such as chilli con carne (£8.25). There's even a breakfast menu, making this an elegant place to start your day. The house wine is £12.50 a bottle. / midnight; no smoking area; no booking.

PizzaExpress £19
154 Victoria St, SW1   7828 1477   2–4C
46 Moreton St, SW1   7592 9488   2–4B
85 Victoria St, SW1   7222 5270   2–4C
10 Dean St, W1   7437 9595   3–1D
13-14 Thayer St, W1   7935 2167   2–1A
133 Baker St, W1   7486 0888   2–1A
20 Greek St, W1   7734 7430   4–2A
21-22 Barrett St, W1   7629 1001   3–1A
23 Bruton Pl, W1   7495 1411   3–2B
29 Wardour St, W1   7437 7215   4–3A
4 Langham Pl, W1   7580 3700   2–1B
6 Upper St James St, W1   7437 4550   3–2D
7-9 Charlotte St, W1   7580 1110   2–1C
30 Coptic St, WC1   7636 3232   2–1C
99 High Holborn, WC1   7831 5305   2–1D
147 Strand, WC2   7836 7716   2–2D
450 The Strand, WC2   7930 8205   2–2C
80-81 St Martins Ln, WC2   7836 8001   4–3B
9-12 Bow St, WC2   7240 3443   4–2D
363 Fulham Rd, SW10   7352 5300   5–3B
150-152 King's Rd, SW3   7351 5031   5–3C
352a King's Rd, SW3   7352 9790   5–3B
6-7 Beauchamp Pl, SW3   7589 2355   5–1C
246 Old Brompton Rd, SW5   7373 4712   5–2A
140 Wandsworth Bridge Rd, SW6   8384 9693   10–1B
895 Fulham Rd, SW6   7731 3117   10–1B
137 Notting Hill Gate, W11   7229 6000   6–2B
7 Rockley Rd, W14   8749 8582   7–1C
26 Porchester Rd, W2   7229 7784   6–1C
252 Chiswick High Rd, W4   8747 0193   7–2A
35 Earls Court Rd, W8   7937 0761   5–1A
335 Upper St, N1   7226 9542   8–3D
30 Highgate High St, N6   8341 3434   8–1B
187 Kentish Town Rd, NW1   7267 0101   8–2B
85-87 Parkway, NW1   7267 2600   8–3B
194 Haverstock Hill, NW3   7794 6777   8–2A
70 Heath St, NW3   7433 1600   8–1A
39-39a Abbey Rd, NW8   7624 5577   8–3A
316 Kennington Rd, SE11   7820 3177   10–1D
4 Borough High St, SE1   7407 2995   9–3C

for updates visit www.hardens.com

PizzaExpress cont'd
9 Belvedere Rd, SE1   7928 4091   2–3D
Cardamom Bldg, Shad Thames, SE1   7403 8484   9–4D
230 Lavender Hill, SW11   7223 5677   10–2C
46 Battersea Br Rd, SW11   7924 2774   5–4C
14 Barnes High St, SW13   8878 1184   10–1A
305 Up Richmond Rd W, SW14   8878 6833   10–2A
144 Upper Richmond Rd, SW15   8789 1948   10–2B
539 Old York Rd, SW18   8877 9812   10–2B
43 Abbeville Rd, SW4   8673 8878   10–2D
2nd Flr, Cabot Place East, E14   7513 0513   11–1C
78-80 Wapping Ln, E1   7481 8436   11–1A
26 Cowcross St, EC1   7490 8025   9–1A
59 Exmouth Mkt, EC1   7713 7264   9–1A
125 London Wall, EC2   7600 8880   9–2B
150 London Wall, EC2   7588 7262   9–2D
49-51 Curtain Rd, EC2   7613 5426   9–1D
Leadenhall Market, EC3   7621 0022   9–2D
7-9 St Bride St, EC4   7583 5126   9–2A
Reliable to the point of 'if you've been to one you've been to them all', this much-loved pizza chain isn't exactly imaginative (and in fact scored rather disappointingly in our survey this year), but thanks to its ubiquitous presence (over 40 locations in central London) you should be able to find a branch within reasonable distance almost anywhere. A comforting combination might be tomato & Mozzarella salad (£3.30) followed by the American Hot – pepperoni & chilli – for £7.70. House wine is £10.95 a bottle. / www.pizzaexpress.co.uk;
11 pm-midnight – City branches earlier; most City branches closed all or part of weekend; most branches don't take bookings.

Pizzeria Castello SE1 £16 A★
20 Walworth Rd   7703 2556   1–3C
This popular pizzeria has long thrived by offering value-for-money, and reliably good pizzas and pastas (£4.70-£6). The menu offers quite a lot besides, with starters such as baked aubergine and Parmesan and tomato (£3.50), and main courses including veal escalope with mixed peppers (£7.90). House wine is £8.90 a bottle. NB: at the time of writing, the place is located by the Elephant & Castle roundabout, but look out for a move in early-2003, as the much-needed redevelopment of the area progresses. / 11 pm, Fri & Sat 11.30 pm; closed Sat L & Sun.

Pizzeria Condotti W1 £18
4 Mill St   7499 1308   3–2C
Though it has a certain amount in common with your typical PizzaExpress, this Mayfair branch has that dash of extra chic you'd hope for from a place a short step from Savile Row. Especially in the evenings, it's a useful rendezvous for a light meal in calm and civilised surroundings. On the culinary front, it offers some salads and pasta dishes in addition to the usual pizzas (all around the £8 mark), and house wine at £11.50 a bottle. / midnight; closed Sun.

sign up for the survey at www.hardens.com

The Place Below EC2 £13 A★
St Mary-le-Bow, Cheapside   7329 0789   9–2C
This well-established vegetarian, intriguingly located in the crypt of the impressive St Mary-le-Bow, is a popular and crowded City lunching destination. The fare is quite innovative, but priced for the affluent local market – a grilled sandwich, perhaps roast leeks and Gruyère is £4 (take away) or a pound more for a 'bake', such as lentil, leek and Parmesan. Unlicensed – juices and coffee are around the £1.50 mark. / www.theplacebelow.co.uk; L only, closed Sat & Sun; no Amex; no smoking; need 15+ to book.

The Polish Club SW7 £16* A
55 Prince's Gate, Exhibition Rd   7589 4635   5–1C
As more astute readers may have guessed, this grand, traditional club dining room in South Kensington is run (and mainly frequented) by Poles. It is particularly strong in the atmosphere department, and also has an excellent summer terrace. A further attraction is the fact that there's a simple 3-course menu (£8 members, £10 non-members) available all day long – you might have soup of the day followed by roast salmon, with apple pancakes for pudding. The house wine is £9.90 a bottle. / 11 pm.

Polygon Bar & Grill SW4 £19* A
4 The Polygon   7622 1199   10–2D
This trendy, and quite pricey, modern British brasserie/grill – hidden away in a backstreet – makes a stylish place to kick off a south London night out. To stay within our budget you'll have to go for the early-bird evening special (6pm-7.30pm), when two courses cost £12.50 – these might be seared tuna with aubergine salsa followed by marinated guinea fowl with noodle salad. The house wine is £12 a bottle. / www.thepolygon.co.uk; 10.45 pm; Mon-Thu D only, Fri-Sun open L & D.

Poons WC2 £14
4 Leicester St   7437 1528   4–3A
It's dependable and consistent, so there's always a good flow of regulars at this inexpensive Chinese establishment, which has a particularly convenient location for West End theatre- and cinema-goers, just north of Leicester Square. Varied set meals are available – for £14, two people can share soup, three main dishes and rice, and even à la carte is not much more expensive. House wine is £7.70 a bottle. / 11.30 pm; no smoking area.

for updates visit www.hardens.com 74

Poons, Lisle Street WC2 £13
27 Lisle St   7437 4549   4–3B
A number of establishments bear the Poons name. This Chinatown spot, basic as it is, is the original and still acclaimed by many as the best of the bunch. There may be no pretensions, but this fact is fully reflected by the prices – you might start with spring rolls or crispy seaweed (£2.50 each), followed by one of a wide selection of pork or chicken dishes (from £4.40). The house wine is £7.70 a bottle. / 11.30 pm; no Amex; no smoking area.

Popeseye £20 ★
108 Blythe Rd, W14   7610 4578   7–1C
277 Upper Richmond Rd, SW15   8788 7733   10–2A
These no-frills Brook Green and Putney bistros are not only two of the least expensive steakhouses in London, but also two of the best. The choice is steak, steak or steak. Well-hung Scottish numbers come in varying sizes at very reasonable prices – the eponymous 8oz popeseye (rump) with chips will set you back £9.45. A salad to go with it will set you back £3.45, and the house Rioja is £11.50 a bottle. / 10.30 pm; D only; closed Sun; no credit cards.

Porchetta Pizzeria £12 ★
33 Boswell St, WC1   7242 2434   2–1D
141-142 Upper St, N1   7288 2488   8–3D
147 Stroud Green Rd, N4   7281 2892   8–1D
Sheer value has won a huge following for these north London pizzerias. They really are very inexpensive, with starters under £5, pizzas around £6 and the house wine at £8.50 a litre. If you're looking for a blow-out at a truly budget level, you really won't do much better. / midnight; WC1 closed Sat L & Sun; no Amex; booking: need 5+ to book.

Pret A Manger £6 ★
Branches throughout London
This designer-metallic take-away chain goes from strength to strength, Extremely reliable sandwiches (£1.15-£3.05) are at the heart of its 'offer', but you will also find wraps, baguettes, salads and sushi (£1.99-£5). You might want to finish with a particularly good fruit salad (£1.69) or a slice of cake (£1.15) and a coffee (£1.25). Prices are a little higher if you eat in.
/ www.pret.com; 3.30 pm-11 pm; closed Sun (except some central branches); no credit cards; no smoking areas; no booking.

The Prince Bonaparte W2 £18
80 Chepstow Rd   7313 9491   6–1B
This was once a very grotty Bayswater boozer, but it has been tarted up (a bit) in recent years, and nowadays attracts a large and devoted younger following thanks to the quality of its satisfying grub. You might have the soup of the day (£4), followed by sausages and mash (£8.50) – washed down by a bottle of the house vino (£11). / 10 pm; no booking.

sign up for the survey at www.hardens.com

Pucci Pizza SW3 £19* 𝔸
205 King's Rd   7352 2134   5–3C
Many competitors have come (and many of those gone) over the years, but this classic hang-out for Chelsea's young and beautiful just goes on and on. Like at so many Italians, you'll have to stick to the pizzas, pastas and salads at this rustic-looking pizzeria if you don't want to blow your budget, but these are all perfectly well done. The house wine is £11.50 a bottle. / 12.30 am; closed Sun L; no credit cards.

QC
Chancery Court Hotel WC1 £20* 𝔸★★
252 High Holborn   7829 7000   2–1D
As long as you don't consume more than the glass of wine included with your 2-course set menu (£14.50) – extra supplies come at a whopping £18 a bottle – you can, amazingly, lunch just about within our budget at this grand former banking hall (located a couple of minutes' walk from Holborn tube). Your selection might be crispy salmon with capers, followed by lamb rump with sweetbreads and tomato couscous. NB: stray into à la carte territory, and you could easily spend three times as much. / www.renaissancehotels.com/loncc; 10.15 pm; closed Sun; no smoking area.

The Queen's NW1 £19
49 Regents Park Rd   7586 0408   8–3B
This impressively-scaled tarted-up boozer is something of a Primrose Hill landmark, and it's one that's well worth a visit, too, if you're looking for reliable gastropub staples such as Cumberland sausages with mash and shallot gravy (£8.95), and apple tart (£4.95). The house wine is £9.90 a bottle. / 9.45 pm; no Amex.

Quiet Revolution £17 𝔸★
28-29 Marylebone High St, W1   7487 5683   2–1B
49 Old St, EC1   7253 5556   9–1B
There's nothing pianissimo about the decent, light dishes – using organic ingredients – which are the forte of this café duo, and their surroundings are pleasant, too (especially at the Marylebone branch). Interesting salads (£4.95-£7.95) and cakes (£2.50-£3.50) are typical of the fare on offer. Organic house wine is available at £15 a bottle, or you might go for one of the healthy juices (£3-£5). / www.quietrevolution.co.uk; W1 6 pm – EC1 9 pm; W1 closed Sat – EC1 closed Sat & Sun; no smoking.

Ragam W1 £13 ★
57 Cleveland St   7636 9098   2–1B
This place certainly isn't anything to look at, but if you're looking for a haven of good-quality cooking in the culinary wasteland overshadowed by the Telecom Tower, this long-established South Indian restaurant is well worth seeking out. Most dishes are under a fiver and the house wine is £9 a bottle, so you would have some difficulty exceeding our budget. / 10.30 pm.

for updates visit www.hardens.com

Raks W1 £12*
4 Heddon St   7439 2929   3–2C
A top destination for a shopping lunch – and a good place for a light evening snack, too – this bare but trendy Turkish establishment has a handy location just a few yards off Regent Street. At lunchtime, there's a good-value 2-course menu (£6.95), from which you might choose soup followed by a chicken kebab. In the evenings, you might have bar snacks (under a fiver) such as meze, washed down by the house wine at £11.50 a bottle. / midnight.

Rani N3 £15 ★
7 Long Ln   8349 4386   1–1B
This Finchley spot is something of a veteran of the Indian veggie world, and it offers a menu of interesting and fresh-tasting dishes. One good-value option is the 2-course menu (£13), though the à la carte dishes are also within our budget, with starters costing about £3 and mains around £5. House wine is £9.70 a bottle. / www.raniuk.com; 10 pm; D only; no smoking area.

Ranoush W2 £14 ★
43 Edgware Rd   7723 5929   6–1D
For a late-night kebab after a night on the town – last orders are at 2.45am – there isn't anywhere better than this Lebanese diner in Bayswater. You might have a snack such as houmous (£3.50) or a plate of lamb with salad and pitta bread (£9). There's no alcohol, but you could have a fresh mango and melon juice (£1.75) instead. / www.maroush.com; 2.45 am; no credit cards.

Raoul's Café W9 £19
13 Clifton Rd   7289 7313   8–4A
On sunny days, the pavement outside this informal bistro/pâtisserie is packed with locals. You can pop in for a croissant and a cup of coffee, or for something more substantial try the soup of the day (£3.95) followed perhaps by an organic hamburger – at £9.95, the same price as a bottle of the house vino. Alternatively, you can take away from Raoul's Express, across the road. / 10.30 pm; no smoking area; no booking at L.

Rasa £19* ★★
6 Dering St, W1   7629 1346   3–2B
55 Stoke Newington Church St, N16   7249 0344   1–1C
It's no great surprise that, for top value, you have to seek out the Stoke Newington original of this dynamic southern Indian duo in preference to its glossier Mayfair offshoot. At the former, starters are £2.50, main dishes are around a fiver, and the house wine £8.95 a bottle. At the latter, you'd need to exercise a little care to remain comfortably within our price-limit, but both sites offer equally good, well-spiced veggie fare.
/ www.rasarestaurants.com; 10.30 pm; N16 closed Mon L-Thu L – W1 closed Sun; no smoking.

sign up for the survey at www.hardens.com

Rasa Travancore N16   £16   ★
56 Stoke Newington Church St   7249 1340   1–1C
The Rasa chain is something of a byword for quality and good-value Indian cooking – see above. What singles this (cramped but welcoming) Stoke Newington branch out is that carnivores are fully catered-for, too. As ever, prices are reasonable – starters (perhaps seafood soup or lamb rice balls) are under a fiver, and curries (for example, Keralan chicken curry with paratha and lemon rice) are around £7 – with veggie options particularly inexpensive. The house wine is £9.50 a bottle. / www.rasarestaurants.com; 10.45 pm; D only, ex Sun open L & D; no smoking.

The Real Greek N1   £19*   ★
15 Hoxton Market   7739 8212   9–1D
Theodore Kyriakou is London's leading exponent of authentic Greek cuisine, and his restaurant is considerably beyond the budget of this guide. However, there are two possibilities for Hellenophiles wanting to try the place – the set lunch (and pre-theatre) menu is a mere £10 for two courses, and the 'Mezedopolio' meze bar attached to the restaurant has dishes ranging from £1.90-£6. Wine, from an all-Greek list, is £11.75 a bottle, and Greek Mythos beer is £3. / www.therealgreek.co.uk; 10.30 pm; closed Sun; no Amex.

Rebato's SW8   £17   🅐
169 South Lambeth Rd   7735 6388   10–1D
Accommodating staff and reliable cooking make this jolly Spanish outfit not far from the Oval a firm favourite with young and old alike. The tapas bar at the front – where tasty and affordable dishes (£3-£5) are served up in a festive atmosphere – is where the budget diner should head. The restaurant at the back – a little out of our budget – makes a good party venue. House wine is £9.75 a bottle. / www.rebatos.com; 10.45 pm; closed Sat L & Sun.

The Red Pepper W9   £19   ★
8 Formosa St   7266 2708   8–4A
It may have a hidden-away Maida Vale backstreet location, but this bare (and somewhat dowdy) pizzeria has quite a reputation. It's all thanks to the quality of the pizzas from the wood-burning oven (£5-£10), and other dishes such as tagliatelle with vegetables and Scamorza cheese (£8). The house wine is £12 a bottle. / 11 pm; closed weekday L; no Amex.

Riccardo's SW3   £17
126 Fulham Rd   7370 6656   5–3B
This 'Italian tapas' restaurant has long been a popular 'budget' destination (at least by Chelsea standards). All dishes come in starter-size portions, and most cost around a fiver – choose from a wide selection of salads (such as roast spinach with Parma ham), pasta dishes and pizzas. The house wine is £10.75 a bottle. / 11.30 pm.

for updates visit www.hardens.com

Rocket W1 £17 Ⓐ
4-6 Lancashire Ct   7629 2889   3–2B
Hidden in a mews off Bond Street, this strikingly-decorated loft, above a bustling bar, is a real find for bargain hunters. (An offshoot has recently opened in Putney – it will do well to match the charm of the original.) The Mediterranean menu is pizza-based, but other dishes (fishcakes, big salads, etc) are interesting and well-realised. Wood-fired pizzas are around £7.50, and a dessert, such as hot chocolate fudge brownie, will set you back about £4. The house wine is £12 a bottle.
/ 11.30 pm; closed Sun.

The Rôtisserie £18* ★★
56 Uxbridge Rd, W12   8743 3028   7–1C
134 Upper St, N1   7226 0122   8–3D
The 2-course set menus (always available, except Sat after 7.50pm) make these pleasantly unpretentious rôtisserie-bistros really top-value destinations. A mere £12.50 buys you the sort of protein-intensive fare that often can't be found within our price range – perhaps tomato, Mozzarella and aubergine salad followed by a rib-eye steak and chips, washed down with house wine at £9.75 a bottle. / www.therotisserie.co.uk; 11 pm; W12 closed Sat L & Sun L – N1 closed Mon L & Tue L.

Rôtisserie Jules £16
6-8 Bute St, SW7   7584 0600   5–2B
133 Notting Hill Gate, W11   7221 3331   6–2B
These simple Gallic rotisseries may not be designed to encourage you to linger, but do offer quality protein very cheaply. The choice is generally chicken, chicken or chicken – a quarter-bird (plus a side dish) is £7.25, or a half is £6.50 – accompanied by fries (£2) or a salad (£2.50). For a party – if you give them advance notice – they will roast a leg of lamb for you (£29, serves 5-8 people). A bottle of the house wine is £7.50. / 11 pm.

Royal China £20* ★★
40 Baker St, W1   7487 4688   2–1A
13 Queensway, W2   7221 2535   6–2C
68 Queen's Grove, NW8   7586 4280   8–3A
30 Westferry Circus, E14   7719 0888   11–1C
They may be garishly decorated in '70s disco style (even the new branches!), but these large establishments are generally accepted as the capital's benchmark for quality Chinese cooking. Great-value lunchtime dim sum (£1.90-£2.30 a dish) are a special attraction. A la carte dishes kick off at about £5, but – with house wine at £13.50 a bottle – it would not be at all difficult to spend beyond our budget. The Bayswater and Marylebone branches are especially worth seeking out.
/ 10.45 pm, Fri & Sat 11.30 pm.

sign up for the survey at www.hardens.com

Royal Court Bar SW1 £15
Sloane Sq   7565 5061   5–2D
It's for sheer handiness that we include this 'zoo' of a bar, beneath Sloane Square. Though it's notionally attached to the famous theatre, it has a life quite of its own (though it's obviously best to avoid the hectic pre-curtain-up hour if you can). Snacks such as chicken liver pâté (£5.50) or soup (£4.25) are the forte, washed down with house wine at £11.50 a bottle. / 10.30 pm; closed Sun; no smoking area.

La Rueda SW4 £19*   Ⓐ
66-68 Clapham High St   7627 2173   10–2D
Skip the restaurant, and settle yourself in to the famous bottle-lined bar of this famous Clapham establishment with a jug of sangria and a couple of tapas. This is where you'll get the vibrant atmosphere, and it's much better value. Most tapas are between £4-£5, sangria is £11 a jug, and a bottle of house wine is £9.50. / 11 pm; no booking in bar.

Rupee Room EC2 £17
10 Copthall Ave   7628 1555   9–2C
This opulently-decorated basement Indian near London Wall is one of the few places you can sit down for a proper meal in the heart of the City and keep within our budget. Starters are around £3.50 and main courses start from £7, but, as so often happens with curry houses, the extras can quickly mount up, so you'll have to exercise some caution. House wine is reasonable, considering, at £7.95 a bottle. / 11 pm; closed Sat & Sun.

Sabai Sabai W6 £15*   ★
270-272 King St   8748 7363   7–2B
It may lack atmosphere to a signal extent, but this Hammersmith restaurant makes up for it with some very tasty Thai cooking. Starters are around £4, and most curries are £6-£8. For top value, however, go for the 2-course lunch menu (£7.95), from which your choice might be spring rolls followed by sweet and sour pork or green chicken curry, washed down with house wine at £8.50 a bottle. / 11.30 pm; closed Sun L; no smoking area.

Sabras NW10 £12   ★★
263 High Rd   8459 0340   1–1A
Willesden Green is hardly oversupplied with good eating venues, making this venerable veggie Indian all the more worth knowing about. Its extensive menu incorporates southern specialities such as bhel poori (£3.25) and dhosas (£6.50-£7.50). The house wine is £10 a bottle. / 10.30 pm; D only, closed Mon; no smoking area.

for updates visit www.hardens.com

St John EC1 £19* ★
26 St John St   7251 0848   9–1B
This converted smokehouse near Smithfield meat market is renowned for the carnivorous treats (which the chef calls 'nose-to-tail eating') served in its restaurant. A full meal would easily take you beyond our price-limit, but if you are intrigued by such things as roast bone marrow and parsley salad (£6.20), or chitterlings with radishes (£6), the bar menu offers snacks at prices that won't quite break the bank, even with house wine at £14.50 a bottle. / www.stjohnrestaurant.co.uk; 11 pm; closed Sat L & Sun.

Sakonis HA0 £13 ★★
129 Ealing Rd   8903 9601   1–1A
For brilliant and cheap Indian cooking, it's difficult to match this large vegetarian canteen in Wembley. The varied menu – which includes some Chinese dishes – can seem rather daunting at first, but nothing costs very much, and most of it is delicious. You might have spring rolls (£5) followed by mushroom biryani (£4.25), with kulfi to finish. Budgeting is assisted by the fact that you can't waste your money on alcohol. / 9.30 pm; no Amex; no smoking.

The Salusbury NW6 £20 ★
50-52 Salusbury Rd   7328 3286   1–2B
The functions of pub and dining room are divided between two parallel rooms at this cosy old Queen's Park boozer, which has been revitalised in recent times. Superior snacks and a hot dish of the day are dispensed from the bar, while the restaurant serves simple Mediterranean food, such as risotti and pastas (£6.50 small; £9 large), plus a few heartier dishes such as roast pork belly and pepperonata (£10) and some classic desserts. The house wine is £10 a bottle. / 10.15 pm; closed Mon L; no Amex.

Sarastro WC2 £17* 𝔸
126 Drury Ln   7836 0101   2–2D
It's technically possible to stay within price-limit at this madcap Theatreland institution – but only if you opt for the set lunch or pre-theatre menus (available noon-6.30pm) which offer two courses for £10. The (notionally Turkish) cooking, however, is really not the point of the place – people come for the wildly Baroque décor and theatrical atmosphere, which make it ideal for boisterous groups (when you'll probably seriously blow the budget). The house wine is £10.75 a bottle.
/ www.sarastro-restaurant.com; 11.30 pm.

sign up for the survey at www.hardens.com

Sarkhel's SW18 £18 ★★
199 Replingham Rd   8870 1483   10–2B
Southfields locals are indeed lucky to be offered Udit Sarkhel's accomplished Indian cooking at such reasonable prices. The set lunch menu (also served until 8pm) offers three courses for £9.95. A la carte, a fairly standard list is supplemented by unusual specials such as chicken tikka makhani (£7.25), washed down with house wine at £10.90 a bottle.
/ www.sarkhels.com; 10.30 pm, Fri & Sat 11 pm; closed Mon; no smoking area.

Satsuma W1 £18
56 Wardour St   7437 8338   3–2D
This stylish Japanese diner in Soho serves up healthy food at refectory tables – it's a popular place, and there's often a queue. Apart from noodles (miso ramen, £5.80), there are good sushi and sashimi, which may tempt one to go over budget. Bento boxes (complete with rice, miso soup and pickles) range from £9.50 for tofu to £15.50 for prawn tempura. Kirin beer is £3.80 for a large bottle.
/ www.osatsuma.com; 11 pm, Wed & Thu 11.30 pm, Fri & Sat 11.45pm; no smoking; no booking.

Scuzi £20
37 Westferry Circus, E14   7519 6699   11–1C
West India Quay, E14   7001 0991   11–1C
2 Creechurch Ln, EC3   7623 3444   9–2D
This smart pizza chain is already making a name for standards at least as good as many of the others trying to occupy the same (much-contested) market 'space'. You need to take some care to stay within budget, perhaps having bruschetta (£2-£4.25) followed by black linguine with prawns (£8.95), washed down with house wine at £10.50 a bottle. / 11.30 pm; EC1 closed Sat & Sun; EC3 & E14 no smoking areas.

Seashell NW1 £18 ★
49 Lisson Grove   7224 9000   8–4A
This famous chippy near Marylebone Station has become a firm fixture on the tourist map, so it's more often than not crammed with coach parties eating our National Dish (£8.50) with an equally traditional pud such as treacle sponge (£3) for 'afters'. This goes on until 7pm, after which the atmosphere mellows and the prices rise. House wine is £10 a bottle.
/ 10.30 pm; closed Sun; no smoking area.

Sedir N1 £15
4 Theberton St   7226 5489   8–3D
This pleasant Turkish bistro, just off the glitzier part of Upper Street, offers inexpensive fare in unpretentious surroundings. Mixed meze (£5.75) followed by the 'chef's special' selection of cooked meats, with salad and rice (£7.50) will easily feed two people, and still leave plenty in the budget for a bottle of the house vino (£8.95). / 11.30 pm, Fri & Sat midnight.

for updates visit www.hardens.com

Shampers W1 £19* Ⓐ
4 Kingly St   7437 1692   3–2D
This friendly, slightly shabby wine bar is only five minutes' walk from Piccadilly Circus, and it's of special note as somewhere where it's dinner which is the 'bargain meal' of the day. Even so, you'll have to choose pretty carefully if you're to stay within our price-limit, perhaps grilled aubergine with pesto and Parmesan (£4.50), followed by pan-fried oyster mushrooms with ginger and pak choy (£8.50). There's quite an impressive wine list, which kicks off at £11.50 a bottle. / 11 pm; closed Sun (& Sat in Aug).

Shanghai E8 £17 Ⓐ
41 Kingsland High St   7254 2878   1–1C
The tiled premises of what was once Dalston's premier pie 'n' eel emporium, tastefully restored, now provide quite an impressive setting for this good-quality Chinese restaurant. The booths at the front are the place to sit, so make sure you arrive early for lunchtime dim sum. At other times there's a fairly standard menu, from which you should be able to choose relatively comfortably within our price limit. The house wine is £9.10 a bottle. / 11 pm; no Amex.

J Sheekey WC2 £20* Ⓐ★★
28-32 St Martin's Ct   7240 2565   4–3B
Believe it or not, one can indeed eat at this smartly-revamped Theatreland fish parlour within our budget – the trick is to eat in the bar, thus avoiding the restaurant's £1.50 cover charge. The weekend set lunch, offering two courses for £13.75, is great value (and the only real option within our price-limit) – you might have smoked haddock & quails egg tart followed by Sheekey's fish pie. House wine is £11.50 a bottle. / midnight.

Shish NW2 £15 ★
2-6 Station Pde   8208 9292   1–1A
Even Willesden Green's greatest supporters might concede that it's not the jazziest place in town, so this funkily-designed newcomer has made quite a stir in the locality. This spot is all the more remarkable as its staple dish is the decidedly un-funky kebab. Downstairs, you can consume a chicken shish (£5.95-£6.75) – preceded perhaps by cold meze (£1.95) – washed down with house wine at £10.90 a bottle or a pint of Stella for £3. Upstairs, there's a popular bar. / 11.15 pm; no Amex; no smoking area; no booking.

sign up for the survey at www.hardens.com

Le Shop SW3 £18
329 King's Rd   7352 3891   5–3B
A fixed point around which the ever-changing King's Road scene revolves, this cheap and cheerful crêperie still resounds to its trademark booming classical 'background' music as it has since it opened over 30 years ago. Pancakes with savoury fillings such as chicken & ratatouille or ham & cheese (around £6.50) are good, but make sure you leave space to try the legendary banana and Nutella version (£5.50). The house wine is £11.95 a bottle. / www.leshop-chelsea.co.uk; midnight; no Amex.

Simpson's Tavern EC3 £14   Ⓐ
38 1/2 Cornhill   7626 9985   9–2C
This splendid chop-house, hidden away in a City back-alley, is probably the closest you will get to the feel of eating in London two hundred years ago. It still attracts a great crush of younger bankers and stockbrokers, who are happy to queue for such solid delights as pork chops or steak and kidney pie (both around a fiver), washed down with house wine at £11 a litre. Concluding with a savoury instead of a sweet – stewed cheese (£2.60) is recommended. / 3 pm; L only, closed Sat & Sun; no booking.

Singapore Garden NW6 £17*   ★
83-83a Fairfax Rd   7328 5314   8–2A
You'd have to scrimp a bit to dine comfortably within our price range at this long-established (and rather tacky) Swiss Cottage pan-oriental. The lunch menu (£8.50), however, offers top value – you might have the likes of satay, followed by Malay chicken curry, and then toffee banana. The house wine is £12 a bottle. / 10.45 pm, Fri & Sat 11.15 pm.

Ground Floor
Smiths of Smithfield EC1 £15*   Ⓐ★
67-77 Charterhouse St   7251 7997   9–1A
There are three floors of dining possibilities at this impressively-converted warehouse, overlooking Smithfield meat market. Prices rise with altitude, so the budget diner is best sticking to the bar area on the ground floor, where breakfast-type dishes such as the 'Full English' (£6.50) are served all day – weekends are especially busy. There are also daily lunchtime 'market specials', such as bangers & mash, pies and quiches (£6 including a drink). If you have room, a Portuguese custard tart would make a fine dessert for around £2. The house wine is £11.75 a bottle.
/ www.smithsofsmithfield.co.uk; 10.30 pm; no booking.

for updates visit www.hardens.com

Soho Spice W1 £20*
124-126 Wardour St   7434 0808   3–1D
Prices at this brightly-decorated modern curry house in Soho are better value than they might seem, as most dishes are in effect complete meals. Tandoori salmon, for instance, comes with rice, vegetables, lentils and naan bread (£11.95). With house wine at £12.95 a bottle, you will need to take a certain amount of care to stay within our budget. / www.sohospice.co.uk; 11.30 pm, Fri & Sat 3 am; no smoking area; need 4+ to book at L, 6+ at D.

Solly's Exclusive NW11 £18*
148 Golders Green Rd   8455 0004   1–1B
There's a more expensive (but superbly kitsch) upstairs restaurant, but for top value seek out the downstairs, diner-style section of this kosher institution in Golders Green. Houmous (£3.25) and lamb shawarma (£9.25), washed down with house wine at £13 a bottle are typical of the fare on offer. / 10.45 pm; closed Fri D & Sat; no Amex; no smoking area.

So.uk SW4 £18   Ⓐ
165 Clapham High St   7622 4004   10–2D
This is really an 'atmosphere' recommendation, as food is far from being the main point of this loungey Moroccan joint in Clapham. If you're looking for a place to hang out with a bottle of house vino (£12.50) and a few tapas-type dishes (£2.50-£5, or a platter for two costs from £12), you won't find many places hereabouts with a better vibe. / 9.45 pm; closed weekday L; no booking.

Souk WC2 £19   Ⓐ
27 Litchfield St   7240 1796   4–3B
It's as a central party venue that this cosy, low-lit and atmospheric Moroccan is especially worth seeking out. The food is rather incidental, but it's also within our budget, even à la carte – couscous with lamb sausage, for example, is £8.95. For top value, however, visit at lunch time, when there's a 3-course set menu for £12.50 including mint tea. The house wine is £12 a bottle. / 11.30 pm.

Soup Opera £8   ★
2 Hanover St, W1   7629 0174   3–2C
6 Market Pl, W1   7637 7882   3–1C
17 Kingsway, WC2   7379 1333   2–2D
Concourse Level, Cabot Pl East, E14   7513 0880   11–1C
18 Bloomfield St, EC2   7588 9188   9–2C
56-57 Cornhill, EC3   7621 0065   9–2C
The name says it all about this makes-a-change-from-sandwiches chain. To blow away the winter blues on a cold day, it's difficult to beat the delights of a quick cup of, perhaps, smoked haddock chowder, complete with bread and a piece of fruit (£4.20, or £6.50 for a seriously large portion). Puddings (fruit salad and the like) are around £1.75, and a coffee will set you back £1.20. / www.soupopera.co.uk; 4 pm-6 pm; closed Sat & Sun – central branches closed Sun; no credit cards; no smoking; no booking.

sign up for the survey at www.hardens.com

Southeast W9 £17
239 Elgin Ave   7328 8883   1–2B
An inexpensive Maida Vale café which serves a pan-Asian menu encompassing such starters as chicken satay and prawn & sweetcorn cakes (both £4.95), with a selection of curries (from £6.95) and so on to follow. House wine is £10.75 a bottle, and Tiger beer £2.75. / 11 pm; no smoking area.

Spago SW7 £17
6 Glendower Pl   7225 2407   5–2B
Conveniently-located only a couple of minutes' walk from the tube station in pricey South Kensington, this well-established pit stop is a perennially popular destination for the local 'Euros'. Hearty portions of pizza and pasta are the culinary attraction – starters cost around £5 and most main dishes are £7. The house wine is £9.80 a bottle. / 11.30 pm; no credit cards.

La Spighetta W1 £20 ★
43 Blandford St   7486 7340   2–1A
There's not a great deal of choice for those on a budget in the area around Baker Street, so it's worth remembering this sparsely-furnished (and rather noisy) basement trattoria, which offers a solid, if basic, pizza and pasta menu. Starters, such as bruschetta, cost around £4, while main courses, like spaghetti bolognaise, are £7.50. House wine is £11.50 a bottle.
/ 10.30 pm; closed weekend L (& Sun D in Aug); no smoking area.

Spread Eagle SE10 £20* A★
2 Stockwell St   8853 2333   1–3D
We have long wrongly overlooked this heart-of-Greenwich ancient pub-conversion (mainly because it gives the impression of trading on Olde Englishness), but it is in fact a surprisingly good restaurant serving up-to-date Gallic cooking. It only falls within our budget (just) for the £13.50, 2-course set lunch (not Sun; also pre-theatre Mon-Thu), which might comprise the likes of duck & lentil terrine, followed by snapper with red onion mash, washed down with house wine at £13 a bottle.
/ www.spreadeagle.org; 10.30 pm; closed Sun D.

Sree Krishna SW17 £13 ★★
192-194 Tooting High St   8672 4250   10–2D
It may not be an exciting place to look at, but those in search of real value crowd out this Tooting South Indian. The fare is mainly vegetarian and, as so often, starters (£1.95-£4.50) are a special strength. The main dishes are £3.95-£6.95, and the house wine is £9 a bottle. / www.sreekrishna.co.uk; 10.45 pm.

for updates visit www.hardens.com

Standard Tandoori W2 £12
21-23 Westbourne Grove   7229 0600   6–1C
Names don't come much more apt than that of this Bayswater curry house, whose formula has changed little since the '60s. Starters are generally less than £4, curries under £6, and the house wine £8 a bottle. / 11.45 pm; no smoking area.

Star Café W1 £13
22 Gt Chapel St   7437 8778   3–1D
Slightly off the beaten track in Soho, this classic caff serves a first-rate full English breakfast for a fiver from 7am (Mon-Fri). Later in the day the emphasis changes to soups (£2.60), omelettes, pasta dishes and daily specials, such as char-grilled chicken (£6.50). The house wine is £9.50 a bottle.
/ www.thestarcafesoho.co.uk; 3.30 pm; closed Sat & Sun; no credit cards; no smoking area.

The Stepping Stone SW8 £20*   Ⓐ★★
123 Queenstown Rd   7622 0555   10–1C
This stylish spot is one of the Battersea's most popular 'local' restaurants. It's no surprise that it's beyond our price-limit in the evening, but its loss-leading lunchtime menu offers the bargain of two courses for £13 – well worth a (short) drive over Chelsea Bridge! Your choice might be lentil and sorrel soup, followed by roast mallard and vegetables, washed down with house wine at £12.50 a bottle. / 11 pm, Mon 10.30 pm; closed Sat L & Sun D; no Amex; no smoking area.

Stick & Bowl W8 £10   ★
31 Kensington High St   7937 2778   5–1A
The simple name speaks volumes about this quick, absolutely-no-refinements oriental diner. At prices like these though – hot & sour soup is £2, special fried noodles £4.60 and a bottle of the house wine only £7.95 – it's difficult to beat its attractions as a pit stop, or a respite from Kensington shopping. That's certainly what the constant crowd suggests.
/ 10.45 pm; no credit cards; no booking.

Stone Mason's Arms W6 £18   Ⓐ
54 Cambridge Grove   8748 1397   7–2C
Despite its un-lovely location on a busy Hammersmith highway, this popular gastropub enjoys a strong following for its adventurous cooking – main courses include such delights as seared ostrich steak (£9.75). The desserts –such as sticky toffee pudding (£3.75) – tend to be more familiar. The house wine is £10 a bottle. / 9.45 pm.

sign up for the survey at www.hardens.com

Strada £19
15-16 New Burlington St, W1   7287 5967   3–2C
9-10 Market Pl, W1   7580 4644   3–1C
6 Great Queen St, WC2   7405 6295   4–1D
237 Earl's Court Rd, SW5   7835 1180   5–2A
175 New King's Rd, SW6   7731 6404   10–1B
105 Upper St, N1   7276 9742   8–3D
11-13 Battersea Rise, SW11   7801 0794   10–2C
102-104 Clapham High St, SW4   7720 9596   10–2D
70 Exmouth Mkt, EC1   7278 0800   9–1A

This chain of basic but solid (and more-stylish-than-average) Italian restaurants is, for the moment at least, managing the difficult trick of maintaining standards as it continues to grow at quite a rate, although service can suffer at busy times. Starters are around £5-£7 and pizza or pasta dishes shouldn't set you back more than about £9 (with meat and fish dishes rather more expensive). The house wine is £6.60 for half a litre. / www.strada.co.uk; 11 pm.

Stratford's W8 £17* ★
7 Stratford Rd   7937 6388   5–2A

Hidden away in the backstreets of Kensington, this Gallic fish restaurant has little natural daytime traffic – budget diners will know that such establishments can offer rich pickings for those prepared to make a bit of effort to seek out lunchtime value. For £10.50, the 2-course set menu (also available 6pm-7.30pm) might offer such delights as herring salad, followed by sirloin steak, washed down by house wine at £10.80 a bottle. / www.stratfords-restaurant.com; 11 pm, Thu-Sat 11.30 pm.

The Sun & Doves SE5 £18
61 Coldharbour Ln   7733 1525   1–4C

This bright, breezy and determinedly Bohemian Denmark Hill gastropub is a perennially popular local hang-out (especially in summer, when the large garden comes into its own). The modish, Mediterranean-influenced food sustains interest, too, including dishes such as Spanish meatballs (£4.50), or Moroccan lamb and chick pea stew (£7.95). House wine is £9.75 a bottle. / www.sundoves.com; 10.30 pm; closed Sun D; no smoking area; no booking.

Sushi-Say NW2 £18 ★
33b Walm Ln   8459 7512   1–1A

With a reputation spread much wider than among the Japanese community based around Willesden Green, this family-run café is renowned not only for the impeccable sushi, but also for more humble and affordable cooking, particularly at weekend lunch times when three courses cost only £7.90. Even at other times, it's perfectly possible, with a degree of care, to remain within our budget. House wine is £9.80 a bottle, or drink tea for 60p. / 10.30 pm; closed Mon, Tue-Fri D only, Sat & Sun open L & D; no smoking area.

for updates visit www.hardens.com

Sweetings EC4 £14* Ⓐ
39 Queen Victoria St   7248 3062   9–3B
This one's a bit of a cheat – you couldn't really accommodate the good-but-simple fish cooking at this City-institution seafood bar within our budget. But if you're prepared to slum it standing at the bar with a generously-filled sandwich (£3.95-£5.50) and a bottle of the house wine (£14), you won't find a more characteristic place for a convivial lunch. Don't forget to wear your pinstripes. / L only, closed Sat & Sun; no booking.

Tajine W1 £20
7a Dorset St   7935 1545   2–1A
Just a good-all-round, inexpensive place – this friendly (and rather cramped) Marylebone Moroccan café offers such delights as aubergine zaalouk (£3.95) and lamb tajine with pears (£10.75), washed down with house wine at £11.95 a bottle. / 10.30 pm; closed Sat L & Sun; no Amex.

Talad Thai SW15 £13   ★★
320 Upper Richmond Rd   8789 8084   10–2A
The queues at this popular Putney-fringe Thai restaurant say it all – the food's great and so are the prices. Eating is communal and there are few frills on the ambience front, but you're guaranteed a great meal that won't cost the earth. Standard dishes like spring rolls and green curry cost around £4.45 each. House wine is £9.50 a bottle, or you can BYO if you're prepared to pay the (somewhat excessive) £5 corkage. / 10 pm; no credit cards; no smoking; no booking.

Tandoori Lane SW6 £18   ★
131a Munster Rd   7371 0440   10–1B
The menu at Fulham's most reliable curry house is hardly innovative and isn't notably cheap (with main courses costing around £7 and side dishes about £3), but exceptional service and a cosy, almost seductive, atmosphere ensure that you'll enjoy well-prepared curries and tandoori dishes in a comfortable setting. House wine is £10.95 a bottle, or drink bottled beers (from £2.10). / 11 pm; no Amex.

**Tapa Room
The Providores W1** £19*   Ⓐ★
109 Marylebone High St   7935 6175   2–1A
Especially if you're looking for somewhere for an interesting breakfast or brunch, this odd-but-interesting Marylebone newcomer – the latest project from the man who established the famous Sugar Club – is well worth seeking out. During the week, English breakfasts (£7.60) are served (9am-11.30am), or at weekends, brunch (highly recommended) is available from 10am-3pm. At other times, the likes of mixed antipasti will set you back £9, washed down with house wine at £12.50 a bottle.
/ www.theprovidores.co.uk; 10.30 pm.

sign up for the survey at www.hardens.com

Tartuf £15 ★
88 Upper St, N1   7288 0954   8–3D
169 Clapham High St, SW4   7622 8169   10–2D
Pizza-like 'tartes flambées' with savoury and sweet toppings are the speciality (from Alsace) which are helping make a big success of this small chain (although exceptionally friendly service may also play a part). You can eat as much as you like for £10.80 (and 5.45pm-7.15pm bills are reduced by 15%), while a 2-course lunch is only £4.90. House wine is £10.95 a bottle. / *midnight; no Amex.*

Tas £16   𝔸★
33 The Cut, SE1   7928 2111   9–4A
72 Borough High St, SE1   7403 7200   9–4C
The opening of Southwark tube station spawned a clutch of new restaurants along the Cut, including a large and loud but attractive Turkish establishment that's always very busy (and deservedly so). The second branch (with café) in Borough is equally bustling at all hours. The 2-course set menu (£7.45) is the most economical option, but the joy of this place is that you really can 'let yourself go', and be pretty confident of staying within budget. The house wine is £10.50 a bottle. / *11.30 pm.*

Level 7 Café
Tate Modern SE1 £20   𝔸
Bankside   7401 5020   9–3B
Even if you don't want to visit the gallery, the City view from Tate Modern's stark 7th-floor café makes it a destination worth seeking out. The modern British cuisine – perhaps onion and cider soup (£4.25) followed by fish & chips (£8.95), and washed down by house wine at £12.50 a bottle – is hardly earth-shattering, but it is reasonably priced. / *www.tate.org.uk; 5.30 pm, Fri & Sat 9 pm; L only, except Fri & Sat open L & D; no smoking.*

Tawana W2 £18   ★
3 Westbourne Grove   7229 3785   6–1C
It's the quality of the cooking that keeps this otherwise bland ten-year-old Thai so popular that it can afford to impose a minimum charge of £10 per person. However, starters and main courses are both around the £5-£7 mark, so it's not too difficult to keep within our budget, and the cooking – fishcakes and pad Thai, for example – is reliably well prepared. House wine is £9.50 a bottle. / *11 pm.*

Tbilisi N7 £15
91 Holloway Rd   7607 2536   8–2D
If you've tired of all the more 'obvious' cuisines, why not check out this Georgian (that's the East European one, not the American state) spot in Holloway? It's not what you'd call an exciting place, but the realisation of such comforting dishes as aubergine salad and chicken in walnut sauce (£4-£7) is pretty solid. The house wine (from Georgia, naturally) is £10 a bottle. / *11 pm; D only.*

for updates visit www.hardens.com

Thai Bistro W4   £17   ★
99 Chiswick High Rd   8995 5774   7–2B
Good quality Thai grub is unceremoniously served at this popular Chiswick refectory, where customers sit at shared tables to enjoy regional specialities, including a plethora of veggie options. Starters, including spring rolls and fishcakes, are all priced around £4.50, with curries at £5.95 and rice at £1.50. House wine is £10.50 a bottle, or swig Thai beers from £2.75. / 11 pm; closed Tue L & Thu L; no Amex; no smoking.

Thai Break W8   £16   ★
30 Uxbridge St   7229 4332   6–2B
It's nothing to look at, but this handily-located oriental, a minute's walk from Notting Hill Gate tube, offers all the standard Thai dishes at a cost that seems especially reasonable in this fashionable part of town. Chicken with cashew nuts, for example, is £6.30, and the house wine is £9.95 a bottle. / 11 pm; closed Sun L.

Thai Café SW1   £16
22 Charlwood St   7592 9584   2–4C
They don't stand much on ceremony at this Pimlico corner café, but – the area hardly being awash with tolerable places to eat, at any price level – it attracts a steady following with its menu of oriental staples at reasonable prices. Most starters are around the £4 mark, and most main courses around £5-£6. The house wine is £9.25 a bottle. / 10.30 pm; closed Sat L & Sun L; no smoking area.

Thai Canteen W6   £12
206 King St   8742 6661   7–2B
This simple newcomer a short walk from the UCI Hammersmith inherits long thin premises that have been through numerous former incarnations. As the name hints, the selection here is of curries and noodle dishes which are not art but which are tasty, prepared with a fair degree of care, and very affordable. You might have duck spring rolls (£3.50) followed by chilli fish curry (£5), washed down with strong Thai beer (£1.70 per bottle), which is the only alcohol sold – but you can BYO for 50p corkage. / 10 pm, Fri & Sat 10.30 pm; closed Mon D & Sun; no credit cards.

Thai Corner Café SE22   £13   ★
44 North Cross Rd   8299 4041   1–4D
A bit of a local fave down East Dulwich way, this unpretentious spot offers all the standard Thai dishes at prices made all the more reasonable by the fact that it's a BYO place. Most main courses are around £5.50, with starters and desserts both at £3.25. / 10.30 pm; no credit cards.

sign up for the survey at www.hardens.com

Thai Garden SW11 £17
58 Battersea Rise 7738 0380 10–2C
Although it's been here for a number of years, this airy Battersea Thai now has a new façade, presenting a fresher face to the world. Service is friendly, too, so it's well worth checking out the long menu which offers extensive permutations of the standard repertoire – most curries are around the £7 mark, and the house wine is £9.95 a bottle. / 11 pm, Fri & Sat 11.30 pm; D only, except Sun open L & D; no Amex.

Thai Noodle Bar SW10 £17 Ⓐ
7 Park Walk 7352 7222 5–3B
Useful for a satisfying meal in an area that can be pretty pricey – just off Chelsea's 'Beach' – this smartly-furnished new oriental does just what its name suggests. With main-course dishes such as duck with jasmine rice (£7.95) or tiger prawn curry (£8.95), it's within our budget at any time, but the 2-course set lunch (£8.50, including coffee) is the top deal. The house wine is £10.80 a bottle. / 11 pm.

Thai on the River SW10 £17* Ⓐ★
15 Lots Rd 7351 1151 5–4B
Go to this swanky Chelsea Thai for the fabulous river view and the bargain 2-course set lunch (Tue-Fri, £7.95) from which you might choose crispy spring rolls followed by green chicken curry or roast duck in sweet tamarind sauce. The house wine is an astounding £18 a bottle, but a glass should be just within budget at £3.75, or drink beer at £3.50 a bottle.
/ www.thaiontheriver.co.uk; 11 pm, Fri & Sat 11.30 pm; closed Mon L & Sat L.

Thai Pot £17
5 Princes St, W1 7499 3333 3–1C
1 Bedfordbury, WC2 7379 4580 4–4C
148 Strand, WC2 7497 0904 2–2D
If you had to sum up these handily-located West End Thais, 'commercial' is perhaps the word which best captures their rather bland efficiency. When it comes to cooking, though, they do what they do pretty well, and prices are quite reasonable – standard curries, for example, are £5.95, and there are satisfying set menus (for two people or more) from £12 a head. The house wine is £9.50 a bottle. / www.thaipot.co.uk; 11.15 pm; closed Sun; no smoking area at Bedfordbury.

Thailand SE14 £9* ★★
15 Lewisham Way 8691 4040 1–3D
Probably still the best Thai cooking in town is to be found at this rather unprepossessing Lewisham spot. A la carte, you'd scrimp to stay within our price range, but if you want to check out the quality of the cooking it's worth making a bit of a detour for the £3.95, 2-course set lunch. House wine is £10 a bottle. / 11 pm; closed Mon, Sat L & Sun L; no Amex; no smoking.

for updates visit www.hardens.com

The Thatched House W6 £19 Ⓐ
115 Dalling Rd   7748 6174   7–1B
This agreeable Hammersmith gastropub (complete with conservatory) is a reliable, if not super-budget, local destination. Apart from filled baguettes, the cheapest main courses are the likes of pork chops with red onions and mash (£8.95), and the house wine is £9.95 a bottle. / www.establishment.ltd.uk; 10 pm; closed Mon, Tue & Sun D; no Amex.

Timo W8 £20* ★
343 Kensington High St   7603 3888   7–1D
It's as a 'value' destination that this efficient new Kensington Italian has garnered a lot of favourable press comment. It's still a touch outside our price-limit à la carte (if not by very much), but at lunchtime you should just about manage to stay within it. The house wine is £9.50 a bottle. / 11 pm; booking: max 8.

Toff's N10 £14
38 Muswell Hill Broadway   8883 8656   1–1B
This Muswell Hill chippy was once (justifiably) perhaps the most famous in north London. It's been through some ups and downs following a change of ownership, but now seems to be re-establishing itself as a destination of some note. Cod 'n' chips, complete with coffee and bread & butter, will set you back only £7.50 before 5.30pm – thereafter, it's £8.95, the same price as a bottle of the house vino. / 10 pm; closed Sun; no smoking area; no booking, Sat.

Tokyo City EC2 £19 ★
46 Gresham St   7726 0308   9–2B
Handily-located for a light City lunch – not far from the Bank of England – this Japanese snackery offers such budget possibilities as bento boxes (£6.50-£13.50) as well as sushi (£1.50-£2.80 a piece), with house wine at £10.80 a bottle. You could, of course, spend quite a lot more if you pushed the boat out. / 10 pm; closed Sat & Sun.

Tom's W11 £17*
226 Westbourne Grove   7221 8818   6–1B
Tom Conran's fashionable upmarket deli offers a range of snacks which can be taken away, or eaten 'in', if you are prepared to queue. Soups (£3.25) and pastries, such as roast onion & red pepper tart (£6.95), plus a few more hearty dishes are always available. Buy wines from the basement shop, or BYO and pay corkage at £1.50 per bottle. / 8 pm; closed Sun D; no Amex; no smoking; no booking.

Touzai EC2 £15
147-149 Curtain Rd   7739 4505   9–1D
If you're looking for a place to fuel up before hanging out in Hoxton, this busy oriental canteen is one of the better choices. Noodle dishes (mostly under £6) are the speciality, washed down with house wine at £9.50 a bottle. / www.touzai.co.uk; 11 pm; no Amex; no smoking area.

sign up for the survey at www.hardens.com

The Trafalgar Tavern SE10 — £20 Ⓐ
Park Row   8858 2437   1–3D

There is no doubting the sense of occasion on visiting this large and historic Greenwich inn, which occupies a superb Thames-side location and is blessed with some magnificent views. The good old-fashioned pub grub includes the likes of steak & mushroom pie (£8.25), but there are also more modern flourishes, such as char-grilled squid (£4.95). House wine is £10 a bottle, or drink lager from £2.50 a pint.
/ www.trafalgartavern.co.uk; 9 pm; closed Mon D & Sun D; no Amex; no booking at weekends.

Troubadour SW5 — £17 Ⓐ
265 Old Brompton Rd   7370 1434   5–3A

It's been much expanded in recent times, but this (rare example of a) south west London coffee shop of note has retained most of its Bohemian charm. Its Earl's Court premises remain particularly popular as a breakfast destination – a full English is £5.45 – and it's also fine for a light lunch. We would recommend it less strongly for dinner (when it's really more of interest as a buzzy bar, often with live music). / 11 pm; no Amex.

Tsunami SW4 — £20* ★
Unit 3, 1-7 Voltaire Rd   7978 1610   10–1D

Good-quality Japanese cooking at reasonable prices has made an immediate name for this Clapham newcomer (located just off the main drag, by the High Street railway station). Main dishes range from £7-£15, so you'll need to exercise a little caution to eat a full meal here within our price-limit. However, you could take friends and share plates of sushi (from £1.80 per piece), tempura (from £1) and skewers (£3.50-£5). Miso soup and rice are both £1.75, and a bottle of house wine is £12. / 10.45 pm, Fri & Sat 11.15 pm; closed Sun L; no smoking area.

Two Brothers N3 — £19 ★
297-303 Regent's Park Rd   8346 0469   1–1B

The Manzi brothers' North Finchley fish 'n' chip shop is probably the most consistently popular in north London. It's not particularly cheap, but worth it for a meal such as marinated herrings (£3.55), followed by cod and chips (£7.95). The house wine is £9.80 a bottle. / www.twobrothers.co.uk; 10.15 pm; closed Mon & Sun; no smoking area; no booking at D.

Uli W11 — £17 ★
16 All Saints Rd   7727 7511   6–1B

This South East Asian café in Notting Hill's hippest restaurant street is living up to its early promise as an unusually good all-rounder (and, for the summer, it boasts a pleasant courtyard at the rear). On the menu you might find the likes of five-spiced pork rolls (£5), vegetable tempura (£4) and shredded chilli beef (£7), to be washed down with house wine at £10 a bottle.
/ www.uli-oriental.co.uk; 11 pm; D only, ex Sun open L & D; no Amex.

for updates visit www.hardens.com

Uno SW1 £16*
1 Denbigh St   7834 1001   2–4B
If you're looking for a 'modern' restaurant in Pimlico, this percussive Italian is one of only two choices hereabouts. You could easily spend beyond our price range, but this is a useful enough venue for pizza and pasta (both from £5.50) – the protein-based main dishes are beyond our budget. A starter of, perhaps, garlic bread with roast vegetables & Pecorino (£3.90) could be followed with a Parma ham & rocket pizza (the most expensive, at £8.90), washed down with house wine at £11.40 a bottle. / 10.45 pm.

The Vale W9 £18* ★
99 Chippenham Rd   7266 0990   1–2B
In the not especially propitious environment of Maida Hill, this neighbourhood restaurant continues to thrive. If you stick to the set menus, you can eat well here within our price range at any time of day. Two courses will set you back £9.50 at lunch or £12 at dinner – you might have the likes of vegetable & Stilton pasty or sardine & potato terrine, followed by roast halibut with crispy noodles or Jerusalem artichoke ravioli, washed down with house wine at £10.50 a bottle. / 11 pm; closed Mon L, Sat L & Sun D; no Amex; no smoking area.

Veeraswamy W1 £20* 𝔸★
Victory House, 99 Regent St   7734 1401   3–3D
You'll have to choose from the useful range of set menus – including a 2-course lunch for £12.75 (also served 5.30pm-6.30pm) – to stay within budget at this innovative subcontinental, conveniently close to Piccadilly Circus. It's on the site of London's longest-running Indian (est.1927), although you'd never know it from the jazzy, contemporary décor. The house wine is £11.50 a bottle. / www.realindianfood.com; 11.30 pm.

Vegia Zena NW1 £14* ★
17 Princess Rd   7483 0192   8–3B
On a good day you can still find Italian cooking of more-than-usual interest at this unpretentious Primrose Hill restaurant. Your selection from the 2-course lunch menu (£8.95) might comprise the likes of pasta with pesto followed by sea bass with watercress salad – you'd have to scrimp a little to dine here within our price limit. The house wine is £9.95 a bottle. / www.vegiazena.com; 11 pm.

sign up for the survey at www.hardens.com

El Vergel SE1 £10 ★★
8 Lant St   7357 0057   9–4B
The name means "The Orchard", and this homely café in a hidden corner of Borough certainly provides a fertile haven of good cheer and fantastically affordable grub. There's no stinting on the portions of robust Spanish and South American fare, and you'd be hard pushed to spend over our budget. Aside from the daily specials board, regular items include home-made corn chips (70p) with salsa (£1.30), large salad bowls (at around £2.50), steak & cheese sandwiches ('churrasco', £3.50), and to finish you might choose cheesecake (£1.50). There's a small wine list starting at £8, or drink San Miguel at £2.30 a bottle. / www.elvergel.co.uk; 3 pm; breakfast & L only, closed Sat & Sun; no credit cards; no smoking; no booking after 12.45 pm.

Viet Hoa E2 £11 ★
70-72 Kingsland Rd   7729 8293   9–1D
This basic but good-quality café, on the Hackney-Shoreditch border, has made quite a name for its good, cheap Vietnamese cooking. With starters from 90p, mains about £5 and puddings costing around £2, you could have several courses and stay within budget. House wine is only £7.99 a bottle, too. / 11.30 pm; no Amex.

Viet-Anh NW1 £11
41 Parkway   7284 4082   8–3B
It's nothing special to look at, but this Vietnamese café in the heart of Camden Town is a friendly place that's made quite a name for the quality of its cooking (even if the 'destination' standards of the early days have not been quite maintained). Most of the main courses are around a fiver, and the house wine a tenner a bottle, so a meal here is always well within our budget. / 11 pm; no Amex; no smoking area.

Vijay NW6 £13 ★★
49 Willesden Ln   7328 1087   1–1B
Although particularly renowned for its vegetarian Southern Indian specialities, none of which cost more than £4, this venerable Kilburn curry house can also be relied upon for the consistently very high standard of its meat and fish-based curries (£4-£7). The house wine is £8.95 a bottle.
/ www.vijayindia.com; 10.45 pm, Fri & Sat 11.45 pm; no smoking area.

Vingt-Quatre SW10 £19
325 Fulham Rd   7376 7224   5–3B
It's for convenience rather than any particular quality that we list Chelsea's only all-hours restaurant, which is ideally located for refuelling after a trendy night out on the 'Beach' (as this particular strip of road is known). There's ample choice within our price range, say, soup (£4.25) followed by fishcakes (£9.25) or Cumberland sausage and mash (£9.50). The house wine is £11 a bottle. / open 24 hours; no booking.

for updates visit www.hardens.com

Vrisaki N22 £ 20 ★
73 Myddleton Rd   8889 8760   1–1C
Those with large appetites will find a journey out to Bounds Green worthwhile, to experience the apparently endless meze served at this large taverna, hidden behind a take-away. The quaffable house wine is a modest £8.50 a bottle, and the meze £16 per head, so you can just about squeeze this experience within our budget. / midnight; closed Sun.

Wagamama £ 16
109-125 Knightsbridge, SW1   7201 8000   5–1D
8 Norris St, SW1   7321 2755   4–4A
101a Wigmore St, W1   7409 0111   3–1A
10a Lexington St, W1   7292 0990   3–2D
4a Streatham St, WC1   7323 9223   2–1C
1 Tavistock St, WC2   7836 3330   4–3D
14a Irving St, WC2   7839 2323   4–4B
26 Kensington High St, W8   7376 1717   5–1A
11 Jamestown Rd, NW1   7428 0800   8–3B
1a Ropemaker St, EC2   7588 2688   9–1C
109 Fleet St, EC4   7583 7889   9–2A
The originators of the no-frills, oriental noodle canteen concept have now spread across London (as have imitators), but they continue to provide good-value ramen dishes (soupy, noodly things) and stir-fries (£5-£8). There are also set meals, of which the top-of-the-range offering, the 'Absolute Wagamama' gives you chicken ramen, dumplings and a Kirin beer for just under a tenner. You'll probably have to queue at peak times.
/ www.wagamama.com; 11 pm; EC4 & EC2 closed Sat & Sun; no smoking; no booking.

The Walmer Castle W11 £ 17   Ⓐ
58 Ledbury Rd   7229 4620   6–1B
The cosy upstairs dining room of a lively Notting Hill pub might be the last place you'd think to look for really tasty Thai cooking, but the results here are in fact surprisingly good. Prices are reasonable, with starters and desserts around the £4 mark and main courses about £7. A typical two-course meal might be green Thai curry followed by mango sorbet, with a bottle of house wine at £9.95. / 10.30 pm; closed weekday L; no booking after 7.30 pm.

White Cross TW9 £ 15   Ⓐ
Water Ln   8940 6844   1–4A
Richmond is such an attractive town that it's a shame it still offers relatively few places for a pleasant and inexpensive lunch. This large Young's pub near Richmond Bridge, with its charming riverside garden, is therefore all the more worth bearing in mind. The food is nothing remarkable, but dishes such as soup of the day (£2.95) and braised lamb in red wine sauce (£6.75) are perfectly well done. The house wine is rather pricey at £16.45 a bottle, but a pint of bitter will set you back £2.20. / www.youngs.co.uk; L only; no Amex; no booking.

sign up for the survey at www.hardens.com

White Horse SW6 £19
1 Parsons Grn 7736 2115 10–1B
Fulham's 'Sloaney Pony' (as the large pub-cum-dining room is affectionately known throughout south west London) is an ever-popular destination that's not content to rest on its laurels – a new, smoke-free, upstairs dining room opened just before we went to press. Realisation of such dishes as hazelnut & pear salad (£6.75) followed, perhaps, by salmon fishcakes (£8.25), is pretty reliable. The house wine is £10.75 a bottle.
/ www.whitehorsesw6.com; 11 pm; no smoking in dining room.

The White House SW4 £20   A
65 Clapham Park Rd 7498 3388 10–2D
Given that the cooking at this Clapham bar/night club is incidental to its primary attractions as a groovy nightspot, it's of quite reasonable quality. Your starter could be chicken satay (£5.50) followed by blackened salmon with wok-fried greens (£8). For top value, arrive early (5.30pm-7.30pm) – before the trendy people, unfortunately – when two courses will set you back £10. The house wine is £12 a bottle.
/ www.thewhitehouselondon.co.uk; 11 pm; D only.

William IV NW10 £19   A★
786 Harrow Rd 8969 5944 1–2B
The one-plate set lunch, which includes a main course plus a glass of wine or beer for £7, and the two course Sunday lunch (£13) are the special attractions for the budget diner at this relaxed and friendly Kensal Green gastropub, which has a charming rear terrace. A la carte you might struggle to keep the prices down, with most main courses around the £10 mark. House wine is £10.75 a bottle, and a pint of London Pride is £2.60. / www.william-iv.co.uk; 10.30 pm, Fri & Sat 11 pm.

Willie Gunn SW18 £20   A
422 Garratt Ln 8946 7773 10–2B
This jolly Earlsfield hang-out continues to be the key rendezvous hereabouts. Thanks to reasonably-priced dishes such as soup of the day with soda bread (£3.75) and smoked salmon fishcakes with fries (£8.50), you can accommodate a meal here within our budget at any time. The house wine is £10 a bottle.
/ 11 pm.

Windsor Castle W8 £18   A
114 Campden Hill Rd 7243 9551 6–2B
For cosy charm, few London pubs can match this quaint Georgian tavern near Notting Hill Gate, whose walled garden is a hugely popular sunny-day attraction. The enjoyable pub grub isn't that cheap, but offers ample choice within our price range, with dishes like steamed mussels or fish 'n' chips costing £7.95. Skip starters and go for the homely puds at £3.45. House wine is £12.45 a bottle, but pints of London Pride are a popular alternative, even at £2.65. / www.windsor-castle-pub.co.uk; 9.30 pm; no smoking area at L; no booking.

for updates visit www.hardens.com

Wine & Kebab SW10   £19*   ★
343 Fulham Rd   7352 0967   5–3B
This friendly taverna has long been a late-night haven for the local Chelsea youth – possibly due to the fact that it's one of the few places in the area with a late licence. The top-value tip is to share the generous meze (£29 for two people), and wash it down with the house wine at £8 a bottle. / 1.30 am; D only.

Wine Factory W11   £18
294 Westbourne Grove   7229 1877   6–1B
As the name might lead one to suppose, the real attraction at this rather sparse Notting Hill eaterie is the excellent-value wine list. The food is rather less of an excitement, but priced reasonably enough for this trendy part of town – Mozzarella & red onion tart (£4.50) followed by one of a good selection of pizzas (£7.50) would make a typical meal. This could be accompanied by a bottle (or two) of house wine at the astonishing price of £7 a time. / 11 pm; closed Sun D; no Amex.

The Wine Library EC3   £20   Ⓐ
43 Trinity Sq   7481 0415   9–3D
Check out these atmospheric City cellars, and for £12.95 you can help yourself to the buffet which includes cheeses, pâtés, quiche, bread, salad, cold meats, fruit and coffee. Then you can let yourself loose on the wines which are the whole point of the place. The selection of bottles is vast (£8-£400), upon which corkage of only £4.50 is charged. So get your pinstripes on – and don't forget to book. / 8 pm; L & early evening only, closed Sat & Sun.

Wódka W8   £18*   Ⓐ★
12 St Alban's Grove   7937 6513   5–1B
It's a little out of our price bracket à la carte, but this Kensington fixture's hidden-away location makes it a very suitable destination for a decadent lunch. The 2-course menu (£11.50) offers such Eastern European delights as krupnik (barley soup with bacon) and bozbash (lamb with saffron and pomegranate), washed down by house wine at £10.50 a bottle. / www.wodka.co.uk; 11.15 pm; closed Sat L & Sun L

Wong Kei W1   £14
41-43 Wardour St   7437 8408   4–3A
The rudeness of its staff is legendary at this massive and brash Chinatown behemoth. Adopt an attitude of Zen-like calm, and you can emerge very quickly and reasonably satisfied by food that is very cheap and actually not bad, considering – just don't try paying in anything other than hard cash. / 11.30 pm; no credit cards; no booking.

sign up for the survey at www.hardens.com

Woodlands £12*
37 Panton St, SW1   7839 7258   4–4A
77 Marylebone Ln, W1   7486 3862   3–1A
The lunchtime buffets (£7.50) at these reliable Indian veggies – one of which has a very central West End location, just off the Haymarket – offer spectacular value, but the set menus (which range from £6-£14.50, and most of which are available at any time) also reward investigation. The house wine is £10 a bottle.
/ www.woodlandsrestaurant.co.uk; 10.30 pm; no Switch.

World Food Café WC2 £16
First Floor, 14 Neal's Yd   7379 0298   4–2C
Open only at lunch, when it is very popular, this Covent Garden café, overlooking Neal's Yard, has a justified reputation for the quality of its global veggie fare. Choices range from falafel or Mexican tortillas (around £6) to Indian thali or Turkish meze (£7.95). Puddings, such as chocolate cake, are £3.25. BYO, or drink fresh juices, from £1.65. / L only, closed Sun; no Amex; no smoking; no booking.

Yas W14 £17
7 Hammersmith Rd   7603 9148   7–1D
Those who claim London as a 24-hour city have the slight problem that finding decent nosh after midnight is still all but impossible in many parts of town. Not at this popular Persian by Olympia, however, where your meal might consist of 'kuku-ye sabzi' (a Persian-style quiche with walnuts and cranberries, £3.95) and stewed lamb with celery and saffron rice (£8.50), washed down with house wine (during licensed hours) at £9.90 a bottle. / www.yasrestaurant.com; 5 am.

Yelo N1 £17
8-9 Hoxton Sq   7729 4626   9–1D
If you want to be at the heart of the Hoxton action, then the outside terrace of this new noodle parlour on the square puts you in pole position. The food – with dishes such as Thai dim sum (£3.95) and fish with tamarind sauce (£4.95) – is well-priced and competently done. The house wine is £8.95 a bottle. / www.yelothai.co.uk; 11 pm, Fri & Sat 11.30 pm; no booking.

Yming W1 £16*   A★★
35-36 Greek St   7734 2721   4–2A
If you're looking for a really good-quality Chinese meal within our budget, avoid the tourist-traps of Chinatown and skip over Shaftesbury Avenue to seek out this still under-appreciated Soho spot. You'd need quite a lot of self-control to stay within our price limit à la carte, but it's certainly possible if you visit from noon-6pm, when you can have three courses – perhaps prawn toast, a meat dish, and lychees, plus coffee – for only £10 (the same price as a bottle of the house wine).
/ www.yming.com; 11.45 pm; closed Sun.

for updates visit www.hardens.com

Yoshino W1 £18* ★★
3 Piccadilly Pl   7287 6622   3–3D
It used to be so authentic that they only did the lunch menu in Japanese, but the attractions of this handily-located café (just by Piccadilly Circus) are now also accessible to those who only speak English. A la carte prices are a little outside our range, but bento boxes – effectively complete meals, with protein, rice, miso soup and vegetables – range in price from only £4.80 at lunchtime (£1 more in the evening) to £12. With house wine at a hefty £13 a bottle, it's best to stick to drinking the complimentary tea. / 10 pm; closed Sun; no smoking.

Yum Yum N16 £17 A★
30 Stoke Newington Church St   7254 6751   1–1C
This ornately-decorated Thai restaurant maintains an eminent position in the much-contested Stoke Newington restaurant scene. Top value is the 2-course set lunch menu (£6.95, including tea or coffee), which might include vegetable spring rolls followed by red duck curry with noodles. Even à la carte, though, and with house wine at £9.95 a bottle, you can eat within our budget at any time. / www.yumyum.co.uk; 10.45 pm, Fri & Sat 11.15 pm.

Zaika W8 £19* A★★
1 Kensington High St   7795 6533   5–1A
It is truly amazing the quality of cooking which the budget luncher can find at the spacious Kensington restaurant, which is one of London's best Indians. You need to stick to the 2-course menu (£11.95) to stay within our price limit – your choice might be tamarind-infused chicken with coriander risotto, followed by swordfish with Kashmiri rogan josh sauce. Alternatively, one-plate specials are available for £8.95, though the house wine will still weigh in at £14.50 a bottle.
/ www.cuisine-collection.co.uk; 10.45 pm; closed Sat L.

Zaika Bazaar SW3 £19 A★
2a Pond Pl   7584 6655   5–2C
The cut-price basement offshoot of one of London's best Indian restaurants (Zaika, see also) offers an exceptionally good-value and wide-ranging menu. With starters such as green chicken tikka (£4.50) and main courses like Mangalore chicken curry (£8.25), and with house wine at £12.95 a bottle, you can always eat here within our budget – pretty remarkable for the environs of Brompton Cross! / www.cuisine-collection.co.uk; 10.45 pm; D only, closed Sun.

sign up for the survey at www.hardens.com

Zamzama NW1 £14 A
161-163 Drummond St   7387 6699   8–4C
If you're looking for Indian food in whizzy modern surroundings, look no further than this futuristic newcomer, not far from Euston station. The setting rather eclipses the food, but the realisation of such dishes as cheese-stuffed chicken with mango sauce (£6.75) or, more prosaically, lamb curry (£5.50) is perfectly competent. The house wine is £7.50 a bottle.
/ www.zamzama.co.uk; 11.30 pm; closed Sat L.

ZeNW3 NW3 £20* ★
83 Hampstead High St   7794 7863   8–2A
Situated in the heart of historic Hampstead, this impressively-minimalist Chinese makes a pleasant venue for the good-quality set lunch (£13.80), which includes two starters and a main course with rice and vegetables – you might have spring rolls, soup and crispy aromatic duck. A la carte, the place is well beyond our budget. The house wine is £12 a bottle. / 11 pm; no Amex.

Zero Degrees SE3 £15 A
29-31 Montpelier Vale   8852 5619   1–4D
There's quite an 'industrial' feel to the impressive modern décor of this Blackheath microbrewery. On the food front, you might go for a wood-fired pizza (around £7), or a sustaining snack such as bruschetta (£2.95), and the excellent house beers start from £2.30 a pint. / www.zerodegrees-microbrewery.co.uk; 11.30 pm.

Zizzi £17 A
110-116 Wigmore St, W1   7935 2336   3–1A
33-41 Charlotte St, W1   7436 9440   2–1C
35-38 Paddington St, W1   7224 1450   2–1A
20 Bow St, WC2   7836 6101   4–2D
73-75 Strand, WC2   7240 1717   4–4D
231 Chiswick High Rd, W4   8747 9400   7–2A
87 Allitsen Rd, NW8   7722 7296   8–3A
35-37 Battersea Rise, SW11   7924 7311   10–2C
This upstart chain of pizza/pasta joints is a serious pretender to the throne which PizzaExpress has long occupied – they have a comfortable, more rustic feel, and portions are generous. A main course of penne with chicken, broccoli and Gorgonzola (£7.25), or grilled aubergine & Parmesan pizza (£6.40), washed down with house wine at £10.15 a bottle would be a typical meal. Finish with the likes of Amaretto-laced apple crumble (£3.85). / www.askcentral.co.uk; 11 pm; no smoking areas; no booking after 7.30 pm.

for updates visit www.hardens.com

INDEXES & CUISINES

INDEXES | BREAKFAST, BYO

BREAKFAST
(with opening times)

Central
Balans: *all branches (8)*
Bank Aldwych *(7 Mon-Fri)*
Bank Westminster *(7 Mon-Fri)*
Bar Italia *(7)*
Bistro 1: *Beak St W1 (11, Sun)*
Carluccio's Caffè: *Market Pl W1 (10); Barrett St W1 (8)*
Food for Thought *(9.30)*
Fortnum's Fountain *(8.30)*
Giraffe: *all branches (8, Sat & Sun 9)*
Maison Bertaux *(8.30)*
Pâtisserie Valerie: *Old Compton St W1 (7.30, Sun 9); Marylebone High St W1 (8, Sun 9); WC2 (9.30, Sun 9)*
Paul: *WC2 (7.30)*
Pizza on the Park *(8.15)*
QC *(7)*
Quiet Revolution: *W1 (9)*
Soup Opera: *all central branches (7.30)*
Star Café *(7)*
Tapa Room (Providores) *(9, Sat & Sun 10)*

West
Adams Café *(7.30, Sat 8.30)*
Balans West: *all branches (8)*
Basilico: *all branches (11)*
Bedlington Café *(8)*
Beirut Express *(7.30)*
Brass. du Marché *(10, Sun 11)*
Café 206 *(8)*
Café Laville *(10)*
Chelsea Bun Diner: *all branches (7)*
La Delizia *(10)*
Fileric *(8)*
Lisboa Patisserie *(7.45)*
Le Metro *(7.30, Sun 8.30)*
Pâtisserie Valerie: *SW3 (7.30, Sun 8)*
Ranoush *(9)*
Raoul's Café *(8.30, Sun 9)*
Le Shop *(10.30)*
Tom's *(8, Sun 10)*
Troubadour *(9)*
Vingt-Quatre *(24 hrs)*

North
Banners *(9, Sat & Sun 10)*
Bar Gansa *(10)*
Café Mozart *(9)*
Chamomile *(7)*
Dartmouth Arms *(11, Sat & Sun 10)*
Gallipoli: *all branches (10.30)*
Giraffe: *all branches (8, Sat & Sun 9)*
Heartstone *(8, Sun 10)*
Shish *(10 Sat & Sun)*

South
Basilico: *all branches (11)*
Boiled Egg *(9, Sun 10)*
Chelsea Bun Diner: *all branches (7)*
Ditto *(noon Sun)*
Eco Brixton: *SW9 (8.30)*
Film Café *(10)*
Gastro *(8)*
Giraffe: *all branches (8, Sat & Sun 9)*
Hudson's *(10 Sat & Sun)*
Konditor & Cook: *The Cut SE1 (8.30)*
La Lanterna *(8, Mon-Sat)*
Tate Modern (Level 7) *(10.15)*
El Vergel *(8.30)*

East
Bar Capitale: *EC4 (6 (coffee only))*
Brick Lane Beigel Bake *(24 hrs)*
Carluccio's Caffè: *E14 (10); EC1 (8)*
Carnevale *(noon (10 for coffee))*
Fox & Anchor *(7)*
Fusion *(7.30)*
Futures *(7.30)*
Hope & Sir Loin *(7 Mon-Fri)*
The Place Below *(7.30)*
Smiths (Ground Floor) *(7am)*
Soup Opera: *all east branches (6.30)*

BYO
(Bring your own wine)

Central
Food for Thought
Fryer's Delight
India Club
Mr Kong

West
Adams Café
Alounak: *all branches*
Bedlington Café
Blah! Blah! Blah!
Café 209
Chelsea Bun Diner: *SW10*
Kandoo
Mawar
Rôtisserie Jules: *SW7*
Tom's

North
Ali Baba
Diwana Bhel-Poori House
Heartstone
Laurent
Seashell

South
Basilico: *SW11*
Eco Brixton: *SW9*
Mirch Masala: *all branches*
Monsieur Max
Polygon Bar & Grill
Spread Eagle
Talad Thai
Thai Corner Café

BYO / CHILDREN | INDEXES

East
Faulkner's
Lahore Kebab House
The Place Below

CHILDREN

**(h – high or special chairs
m – children's menu
p – children's portions
e – weekend entertainments
o – other facilities)**

Central
Abeno *(hp)*
Alfred *(p)*
Aroma II *(hm)*
Ask! Pizza: *all central branches (hp)*
Balans: *all branches (hp)*
Bank Aldwych *(hm)*
Bank Westminster *(hm)*
Bar Italia *(h)*
Benihana: *W1 (h)*
Blues *(o)*
Boudin Blanc *(hp)*
Brahms *(hp)*
La Brasserie Townhouse *(hm)*
Café du Jardin *(p)*
Carluccio's Caffè: *all branches (h)*
China City *(h)*
Chuen Cheng Ku *(h)*
Efes Kebab House: *all branches (hp)*
Fairuz *(h)*
Food for Thought *(p)*
Fortnum's Fountain *(hm)*
Giraffe: *all branches (hm)*
Golden Dragon *(h)*
Gourmet Pizza Co.: *all branches (h)*
Grenadier *(p)*
Hakkasan *(p)*
Harbour City *(h)*
Hard Rock Café *(hmo)*
Italian Kitchen *(m)*
Joy King Lau *(h)*
Malabar Junction *(h)*
Masala Zone *(hp)*
Melati *(h)*
Mr Kong *(hp)*
New Mayflower *(h)*
New World *(h)*
Ozer *(h)*
Paul: *WC2 (he)*
Pizza on the Park *(he)*
PizzaExpress: *Moreton St SW1, Victoria St SW1, Baker St W1, Bruton Pl W1, Charlotte St W1, Greek St W1, Upper St James St W1, Dean St W1, Barrett St W1, Wardour St W1, both WC1, St Martins Ln WC2, Bow St WC2 (h); Langham Pl W1, The Strand WC2 (ho); Victoria St SW1 (o)*
Pizzeria Condotti *(h)*
Poons *(h)*
La Porchetta Pizzeria: *WC1 (h)*
QC *(hm)*

Royal China: *W1 (h)*
Sarastro *(p)*
Satsuma *(h)*
Shampers *(p)*
J Sheekey *(hp)*
Soho Spice *(h)*
Souk *(h)*
Soup Opera: *Hanover St W1 (h)*
La Spighetta *(hp)*
Star Café *(h)*
Strada: *all branches (h)*
Tajine *(h)*
Tapa Room (Providores) *(h)*
Uno *(hm)*
Veeraswamy *(hm)*
Wagamama: *Norris St SW1, both W1, WC1, both WC2 (h)*
World Food Café *(h)*
Zizzi: *Paddington St W1, both WC2 (h)*

West
The Abingdon *(hp)*
Abu Zaad *(h)*
Aglio e Olio *(h)*
Alounak: *W14 (h)*
The Anglesea Arms *(hp)*
Ask! Pizza: *all west branches (hp)*
Balans West: *all branches (hp)*
Bar Japan *(h)*
Beirut Express *(h)*
Ben's Thai *(h)*
Benihana: *SW3 (h)*
Bersagliera *(hm)*
Blue Elephant *(he)*
Blue Lagoon *(h)*
The Brackenbury *(h)*
Brass. du Marché *(hp)*
Brasserie St Quentin *(hm)*
Brilliant *(hp)*
Café 209 *(hp)*
Calzone: *all west branches (hmo)*
Carpaccio's *(hp)*
Chiswick *(hp)*
Le Colombier *(hp)*
Coopers Arms *(p)*
Costa's Fish *(p)*
Coyote Café *(hm)*
La Delizia *(h)*
Frantoio *(hp)*
Galicia *(p)*
The Gate: *W6 (h)*
The Havelock Tavern *(hp)*
Itsu: *SW3 (p)*
Kandoo *(h)*
Khan's *(h)*
Khan's of Kensington *(p)*
Lots Road *(p)*
Lou Pescadou *(hm)*
Lundum's *(p)*
Made in Italy *(h)*
Madhu's Brilliant *(h)*
Malabar *(hp)*
Mandalay *(hp)*

sign up for the survey at www.hardens.com 105

INDEXES | CHILDREN

Mandarin Kitchen (h)
Mediterraneo (h)
Nayaab (h)
Osteria Basilico (h)
Palatino (h)
The Papaya Tree (h)
Parade (he)
Pellicano (h)
Phoenicia (h)
PizzaExpress: SW10, Beauchamp Pl SW3, King's Rd SW3, W11, W14, W2, W4, W8 (h); Fulham Rd SW6 (ho)
The Polish Club (p)
Pucci Pizza (p)
Ranoush (m)
Raoul's Café (h)
Riccardo's (hmo)
Rôtisserie Jules: all branches (hm)
Sabai Sabai (h)
Le Shop (hp)
Spago (h)
Strada: all branches (h)
Thai Noodle Bar (p)
Thai on the River (h)
Timo (h)
Tom's (h)
Troubadour (h)
The Vale (hp)
Wagamama: W8 (h)
The Walmer Castle (hp)
White Horse (hm)
William IV (h)
Yas (hp)
Zaika Bazaar (h)
Zizzi: W4 (hp)

North
Afghan Kitchen (h)
Ali Baba (h)
Anglo Asian Tandoori (h)
Ask! Pizza: N1, Hawley Cr NW1, NW3 (hp)
Banners (hmo)
Bar Gansa (h)
Barracuda (h)
Benihana: NW3 (he)
La Brocca (p)
Bu San (h)
Café de Maya (hp)
Café Mozart (hpe)
Calzone: NW3 (hm); N1 (hmo)
Chamomile (h)
China Dream (hp)
Chutneys (m)
Daphne (hp)
Dartmouth Arms (p)
Don Pepe (hp)
Frederick's (hm)
Furnace (p)
Gallipoli: all branches (h)
The Gate: NW3 (hp)
Geeta (h)
Giraffe: all branches (hm)
Granita (p)

Great Nepalese (p)
Jashan: HA0 (hp)
Lansdowne (h)
Laurent (h)
The Little Bay: NW6 (p)
The Lord Palmerston (p)
Manna (hp)
Marine Ices (hm)
Mesclun (h)
Nautilus (h)
La Piragua (h)
PizzaExpress: all north branches (h)
La Porchetta Pizzeria: all north branches (p)
Rani (hm)
Rôtisserie: N1 (h)
Royal China: NW8 (h)
Sabras (p)
Sakonis (h)
The Salusbury (hm)
Seashell (hp)
Sedir (hp)
Singapore Garden (h)
Solly's Exclusive (h)
Strada: all branches (h)
Tartuf: all branches (h)
Toff's (hm)
Two Brothers (hm)
Vegia Zena (hp)
Vijay (h)
Wagamama: NW1 (h)
Yum Yum (h)
ZeNW3 (h)
Zizzi: NW8 (hp)

South
Alma (hp)
Antipasto & Pasta (h)
Antipasto e Pasta (hp)
Ask! Pizza: all south branches (hp)
Babur Brasserie (hp)
Baltic (hm)
Bankside (h)
Bengal Clipper (h)
Bibo (p)
Boiled Egg (hme)
Bread & Roses (ho)
Buona Sera: SW11 (h)
Butlers Wharf Chop-house (h)
Café Portugal (hp)
Cantina del Ponte (hm)
Cantinetta Venegazzú (hp)
The Castle (hm)
Chez Lindsay (h)
Cinnamon Cay (hm)
Ditto (hm)
don Fernando's (hp)
Eco: SW4 (h)
Film Café (hp)
Fujiyama (h)
Gastro (p)
Giraffe: all branches (hm)

for updates visit www.hardens.com   106

CHILDREN / ENTERTAINMENTS | **INDEXES**

Gourmet Burger Kitchen: *SW11 (h)*
Gourmet Pizza Co.: *all branches (h)*
Indian Ocean *(h)*
Kastoori *(p)*
La Lanterna *(h)*
Ma Goa *(hm)*
Mirch Masala: *all branches (h)*
Need The Dough! *(hmo)*
Niksons *(h)*
O'Zon *(hm)*
The Pepper Tree *(h)*
Phoenix *(h)*
Pizza Metro *(h)*
PizzaExpress: *Cardomom Bldg, Shad Thames SE1, Lavender Hill SW11, SW14, SW15, SW18, SW4 (h); Belvedere Rd SE1, Battersea Br Rd SW11 (ho)*
Pizzeria Castello *(h)*
Polygon Bar & Grill *(hp)*
La Rueda *(hp)*
Sarkhel's *(hm)*
The Stepping Stone *(hmo)*
Strada: *all branches (h)*
The Sun & Doves *(hp)*
Tartuf: *all branches (h)*
Tas: *all branches (h)*
Tate Modern (Level 7) *(hmo)*
Thai Corner Café *(p)*
The Trafalgar Tavern *(hm)*
Willie Gunn *(h)*
Zero Degrees *(h)*
Zizzi: *SW11 (hp)*

East
Alba *(hp)*
Ask! Pizza: *EC1 (h)*
Carluccio's Caffè: *all branches (h)*
Carnevale *(p)*
Faulkner's *(hm)*
Frocks *(hp)*
Gourmet Pizza Co.: *all branches (h)*
Lahore Kebab House *(h)*
Moro *(hp)*
PizzaExpress: *London Wall EC2, EC4 (h); Curtain Rd EC2 (ho); E1, Exmouth Mkt EC1 (o)*
Royal China: *E14 (h)*
St John *(h)*
Scuzi: *both E14 (hm)*
Shanghai *(hp)*
Simpson's Tavern *(p)*
Strada: *all branches (h)*
Viet Hoa *(h)*
Wagamama: *EC2 (h)*

ENTERTAINMENTS
(Check times before you go)

Central
Bank Aldwych *(jazz, Sun)*
Bank Westminster *(DJ, Wed-Sat)*
Brahms *(live music, Sun)*
Café du Jardin *(jazz pianist, nightly)*
Efes Kebab House: *Gt Portland St W1 (belly dancer, nightly)*
Hakkasan *(DJ, Fri & Sat)*
Pizza on the Park *(jazz, nightly)*
PizzaExpress: *Dean St W1 (jazz, nightly)*
Sarastro *(opera, Mon & Sun)*
Soho Spice *(DJ, Fri-Sat)*
Souk *(belly dancer & DJ, Thu-Sat)*

West
Krungtap *(karaoke)*
PizzaExpress: *Beauchamp Pl SW3 (jazz, Sat pm)*
Spago *(band, Fri & singer, Sat)*
Troubadour *(club downstairs)*
William IV *(DJ, Fri & Sat)*

North
Bar Gansa *(flamenco, Mon)*
Barracuda *(jazz, Fri & Sat)*
Benihana: *NW3 (children's ents, Sun)*
La Brocca *(jazz, Thu in bar)*
Don Pepe *(singer & organist, nightly)*
Mesclun *(Jazz, Sat L, Sun LD)*
PizzaExpress: *Kentish Town Rd NW1 (jazz, Wed & Sat pm)*

South
Baltic *(jazz, Sun)*
Bengal Clipper *(pianist, nightly)*
Cantina del Ponte *(live music, Thu)*
Ditto *(big screen sports TV)*
Film Café *(film theatre)*
George II *(DJ, Fri & Sat)*
La Lanterna *(live music, Fri pm)*
Meson don Felipe *(flamenco guitarist, nightly)*
Pizzeria Castello *(salsa, Mon pm)*
Rebato's *(music, Tue-Sat nights)*
La Rueda *(disco, Fri & Sat)*
So.uk *(DJ, Wed-Sat)*
Tas: *Borough High St SE1 (guitarist, nightly); The Cut SE1 (music, nightly)*
The Trafalgar Tavern *(bands, Fri or Sat pm)*
The White House *(DJ, Wed-Sun D)*

East
Cantaloupe *(DJ, Fri & Sat)*
PizzaExpress: *E14 (music, Tue pm)*
Rupee Room *(karaoke)*
Scuzi: *EC3 (music, Tue-Fri); West India Quay E14 (music, Tue-Sat)*
Tokyo City *(Karaoke)*

sign up for the survey at www.hardens.com

INDEXES | LATE, NO-SMOKING

LATE
(open till midnight or later as shown; may be earlier Sunday)

Central
Balans: *W1 (5 am, Sun 1 am)*
Bar Italia *(4 am, Fri & Sat open 24 hours)*
Benihana: *all branches (Fri & Sat only)*
Blues *(Thu-Sat only)*
Boulevard
Café du Jardin
Café Emm *(Fri & Sat only, 12.30 am)*
Efes Kebab House: *Gt Portland St W1 (Fri & Sat only, 3 am)*
Hard Rock Café *(12.30 am, Fri & Sat 1 am)*
Incognico
Itsu: *W1 (midnight, Fri & Sat)*
Melati *(Fri & Sat only, 12.30 am)*
Mr Kong *(2.45 am)*
New Mayflower *(3.45 am)*
Ozer
Pizza on the Park
PizzaExpress: *Moreton St SW1, Victoria St SW1, Baker St W1, Bruton Pl W1, Charlotte St W1, Upper St James St W1, Barrett St W1, Wardour St W1, both WC1, St Martins Ln WC2, The Strand WC2, Bow St WC2; Greek St W1 (midnight); Dean St W1 (midnight, Wed-Sat 1 am)*
Pizzeria Condotti
La Porchetta Pizzeria: *all branches (midnight)*
Rasa: *all branches (Fri & Sat only)*
J Sheekey
Soho Spice *(3 am, Fri & Sat only)*
Soup Opera: *Hanover St W1 (Fri only)*

West
Alounak: *all branches*
Anarkali
Balans: *W8 (1 am); SW5 (1 am)*
Beirut Express *(1.45 am)*
Benihana: *all branches (Fri & Sat only)*
Blue Elephant
Calzone: *all branches (midnight, Fri & Sat 12.30 am)*
Chelsea Bun
Diner: *SW10 (midnight)*
La Delizia
Lou Pescadou
Nayaab
Patio
PizzaExpress: *SW10, all in SW3N, SW5, Wandsworth Bridge Rd SW6, W11, W14, W2, W4, W8*
Pucci Pizza *(12.30 am)*
Ranoush *(3 am)*
Riccardo's
Le Shop
Spago
Vingt-Quatre *(24 hours)*
Wine & Kebab *(2 am)*
Yas *(5 am)*

North
Ali Baba
Banners *(Fri & Sat only)*
Bar Gansa
Benihana: *all branches (Fri & Sat only)*
Calzone: *all branches (midnight, Fri & Sat 12.30 am)*
Don Pepe
The Little Bay: *all branches*
La Piragua
PizzaExpress: *all north branches*
La Porchetta Pizzeria: *all branches (midnight)*
Rasa: *all branches (Fri & Sat only)*
Tartuf: *all branches (midnight)*
Vrisaki

South
Buona Sera: *SW11*
Gastro
PizzaExpress: *Borough High St SE1, Lavender Hill SW11, SW13, SW14, SW15, SW18*
Tartuf: *all branches (midnight)*

East
Brick Lane Beigel Bake *(24 hours)*
Lahore Kebab House
The Little Bay: *all branches*
PizzaExpress: *E1, Curtain Rd EC2*

NO-SMOKING AREAS
(* completely no smoking)

Central
Abeno
La Brasserie Townhouse
Busaba Eathai: *W1**
Chiang Mai
China City
Chuen Cheng Ku
Food for Thought*
Gourmet Pizza Co.: *W1*
Hakkasan
Hard Rock Café
Ikkyu
Kulu Kulu*
Maison Bertaux
Malabar Junction
Masala Zone*
Mela
Mildred's*
New World
Pan-Asian Canteen
Paul: *WC2**
Pizza on the Park
PizzaExpress: *Victoria St SW1*
Poons, Lisle Street
QC
Rasa: *all branches**
Royal Court Bar
Sarastro
Satsuma*
Soho Spice

for updates visit www.hardens.com

NO-SMOKING, OUTSIDE TABLES | INDEXES

La Spighetta
Star Café
Thai Café
Thai Pot: *Bedfordbury WC2*
Wagamama: *both W1, WC1**
World Food Café*
Yoshino

West
Bedlington Café*
Blue Lagoon
Café Laville
Chiswick
Itsu: *SW3**
Khan's
Khan's of Kensington
Mandalay*
Palatino
The Papaya Tree
Phoenicia
Raoul's Café
Sabai Sabai
Southeast
Standard Tandoori
Thai Bistro*
Thai Break
Tom's*
The Vale
White Horse
Windsor Castle

North
Anglo Asian Tandoori
Café de Maya
Café Japan
Café Mozart*
Cantina Italia
Chamomile
Chutneys
Diwana B-P House
Frederick's
Giraffe: *NW3**
Heartstone*
Jashan: *HA0**
The Little Bay: *NW6*
Manna*
Marine Ices
Oriental City
The Parsee
Rani
Rasa: *all branches**
Rasa Travancore*
Sabras
Seashell
Shish
Solly's Exclusive
Sushi-Say
Toff's
Two Brothers
Viet-Anh
Vijay

South
Babur Brasserie
Bankside
Coromandel
Eco: *SW4*
Film Café
Gastro
Gourmet Burger Kitchen: *SW11**
Konditor & Cook: *Stoney St SE1**
The Pepper Tree
Sarkhel's
The Stepping Stone
The Sun & Doves
Talad Thai*
Tate Modern (Level 7)*
Thailand*

East
Arkansas Café*
Brick Lane Beigel Bake*
Café Indiya
Faulkner's
Fusion*
Futures*
Gourmet Pizza Co.: *E14*
K10*
Moshi Moshi: *EC2**
The Place Below*
Touzai

OUTSIDE TABLES
(* particularly recommended)

Central
Alfred
L'Artiste Musclé*
Ask! Pizza: *Grafton Way W1*
Aurora*
Balans: *all branches*
Bank Westminster
Bar Italia
Boudin Blanc*
Boulevard
Brahms*
La Brasserie Townhouse
Café du Jardin
Carluccio's Caffè: *all central branches**
China City
Efes Kebab House: *Gt Titchfield St W1*
Fairuz: *W1*
Giraffe: *W1*
Gordon's Wine Bar*
Hard Rock Café
Hellenik
Italian Kitchen
Jenny Lo's
Maison Bertaux
Masala Zone
Mela
Mildred's
Ozer

sign up for the survey at www.hardens.com

INDEXES | OUTSIDE TABLES

Paolo
Pâtisserie Valerie: *Marylebone High St W1, WC2*
The Perseverance
Pizza on the Park
PizzaExpress: *Moreton St SW1, Baker St W1, Charlotte St W1, Langham Pl W1, Barrett St W1, both WC1, The Strand WC2*
Quiet Revolution: *all branches*
Rocket
Sarastro
Souk
Soup Opera: *both W1*
Star Café
Strada: *Market Pl W1*; New Burlington St W1*
Tajine
Tapa Room (Providores)
Uno
Wagamama: *Irving St WC2*
Zizzi: *Paddington St W1, Bow St WC2*

West
The Abingdon*
The Anglesea Arms
Ask! Pizza: *SW6, Spring St W2, W4*
The Atlas*
Balans West: *all branches*
Bedlington Café
La Bouchée
The Brackenbury*
Brass. du Marché
Brasserie St Quentin
The Builder's Arms
Café 206
Café Laville*
Calzone: *all branches*
Chelsea Bun Diner: *all branches*
Chiswick
Le Colombier*
Costa's Fish
Coyote Café*
La Delizia
Il Falconiere
The Gate: *W6**
Golborne House
The Havelock Tavern
Kandoo
Khan's of Kensington
Khyber Pass
Krungtap
Latymers
Lisboa Patisserie
Lou Pescadou
Lundum's
Made in Italy
Mediterraneo
Le Metro
Old Parr's Head
Osteria Basilico
Palatino*
Pâtisserie Valerie: *SW3*
Pellicano

The Pilot*
PizzaExpress: *King's Rd SW3*; both SW6, W14, W2, W4, W8*
The Polish Club*
Pucci Pizza
Raoul's Café
The Red Pepper
Riccardo's
Rôtisserie Jules: *SW7*
Le Shop
Southeast
Spago
Stone Mason's Arms
Thai Noodle Bar
Thai on the River*
The Thatched House*
Tom's*
Troubadour
Uli
Vingt-Quatre
White Horse
William IV*
Windsor Castle*
Wine Factory
Wódka
Yas
Zizzi: *W4*

North
Ask! Pizza: *N1, NW3*
Bar Gansa
Barracuda*
Benihana: *NW3*
La Brocca
Café Mozart*
Calzone: *all branches*
Chamomile
The Chapel
Daphne*
Dartmouth Arms
Frederick's*
Gallipoli: *all branches*
The Gate: *NW3*
Gourmet Burger Kitchen: *NW6*
Lansdowne
Laurent
Lemonia
The Little Bay: *all branches*
The Lord Palmerston
Mango Room
Manna
North Sea Fish
Odette's
Petit Auberge
La Piragua
PizzaExpress: *Parkway NW1, Haverstock Hill NW3, NW8*
The Queen's
The Real Greek
Rôtisserie: *N1*
The Salusbury
Singapore Garden
Solly's Exclusive

for updates visit www.hardens.com

OUTSIDE TABLES, PRE/POST THEATRE | INDEXES

Tartuf: *all branches*
Tbilisi
Vegia Zena
Viet-Anh
Yelo

South
Antipasto & Pasta
Antipasto e Pasta
Arancia
Ask! Pizza: *SE1*
Baltic
Boiled Egg*
Bread & Roses
Buona Sera: *SW11*
Butlers Wharf
 Chop-house*
Cantina del Ponte*
Cantinetta Venegazzú*
The Castle*
Chelsea Bun Diner: *all branches*
Cinnamon Cay
don Fernando's
Film Café
Gastro
Giraffe: *SW11*
Gourmet Burger
 Kitchen: *SW11*
Gourmet Pizza Co.: *SE1**
Hudson's
Kennington Lane*
Konditor & Cook: *Stoney St SE1*
La Lanterna
Need The Dough!
Niksons
O'Zon
The Pepper Tree
Phoenix
Pizza Metro
PizzaExpress: *SW14, SW15, SW4*
Popeseye: *SW15*
La Rueda
Spread Eagle
Strada: *SW11*
The Sun & Doves*
Tartuf: *all branches*
White Cross*
The White House
Zizzi: *SW11*

East
Arkansas Café
Ask! Pizza: *EC1*
Bar Capitale: *all branches*
Café Indiya
Cantaloupe
Carluccio's Caffè: *EC1*
Carnevale*
The Eagle
Fox & Anchor
Frocks*
Gourmet Pizza Co.: *E14*
The Little Bay: *all branches*

LMNT
Moro
Moshi Moshi: *EC4*
PizzaExpress: *Exmouth Mkt EC1*
The Place Below*
Quiet Revolution: *all branches*
Royal China: *E14*
Scuzi: *both E14*

PRE/POST THEATRE
(evening opening times are given;
* open all day)

Central
Alfred *(6 pm)*
L'Artiste Musclé *(6 pm)*
Blues*
Boudin Blanc *(6 pm)*
Café du Jardin *(5.30 pm)*
Chiang Mai *(6 pm)*
Chuen Cheng Ku*
Gopal's of Soho *(6 pm)*
Gordon's Wine Bar*
Harbour City*
Italian Kitchen*
Melati*
Mon Plaisir *(5.45 pm)*
Mr Kong*
New World*
PizzaExpress: *Baker St W1, Bruton Pl W1, Charlotte St W1, Greek St W1, Dean St W1, Barrett St W1, Wardour St W1, Coptic St WC1, Bow St WC2**
Pizzeria Condotti*
Poons*
Poons, Lisle Street*
Shampers*
Wagamama: *WC1**
Wong Kei*

North
Frederick's *(5.45 pm)*

East
Alba *(6 pm)*

PRIVATE ROOMS
(for the most comprehensive
listing of venues for functions –
from palaces to pubs – see
Harden's Party Guide for London,
available in all good bookshops)
* particularly recommended

Central
Alfred *(15-20)*
Aperitivo *(30)*
Aroma II *(40)*
L'Artiste Musclé *(25)*
Aurora *(20)*
Bank Westminster *(20,20)**
Benihana: *W1 (10)*
Bistro 1: *Beak St W1 (25)*
Blues *(40)*
Boudin Blanc *(20,20)*

sign up for the survey at www.hardens.com

INDEXES | PRIVATE ROOMS

Boulevard (80)
La Brasserie Townhouse (20)
Café du Jardin (60)
Chiang Mai (30)
China City (10,20,30,40)
Chuen Cheng Ku (56)
Deca (16)
Efes Kebab House: Gt Titchfield St W1 (45)
L'Estaminet (16)
Fairuz: W1 (25)
Fortnum's Fountain (56)
Giraffe: W1 (80)
Golden Dragon (40)
Gopal's of Soho (20)
Harbour City (80,60,40)
Ikkyu (10)
Italian Kitchen (10)
Jenny Lo's (20)
Joy King Lau (60)
Mela (40)
Melati (35)
Mon Plaisir (28)
Mr Kong (40)
New World (200)
Pan-Asian Canteen (41)
The Perseverance (24)
Pizza on the Park (100)
PizzaExpress: Baker St W1 (100); Wardour St W1 (30); Moreton St SW1, Charlotte St W1 (35); Coptic St WC1, St Martins Ln WC2 (40); Bruton Pl W1 (45); Upper St W1, Bow St WC2 (50); High Holborn WC1 (55); Dean St W1, Barrett St W1 (70)
Pizzeria Condotti (40)
Poons (24)
Poons, Lisle Street (15,35)
Ragam (15)
Raks (20)
Rasa: W1 (85)
Rocket (10,30)
Royal China: W1 (12)
Royal Court Bar (12)
Shampers (45)
Soho Spice (30)
Souk (20,35)
Star Café (35)
Strada: Market Pl W1 (?)
Tajine (40)
Thai Café (22)
Veeraswamy (36)
Yming (1)
Yoshino (20)

West
The Abingdon (70)
Abu Zaad (25)
Adams Café (24)
Anarkali (40)
The Atlas (40)
Bar Japan (6)
Ben's Thai (20)
Benihana: SW3 (12)
Blah! Blah! Blah! (30)

Blue Elephant (200)
Blue Lagoon (30)
The Brackenbury (30)
Brass. du Marché (50)
Brasserie St Quentin (25)
Brilliant (125)
Carpaccio's (45)
Chelsea Bun Diner: SW10 (50)
Le Colombier (28)
Coopers Arms (25)
The Cow (Dining Room) (35)
Il Falconiere (35)
Golborne House (35)
Good Earth (40)
The Ifield (23)
Khan's (200)
Khan's of Kensington (30)
Krungtap (30)
Lomo (20)
Lou Pescadou (45)
Made in Italy (20)
Madhu's Brilliant (50)
Malabar (35)
Nayaab (45)
Parade (40)
Patio (50)
Pellicano (25)
Phoenicia (36)
PizzaExpress: Beauchamp Pl SW3 (16); SW10 (50); King's Rd SW3 (60)
The Polish Club (20,50)
Pucci Pizza (50)
Raoul's Café (18)
Riccardo's (8)
Rôtisserie Jules: SW7 (28); W11 (56)
Royal China: W2 (15,20)
Le Shop (35)
Southeast (25)
Spago (40)
Standard Tandoori (55)
Stick & Bowl (20)
Stratford's (32)
Tawana (40)
Thai Noodle Bar (25)
Thai on the River (90 (+90 outside))
The Thatched House (30)
Timo (18)
Troubadour (30)
Uli (32)
The Vale (14,30,40)
White Horse (45)
William IV (35)
Wine Factory (45)
Wódka (30)
Yas (34)
Zaika (16)

North
Afghan Kitchen (25)
Anglo Asian Tandoori (30-40)
Barracuda (35)

for updates visit www.hardens.com

PRIVATE ROOMS | INDEXES

The Chapel (30)
China Dream (30)
Chutneys (60,35)
Daphne (50)
Diwana B-P House (35)
Frederick's (18,32)
Geeta (36)
Giraffe: NW3 (45); N1 (70)
Great Nepalese (32)
Gung-Ho (24)
Lemonia (40)
The Little Bay: NW6 (60)
The Lord Palmerston (30)
Mango Room (30)
North Sea Fish (40)
Odette's (8,30)*
The Parsee (18)
Petit Auberge (45)
La Piragua (70)
PizzaExpress: Kentish Town Rd NW1 (25); Heath St NW3 (30); Haverstock Hill NW3 (40); NW8 (55); N1 (70)
Rasa: N16 (45)
The Real Greek (8,20)
Royal China: NW8 (15,20)
Sedir (42)
Singapore Garden (6)
Solly's Exclusive (100)
Sushi-Say (6)
Tartuf: N1 (40)
Tbilisi (30)
Vegia Zena (20)
Vrisaki (14)
Yum Yum (30)
Zamzama (40)
ZeNW3 (24)

South
Alma (70)
Antipasto & Pasta (30)
Arancia (8)
Baltic (35)
Bankside (70)
Bread & Roses (50)
The Castle (30)
Chez Lindsay (36)
Coromandel (30)
Ditto (20)
don Fernando's (100)
Fish in a Tie (40)
Fujiyama (25)
George II (40)
Hudson's (12)
Kennington Lane (40)
La Lanterna (85,50)
Ma Goa (35)
Niksons (38)
Pizza Metro (50)
PizzaExpress: SW15 (30); Borough High St SE1 (40); SE11, SW18 (50)
Pizzeria Castello (80)
So.uk (30)
Spread Eagle (25)
Sree Krishna (50,60)
Tas: The Cut SE1 (35); Borough High St SE1 (80)
Thailand (28)
The Trafalgar Tavern (200)*
White Cross (30)
The White House (8,26)
Zero Degrees (50)

East
Alba (30)
Arkansas Café (50)
Café Indiya (50)
Cantaloupe (20)
Fox & Anchor (24)
Frocks (30)
Hope & Sir Loin (20)
Moro (12)
Moshi Moshi: EC4 (60)
PizzaExpress: London Wall EC2 (250); Cowcross St EC1, Curtain Rd EC2 (60); E1 (76)
Royal China: E14 (15,20)
St John (18)
Shanghai (40,40)

sign up for the survey at www.hardens.com

CUISINES | EUROPE

ALSATIAN

★
Tartuf (N1, SW4)

BRITISH, MODERN

Ⓐ★★
Frederick's (N1)
The Havelock Tavern (W14)
Kennington Lane (SE11)
Odette's (NW1)
QC (WC1)
The Stepping Stone (SW8)

★★
The Anglesea Arms (W6)
Konditor & Cook (SE1)

Ⓐ★
Bank Aldwych (WC2)
Bank Westminster (SW1)
Blues (W1)
Café du Jardin (WC2)
Le Deuxième (WC2)
Ditto (SW18)
Mango Room (NW1)
Niksons (SW11)
Parade (W5)
Phoenix (SW15)
William IV (NW10)

★
Alfred (WC2)
Bradley's (NW3)
The Castle (SW11)
Chiswick (W4)
George II (SW11)
Granita (N1)
St John (EC1)
The Vale (W9)

Ⓐ
Aurora (W1)
The Builder's Arms (SW3)
Cantaloupe (EC2)
Coopers Arms (SW3)
Fortnum's Fountain (W1)
Frocks (E9)
Golborne House (W10)
The Ifield (SW10)
Lansdowne (NW1)
LMNT (E8)
Lots Road (SW10)
Stone Mason's Arms (W6)
The Thatched House (W6)
Willie Gunn (SW18)

-
The Abingdon (W8)
Bankside (SE1)
The Brackenbury (W6)
The Chapel (NW1)
The Cow
  (Dining Room) (W2)
Dartmouth Arms (NW5)
The Lord Palmerston (NW5)
Mesclun (N16)
Le Metro (SW3)
The Perseverance (WC1)
The Pilot (W4)
The Prince Bonaparte (W2)
The Queen's (NW1)
Raoul's Café (W9)
The Sun & Doves (SE5)
Vingt-Quatre (SW10)
White Horse (SW6)

BRITISH, TRADITIONAL

Ⓐ★
Butlers Wharf
  Chop-house (SE1)
Smiths of Smithfield
  (Ground Floor) (EC1)

Ⓐ
Ffiona's (W8)
Grenadier (SW1)
Simpson's Tavern (EC3)
The Trafalgar Tavern (SE10)
Windsor Castle (W8)
The Wine Library (EC3)

-
Fox & Anchor (EC1)
Hope & Sir Loin (EC1)

DANISH

Ⓐ★★
Lundum's (SW7)

EAST & CENTRAL EUROPEAN

Ⓐ
Café Mozart (N6)

FRENCH

Ⓐ★★
Deca (W1)

★★
Brasserie St Quentin (SW3)
Incognico (WC2)

Ⓐ★
Boudin Blanc (W1)
Chez Lindsay (TW10)
Le Colombier (SW3)
L'Estaminet (WC2)

for updates visit www.hardens.com

EUROPE | CUISINES

Mon Plaisir *(WC2)*
Spread Eagle *(SE10)*

★
La Brasserie
  Townhouse *(WC1)*
Granita *(N1)*

Ⓐ
L'Artiste Musclé *(W1)*
La Bouchée *(SW7)*
Brass. du Marché *(W10)*
Gastro *(SW4)*

-
Petit Auberge *(N1)*

GEORGIAN

-
Tbilisi *(N7)*

GREEK

Ⓐ★
Hellenik *(W1)*

★
The Real Greek *(N1)*
Vrisaki *(N22)*
Wine & Kebab *(SW10)*

Ⓐ
Lemonia *(NW1)*

-
Daphne *(NW1)*

ITALIAN

Ⓐ★
Arancia *(SE16)*
Bibo *(SW13)*
Carpaccio's *(SW3)*
Frantoio *(SW10)*
Made in Italy *(SW3)*
Osteria Basilico *(W11)*

★
Aglio e Olio *(SW10)*
Alba *(EC1)*
Antipasto e Pasta *(SW4)*
Cantinetta Venegazzú *(SW11)*
Palatino *(W4)*
Pellicano *(SW3)*
La Porchetta Pizzeria *(N1, N4, WC1)*
The Red Pepper *(W9)*
The Salusbury *(NW6)*
La Spighetta *(W1)*
Timo *(W8)*
Vegia Zena *(NW1)*

Ⓐ
Aperitivo *(W1)*
La Brocca *(NW6)*
Buona Sera *(SW11, SW3)*
Café 206 *(W11)*
Cantina del Ponte *(SE1)*
Pizza on the Park *(SW1)*
Zizzi *(NW8, SW11, W1, W4, WC2)*

-
Antipasto & Pasta *(SW11)*
Bersagliera *(SW3)*
Cantina Italia *(N1)*
Carluccio's Caffè *(E14, EC1, W1)*
La Delizia *(SW3)*
Il Falconiere *(SW7)*
Il Forno *(W1)*
Italian Kitchen *(WC1)*
La Lanterna *(SE1)*
Marine Ices *(NW3)*
Need The Dough! *(SW11)*
Paolo *(W1)*
Riccardo's *(SW3)*
Spago *(SW7)*
Strada *(EC1, N1, SW11, SW4, SW5, SW6, W1, WC2)*
Uno *(SW1)*
Wine Factory *(W11)*

MEDITERRANEAN

★★
El Vergel *(SE1)*

Ⓐ★
The Eagle *(EC1)*
Made in Italy *(SW3)*
Mediterraneo *(W11)*

Ⓐ
The Atlas *(SW6)*
Bistro 1 *(W1, WC2)*
Fish in a Tie *(SW11)*
The Little Bay *(EC1, NW6)*
Rocket *(W1)*

-
Errays *(N1)*
Raks *(W1)*
Tom's *(W11)*

POLISH

Ⓐ★
Wódka *(W8)*

Ⓐ
Baltic *(SE1)*
The Polish Club *(SW7)*

-
Patio *(W12)*

CUISINES | EUROPE/AMERICAS/MISCELLANEOUS

PORTUGUESE

Ⓐ
Café Portugal *(SW8)*

SPANISH

Ⓐ★★
Moro *(EC1)*

Ⓐ
Bar Gansa *(NW1)*
don Fernando's *(TW9)*
Lomo *(SW10)*
Meson don Felipe *(SE1)*
Rebato's *(SW8)*
La Rueda *(SW4)*

-
Don Pepe *(NW8)*
Galicia *(W10)*

AMERICAN

★
Arkansas Café *(E1)*

-
Coyote Café *(W4)*

MEXICAN/TEXMEX

-
Coyote Café *(W4)*

SOUTH AMERICAN

★★
El Vergel *(SE1)*

-
La Piragua *(N1)*

INTERNATIONAL

Ⓐ
Alma *(SW18)*
Barracuda *(N16)*
Bread & Roses *(SW4)*
Café Laville *(W2)*
Coopers Arms *(SW3)*
Giraffe *(N1, NW3, SW11, W1)*
Gordon's Wine Bar *(WC2)*
Hudson's *(SW15)*
Sarastro *(WC2)*
Shampers *(W1)*
Tate Modern (Level 7) *(SE1)*
White Cross *(TW9)*
The White House *(SW4)*
Windsor Castle *(W8)*

-
Balans West *(SW5, W1, W8)*
Banners *(N8)*
Boulevard *(WC2)*
Brahms *(SW1)*
Café Emm *(W1)*
Chelsea Bun Diner *(SW10, SW11)*
Film Café *(SE1)*
Horse *(SE1)*
Royal Court Bar *(SW1)*
Star Café *(W1)*

EAST/WEST

Ⓐ★
Cinnamon Cay *(SW11)*
Tapa Room (Providores) *(W1)*

★
Tsunami *(SW4)*

FISH & SEAFOOD

Ⓐ★★
J Sheekey *(WC2)*

★★
Chez Liline *(N4)*
Mandarin Kitchen *(W2)*

★
Bradley's *(NW3)*
Lou Pescadou *(SW5)*
Stratford's *(W8)*

Ⓐ
Gastro *(SW4)*
Polygon Bar & Grill *(SW4)*
Sweetings *(EC4)*

STEAKS & GRILLS

★★
Rôtisserie *(N1, W12)*

★
Arkansas Café *(E1)*
Popeseye *(SW15, W14)*

Ⓐ
Polygon Bar & Grill *(SW4)*
Simpson's Tavern *(EC3)*

-
Field & Forest *(WC2)*
Fox & Anchor *(EC1)*
Hope & Sir Loin *(EC1)*
Rôtisserie Jules *(SW7, W11)*

for updates visit www.hardens.com

MICELLANEOUS | CUISINES

ORGANIC

Ⓐ★
Quiet Revolution (EC1, W1)

★
Heartstone (NW1)

VEGETARIAN

Ⓐ★★
The Gate (NW3, W6)

★★
Blah! Blah! Blah! (W12)
Chiang Mai (W1)
Geeta (NW6)
Kastoori (SW17)
Rasa (N16, W1)
Sabras (NW10)
Sree Krishna (SW17)
Vijay (NW6)

Ⓐ★
Blue Elephant (SW6)
The Place Below (EC2)

★
Bu San (N7)
Carnevale (EC1)
Chutneys (NW1)
Diwana Bhel
 -Poori House (NW1)
Food for Thought (WC2)
Futures (EC3)
Jashan (HA0, N8)
Malabar Junction (WC1)
Manna (NW3)
Mildred's (W1)
Ragam (W1)
Rani (N3)

-
Blue Lagoon (W14)
India Club (WC2)
Masala Zone (W1)
Sedir (N1)
Woodlands (SW1, W1)
World Food Café (WC2)

AFTERNOON TEA

Ⓐ
Aurora (W1)

-
Pâtisserie Valerie (SW3, W1, WC2)

BURGERS, ETC

★
Arkansas Café (E1)
Gourmet Burger
 Kitchen (NW6, SW11, SW15)

Ⓐ
Hard Rock Café (W1)

CREPES

Ⓐ★
Chez Lindsay (TW10)

-
Le Shop (SW3)

FISH & CHIPS

★★
Faulkner's (E8)

★
Brady's (SW18)
Costa's Fish (W8)
Nautilus (NW6)
North Sea Fish (WC1)
Seashell (NW1)
Two Brothers (N3)

-
Fryer's Delight (WC1)
Toff's (N10)

ICE CREAM

-
Marine Ices (NW3)

PIZZA

Ⓐ★★
Pizza Metro (SW11)

★★
Basilico (SW11, SW15, SW6)

Ⓐ★
Bibo (SW13)
Made in Italy (SW3)
Osteria Basilico (W11)
Pizzeria Castello (SE1)

★
Bar Capitale (EC2, EC4)
Eco (SW4)
Eco Brixton (SW9)
Furnace (N1)
Porchetta Pizzeria (N1, N4, WC1)
The Red Pepper (W9)
La Spighetta (W1)

sign up for the survey at www.hardens.com

CUISINES | MISC./AFRICA/MIDDLE EAST

Ⓐ
Ask! Pizza *(EC1, N1, NW1, NW3, SE1, SW1, SW13, SW3, SW6, SW7, W1, W11, W2, W4, W8)*
La Brocca *(NW6)*
Buona Sera *(SW11, SW3)*
Pizza on the Park *(SW1)*
Pucci Pizza *(SW3)*
Rocket *(W1)*
Zero Degrees *(SE3)*
Zizzi *(NW8, SW11, W1, W4, WC2)*

-

Bersagliera *(SW3)*
Calzone *(N1, NW3, SW10, W11)*
Cantina Italia *(N1)*
La Delizia *(SW3)*
Gourmet Pizza Co. *(E14, SE1, W1)*
La Lanterna *(SE1)*
Marine Ices *(NW3)*
PizzaExpress *(E1, E14, EC1, EC2, EC3, EC4, N1, N6, NW1, NW3, NW8, SE1, SE11, SW1, SW10, SW11, SW13, SW14, SW15, SW18, SW3, SW4, SW5, SW6, W1, W11, W14, W2, W4, W8, WC1, WC2)*
Pizzeria Condotti *(W1)*
Scuzi *(E14, EC3)*
Spago *(SW7)*
Strada *(EC1, N1, SW11, SW4, SW5, SW6, W1, WC2)*
Wine Factory *(W11)*

SANDWICHES, CAKES, ETC

★★
Brick Lane Beigel Bake *(E1)*
Konditor & Cook *(SE1)*
Lisboa Patisserie *(W10)*

Ⓐ★
Maison Bertaux *(W1)*
Paul *(W1, WC2)*

Ⓐ
Bar Italia *(W1)*
Troubadour *(SW5)*

-

Boiled Egg *(SW11)*
Chamomile *(NW3)*
Fileric *(SW7)*
Pâtisserie Valerie *(SW3, W1, WC2)*
Tom's *(W11)*

SOUP

★
Soup Opera *(E14, EC2, EC3, W1, WC2)*

AFRO-CARIBBEAN

Ⓐ★
Mango Room *(NW1)*

-

Banners *(N8)*

MOROCCAN

Ⓐ★★
Moro *(EC1)*

★
Maghreb *(N1)*

-

Adams Café *(W12)*
Tajine *(W1)*

NORTH AFRICAN

★
Laurent *(NW2)*

Ⓐ
Souk *(WC2)*
So.uk *(SW4)*

-

Azou *(W6)*

TUNISIAN

★
Laurent *(NW2)*

-

Adams Café *(W12)*

EGYPTIAN

-

Ali Baba *(NW1)*

ISRAELI

-

Solly's Exclusive *(NW11)*

KOSHER

-

Solly's Exclusive *(NW11)*

LEBANESE

★★
Beirut Express *(W2)*

for updates visit www.hardens.com

MIDDLE EAST/ASIA/INDIA | **CUISINES**

★
Phoenicia *(W8)*
Ranoush *(W2)*

-
Fairuz *(W1, W2)*

MIDDLE EASTERN

★
Abu Zaad *(W12)*
Shish *(NW2)*

-
Gaby's *(WC2)*
Solly's Exclusive *(NW11)*

PERSIAN

★
Alounak *(W14, W2)*
Kandoo *(W2)*
Mohsen *(W14)*

-
Yas *(W14)*

TURKISH

Ⓐ★
Ozer *(W1)*
Tas *(SE1)*

Ⓐ
Gallipoli *(N1)*

-
Efes Kebab House *(W1)*
Raks *(W1)*
Sedir *(N1)*

AFGHANI

★
Afghan Kitchen *(N1)*

BURMESE

★★
Mandalay *(W2)*

CHINESE

Ⓐ★★
Yming *(W1)*

★★
Mandarin Kitchen *(W2)*
Royal China *(E14, W1, NW8, W2)*

Ⓐ★
China Dream *(NW3)*
Gung-Ho *(NW6)*
Hakkasan *(W1)*

★
Aroma II *(W1)*
The Four Seasons *(W2)*
Good Earth *(SW3)*
Jenny Lo's *(SW1)*
Mr Kong *(WC2)*
New Mayflower *(W1)*
Singapore Garden *(NW6)*
Stick & Bowl *(W8)*
ZeNW3 *(NW3)*

Ⓐ
Shanghai *(E8)*

-
China City *(WC2)*
Chuen Cheng Ku *(W1)*
Golden Dragon *(W1)*
Harbour City *(W1)*
Joy King Lau *(W1)*
New World *(W1)*
Poons *(WC2)*
Poons, Lisle Street *(WC2)*
Wong Kei *(W1)*

CHINESE, DIM SUM

★★
Royal China *(E14, W1, NW8, W2)*

Ⓐ
Shanghai *(E8)*

-
Chuen Cheng Ku *(W1)*
Golden Dragon *(W1)*
Harbour City *(W1)*
Joy King Lau *(W1)*
New World *(W1)*

INDIAN

Ⓐ★★
Zaika *(W8)*

★★
Chowki *(W1)*
Geeta *(NW6)*
Kastoori *(SW17)*
Lahore Kebab House *(E1)*
Mirch Masala *(SW16, SW17)*
The Parsee *(N19)*
Rasa *(N16, W1)*
Sakonis *(HA0)*
Sarkhel's *(SW18)*
Sree Krishna *(SW17)*
Vijay *(NW6)*

sign up for the survey at www.hardens.com   *119*

CUISINES | INDIA/ASIA

Ⓐ★
Malabar *(W8)*
Veeraswamy *(W1)*
Zaika Bazaar *(SW3)*

★
Babur Brasserie *(SE23)*
Bengal Clipper *(SE1)*
Brilliant *(UB2)*
Café Indiya *(E1)*
Chutneys *(NW1)*
Diwana B-P House *(NW1)*
Gopal's of Soho *(W1)*
Jashan *(HA0, N8)*
Khan's of Kensington *(SW7)*
Ma Goa *(SW15)*
Madhu's Brilliant *(UB1)*
Malabar Junction *(WC1)*
Mela *(WC2)*
Ophim *(W1)*
Ragam *(W1)*
Rani *(N3)*
Tandoori Lane *(SW6)*

Ⓐ
Zamzama *(NW1)*

-
Anarkali *(W6)*
Anglo Asian Tandoori *(N16)*
Great Nepalese *(NW1)*
India Club *(WC2)*
Indian Ocean *(SW17)*
Khan's *(W2)*
Khyber Pass *(SW7)*
Masala Zone *(W1)*
Nayaab *(SW6)*
Noor Jahan *(SW5)*
Rupee Room *(EC2)*
Soho Spice *(W1)*
Standard Tandoori *(W2)*
Woodlands *(SW1, W1)*

INDIAN, SOUTHERN

★★
Geeta *(NW6)*
Kastoori *(SW17)*
Rasa *(N16, W1)*
Sabras *(NW10)*
Sree Krishna *(SW17)*
Vijay *(NW6)*

★
Chutneys *(NW1)*
Coromandel *(SW11)*
Malabar Junction *(WC1)*
Ragam *(W1)*
Rani *(N3)*
Rasa Travancore *(N16)*

-
India Club *(WC2)*
Woodlands *(SW1, W1)*

INDONESIAN

-
Melati *(W1)*

JAPANESE

★★
Café Japan *(NW11)*
Inaho *(W2)*
Jin Kichi *(NW3)*
Kulu Kulu *(W1)*
Yoshino *(W1)*

Ⓐ★
Benihana *(NW3, SW3, W1)*
Itsu *(SW3, W1)*

★
Abeno *(WC1)*
Bar Japan *(SW5)*
Bu San *(N7)*
Ikkyu *(W1)*
K10 *(EC2)*
Noto *(EC2)*
Sushi-Say *(NW2)*
Tokyo City *(EC2)*
Tsunami *(SW4)*

Ⓐ
Fujiyama *(SW9)*

-
Moshi Moshi *(E14, EC2, EC4)*
Satsuma *(W1)*
Wagamama *(EC2, EC4, NW1, SW1, W1, W8, WC1, WC2)*

KOREAN

★
Bu San *(N7)*

MALAYSIAN

★
Mawar *(W2)*
Singapore Garden *(NW6)*

-
Café de Maya *(NW3)*
Melati *(W1)*

PAKISTANI

★★
Lahore Kebab House *(E1)*
Mirch Masala *(SW16, SW17)*

for updates visit www.hardens.com

ASIA | CUISINES

-
Nayaab (SW6)

PAN-ASIAN

★
Oriental City (NW9)
Pan-Asian Canteen (SW1)
Uli (W11)

-
Fusion (EC2)
O'Zon (TW1)
Southeast (W9)
Touzai (EC2)

THAI

★★
Chiang Mai (W1)
Talad Thai (SW15)
Thailand (SE14)

🅐★
Blue Elephant (SW6)
Busaba Eathai (W1, WC1)
Churchill Arms (W8)
Thai on the River (SW10)
Yum Yum (N16)

★
Bangkok (SW7)
Latymers (W6)
The Papaya Tree (W8)
Sabai Sabai (W6)
Tawana (W2)
Thai Bistro (W4)
Thai Break (W8)
Thai Corner Café (SE22)

🅐
Café 209 (SW6)
The Pepper Tree (SW4)
Thai Noodle Bar (SW10)
The Walmer Castle (W11)

-
Bedlington Café (W4)
Ben's Thai (W9)
Blue Jade (SW1)
Blue Lagoon (W14)
Café de Maya (NW3)
Krungtap (SW10)
Manorom (WC2)
Old Parr's Head (W14)
Thai Café (SW1)
Thai Canteen (W6)
Thai Garden (SW11)
Thai Pot (W1, WC2)
Yelo (N1)

VIETNAMESE

★
Viet Hoa (E2)

-
Viet-Anh (NW1)

sign up for the survey at www.hardens.com

AREA OVERVIEWS

Where the ratings for a restaurant appear in brackets, eg (𝔸★), you can usually keep expenditure within our £20-a-head budget only at certain times of the day, or by sticking to a particular menu. Eating at other times or from the à la carte menu may be much more expensive.

AREA OVERVIEWS | CENTRAL

CENTRAL

Soho, Covent Garden & Bloomsbury
(Parts of W1, all WC2 and WC1)

£20	QC	British, Modern	(Ⓐ★★)
	Bank Aldwych	"	(Ⓐ★)
	Aurora	"	(Ⓐ)
	The Perseverance	"	
	Incognico	French	(★★)
	J Sheekey	Fish & seafood	(Ⓐ★★)
	Aroma II	Chinese	★
	Soho Spice	Indian	(–)
£15+	Blues	British, Modern	(Ⓐ★)
	Café du Jardin	"	(Ⓐ★)
	Le Deuxième	"	(Ⓐ★)
	Alfred	"	(★)
	L'Estaminet	French	(Ⓐ★)
	Aperitivo	Italian	Ⓐ
	Zizzi	"	Ⓐ
	Il Forno	"	
	Strada	"	
	Gordon's Wine Bar	International	Ⓐ
	Sarastro	"	(Ⓐ)
	Shampers	"	(Ⓐ)
	Balans	"	
	Café Emm	"	
	Boulevard	"	(–)
	Mildred's	Vegetarian	★
	World Food Café	"	
	North Sea Fish	Fish & chips	★
	PizzaExpress	Pizza	
	Souk	North African	Ⓐ
	Gaby's	Middle Eastern	
	Yming	Chinese	(Ⓐ★★)
	New Mayflower	"	★
	China City	"	
	Chuen Cheng Ku	"	
	Golden Dragon	"	
	Harbour City	"	
	Joy King Lau	"	
	New World	"	
	Chowki	Indian	★★
	Gopal's of Soho	"	★
	Mela	"	★
	Ophim	"	(★)
	Kulu Kulu	Japanese	★★
	Itsu	"	Ⓐ★
	Satsuma	"	
	Wagamama	"	
	Melati	Malaysian	
	Chiang Mai	Thai	(★★)
	Busaba Eathai	"	Ⓐ★
	Manorom	"	
	Thai Pot	"	

for updates visit www.hardens.com

CENTRAL | **AREA OVERVIEWS**

£10+	Mon Plaisir	French	(𝔸★)
	La Porchetta Pizzeria	Italian	★
	Bistro 1	Mediterranean	𝔸
	Star Café	International	
	Field & Forest	Steaks & grills	(–)
	Food for Thought	Vegetarian	★
	Paul	Sandwiches, cakes, etc	𝔸 ★
	Mr Kong	Chinese	★
	Poons	"	
	Poons, Lisle Street	"	
	Wong Kei	"	
	India Club	Indian	
	Masala Zone	"	
£5+	Fryer's Delight	Fish & chips	
	Maison Bertaux	Sandwiches, cakes, etc	𝔸 ★
	Bar Italia	"	𝔸
	Pâtisserie Valerie	"	
	Soup Opera	Soup	★

Mayfair & St James's
(Parts of W1 and SW1)

£20	Deca	French	(𝔸★★)
	L'Artiste Musclé	"	𝔸
	Hakkasan	Chinese	(𝔸★)
	Veeraswamy	Indian	(𝔸★)
£15+	Fortnum's Fountain	British, Modern	(𝔸)
	Boudin Blanc	French	(𝔸★)
	Strada	Italian	
	Rocket	Mediterranean	𝔸
	Hard Rock Café	Burgers, etc	𝔸
	Ask! Pizza	Pizza	𝔸
	Gourmet Pizza Co.	"	
	PizzaExpress	"	
	Pizzeria Condotti	"	
	Rasa	Indian	(★★)
	Yoshino	Japanese	(★★)
	Benihana	"	(𝔸★)
	Wagamama	"	
	Thai Pot	Thai	
£10+	Raks	Turkish	(–)
	Woodlands	Indian	(–)
£5+	Soup Opera	Soup	★

Fitzrovia & Marylebone
(Part of W1)

£20	La Spighetta	Italian	★
	Giraffe	International	𝔸
	Tajine	Moroccan	
	Fairuz	Lebanese	
	Royal China	Chinese	(★★)
	Malabar Junction	Indian	(★)

sign up for the survey at www.hardens.com

AREA OVERVIEWS | CENTRAL

£15+	La Brasserie Townhouse	*French*	(★)
	Hellenik	*Greek*	(🅐★)
	Zizzi	*Italian*	🅐
	Carluccio's Caffè	"	
	Paolo	"	
	Strada	"	
	Italian Kitchen	"	(–)
	Tapa Room (Providores)	*East/West*	(🅐★)
	Quiet Revolution	*Organic*	🅐★
	Ask! Pizza	*Pizza*	🅐
	PizzaExpress	"	
	Ozer	*Turkish*	(🅐★)
	Efes Kebab House	"	
	Ikkyu	*Japanese*	★
	Wagamama	"	
£10+	Bistro 1	*Mediterranean*	🅐
	Paul	*Sandwiches, cakes, etc*	🅐★
	Ragam	*Indian*	★
	Woodlands	"	(–)
	Abeno	*Japanese*	(★)
£5+	Pâtisserie Valerie	*Sandwiches, cakes, etc*	

Belgravia, Victoria & Pimlico (SW1, except St James's)

£20	Bank Westminster	*British, Modern*	(🅐★)
£15+	Pizza on the Park	*Italian*	🅐
	Uno	"	(–)
	Brahms	*International*	
	Royal Court Bar	"	
	Ask! Pizza	*Pizza*	🅐
	PizzaExpress	"	
	Wagamama	*Japanese*	
	Pan-Asian Canteen	*Pan-Asian*	★
	Blue Jade	*Thai*	
	Thai Café	"	
£10+	Grenadier	*British, Traditional*	(🅐)
	Jenny Lo's	*Chinese*	★

for updates visit www.hardens.com

WEST | **AREA OVERVIEWS**

WEST

Chelsea, South Kensington, Kensington, Earl's Court & Fulham (SW3, SW5, SW6, SW7, SW10 & W8)

£20	The Builder's Arms	British, Modern	𝔸
	The Ifield	"	𝔸
	The Abingdon	"	(–)
	Made in Italy	Italian	𝔸★
	Timo	"	★
	Noor Jahan	Indian	
£15+	Lots Road	British, Modern	𝔸
	Vingt-Quatre	"	
	White Horse	"	
	Le Metro	"	(–)
	Ffiona's	British, Traditional	(𝔸)
	Lundum's	Danish	(𝔸★★)
	Brasserie St Quentin	French	(★★)
	Le Colombier	"	(𝔸★)
	Wine & Kebab	Greek	(★)
	Carpaccio's	Italian	(𝔸★)
	Frantoio	"	(𝔸★)
	Aglio e Olio	"	★
	Pellicano	"	(★)
	Buona Sera	"	𝔸
	Bersagliera	"	
	Riccardo's	"	
	Spago	"	
	Strada	"	
	Il Falconiere	"	(–)
	The Atlas	Mediterranean	𝔸
	Wódka	Polish	(𝔸★)
	The Polish Club	"	(𝔸)
	Lomo	Spanish	𝔸
	Coopers Arms	International	𝔸
	Windsor Castle	"	𝔸
	Balans West	"	
	Balans	"	
	Chelsea Bun Diner	"	
	Lou Pescadou	Fish & seafood	(★)
	Stratford's	"	(★)
	Rôtisserie Jules	Steaks & grills	
	Le Shop	Crêpes	
	Basilico	Pizza	★★
	Ask! Pizza	"	𝔸
	Pucci Pizza	"	(𝔸)
	Calzone	"	
	PizzaExpress	"	
	Troubadour	Sandwiches, cakes, etc	𝔸
	Phoenicia	Lebanese	(★)
	Good Earth	Chinese	(★)
	Zaika	Indian	(𝔸★★)
	Malabar	"	𝔸★
	Zaika Bazaar	"	𝔸★
	Khan's of Kensington	"	★

sign up for the survey at www.hardens.com

AREA OVERVIEWS | WEST

	Tandoori Lane	"	★
	Nayaab	"	
	Itsu	Japanese	Ⓐ★
	Benihana	"	(Ⓐ★)
	Bar Japan	"	(★)
	Wagamama	"	
	Blue Elephant	Thai	(Ⓐ★)
	Thai on the River	"	(Ⓐ★)
	Bangkok	"	★
	The Papaya Tree	"	★
	Thai Break	"	★
	Thai Noodle Bar	"	Ⓐ
£10+	La Bouchée	French	(Ⓐ)
	Costa's Fish	Fish & chips	★
	La Delizia	Pizza	
	Stick & Bowl	Chinese	★
	Khyber Pass	Indian	
	Churchill Arms	Thai	Ⓐ★
	Café 209	"	Ⓐ
	Krungtap	"	
£5+	Fileric	Sandwiches, cakes, etc	
	Pâtisserie Valerie	"	

Notting Hill, Holland Park, Bayswater, North Kensington & Maida Vale (W2, W9, W10, W11)

£20	Golborne House	British, Modern	Ⓐ
	Brass. du Marché	French	(Ⓐ)
	Osteria Basilico	Italian	(Ⓐ★)
	Fairuz	Lebanese	
	Royal China	Chinese	(★★)
£15+	The Vale	British, Modern	(★)
	The Prince Bonaparte	"	
	Raoul's Café	"	
	The Cow (Dining Rm)	"	(–)
	The Red Pepper	Italian	★
	Café 206	"	Ⓐ
	Wine Factory	"	
	Mediterraneo	Mediterranean	(Ⓐ★)
	Galicia	Spanish	
	Café Laville	International	Ⓐ
	Rôtisserie Jules	Steaks & grills	
	Ask! Pizza	Pizza	Ⓐ
	Calzone	"	
	PizzaExpress	"	
	Tom's	Sandwiches, cakes, etc	(–)
	Beirut Express	Lebanese	★★
	Alounak	Persian	★
	Mandarin Kitchen	Chinese	(★★)
	The Four Seasons	"	★
	Inaho	Japanese	(★★)
	Uli	Pan-Asian	★
	Southeast	"	

for updates visit www.hardens.com

WEST | **AREA OVERVIEWS**

	Tawana	*Thai*	★
	The Walmer Castle	"	🄰
	Ben's Thai	"	
£10+	Ranoush	*Lebanese*	★
	Kandoo	*Persian*	★
	Mandalay	*Burmese*	★★
	Khan's	*Indian*	
	Standard Tandoori	"	
	Mawar	*Malaysian*	★
£1+	Lisboa Patisserie	*Sandwiches, cakes, etc*	★★

Hammersmith, Shepherd's Bush Chiswick & Olympia (W4, W5, W6, W12, W14)

£20	The Havelock Tavern	*British, Modern*	(🄰★★)
	The Anglesea Arms	"	★★
	Popeseye	*Steaks & grills*	★
	The Gate	*Vegetarian*	🄰★★
	Azou	*North African*	
£15+	Parade	*British, Modern*	(🄰★)
	Chiswick	"	(★)
	Stone Mason's Arms	"	🄰
	The Thatched House	"	🄰
	The Pilot	"	
	The Brackenbury	"	(–)
	Palatino	*Italian*	(★)
	Zizzi	"	🄰
	Patio	*Polish*	(–)
	Rôtisserie	*Steaks & grills*	(★★)
	Blah! Blah! Blah!	*Vegetarian*	★★
	Coyote Café	*American*	
	Ask! Pizza	*Pizza*	🄰
	PizzaExpress	"	
	Adams Café	*Moroccan*	
	Alounak	*Persian*	★
	Mohsen	"	★
	Yas	"	
	Brilliant	*Indian*	★
	Madhu's Brilliant	"	★
	Thai Bistro	*Thai*	★
	Sabai Sabai	"	(★)
	Bedlington Café	"	
£10+	Abu Zaad	*Middle Eastern*	★
	Anarkali	*Indian*	
	Latymers	*Thai*	★
	Old Parr's Head	"	
	Thai Canteen	"	
	Blue Lagoon	"	(–)

sign up for the survey at www.hardens.com

AREA OVERVIEWS | NORTH

NORTH

Hampstead, West Hampstead, St John's Wood, Regent's Park, Kilburn & Camden Town (NW postcodes)

£20	Odette's	British, Modern	(A★★)
	Lansdowne	"	(A)
	The Chapel	"	
	The Salusbury	Italian	★
	Giraffe	International	A
	The Gate	Vegetarian	A★★
	Mango Room	Afro-Caribbean	A★
	Royal China	Chinese	(★★)
	ZeNW3	"	(★)
	Jin Kichi	Japanese	★★
£15+	William IV	British, Modern	A★
	Bradley's	"	(★)
	Dartmouth Arms	"	
	The Lord Palmerston	"	
	The Queen's	"	
	Lemonia	Greek	A
	La Brocca	Italian	A
	Zizzi	"	A
	Marine Ices	"	
	Bar Gansa	Spanish	A
	Don Pepe	"	
	Heartstone	Organic	★
	Manna	Vegetarian	(★)
	Nautilus	Fish & chips	★
	Seashell	"	★
	Ask! Pizza	Pizza	A
	Calzone	"	
	PizzaExpress	"	
	Laurent	Tunisian	★
	Ali Baba	Egyptian	
	Solly's Exclusive	Israeli	(–)
	Shish	Middle Eastern	★
	China Dream	Chinese	A★
	Gung-Ho	"	A★
	Great Nepalese	Indian	
	Café Japan	Japanese	(★★)
	Benihana	"	(A★)
	Sushi-Say	"	★
	Wagamama	"	
	Singapore Garden	Malaysian	(★)
£10+	Daphne	Greek	
	Vegia Zena	Italian	(★)
	The Little Bay	Mediterranean	A
	Gourmet Burger Kitchen	Burgers, etc	★
	Chamomile	Sandwiches, cakes, etc	
	Geeta	Indian	★★
	Sakonis	"	★★
	Vijay	"	★★
	Chutneys	"	★
	Diwana B-P House	"	★

for updates visit www.hardens.com

NORTH | **AREA OVERVIEWS**

	Jashan	"	★
	Zamzama	"	Ⓐ
	Sabras	Indian, Southern	★★
	Oriental City	Pan-Asian	★
	Café de Maya	Thai	
	Viet-Anh	Vietnamese	

Islington, Highgate, Crouch End, Stoke Newington, Finsbury Park, Muswell Hill & Finchley (N postcodes)

£20	Frederick's	British, Modern	(Ⓐ★★)
	Vrisaki	Greek	★
	Cantina Italia	Italian	(–)
	Giraffe	International	Ⓐ
	The Parsee	Indian	★★
£15+	Café Mozart	East & Central European	Ⓐ
	Tartuf	Alsatian	★
	Petit Auberge	French	
	The Real Greek	Greek	(★)
	Strada	Italian	
	Errays	Mediterranean	
	Barracuda	International	Ⓐ
	Banners	"	
	Chez Liline	Fish & seafood	(★★)
	Rôtisserie	Steaks & grills	(★★)
	Two Brothers	Fish & chips	★
	Furnace	Pizza	★
	Ask! Pizza	"	Ⓐ
	Calzone	"	
	PizzaExpress	"	
	Maghreb	Moroccan	★
	Gallipoli	Turkish	Ⓐ
	Sedir	"	
	Tbilisi	Georgian	
	Rasa	Indian	(★★)
	Rani	"	★
	Anglo Asian Tandoori	"	
	Rasa Travancore	Indian, Southern	★
	Bu San	Korean	★
	Yum Yum	Thai	Ⓐ★
	Yelo	"	
£10+	Granita	British, Modern	(★)
	Mesclun	"	(–)
	La Porchetta Pizzeria	Italian	★
	La Piragua	South American	
	Toff's	Fish & chips	
	Afghan Kitchen	Afghani	★
	Jashan	Indian	★

sign up for the survey at www.hardens.com

AREA OVERVIEWS | SOUTH

SOUTH

South Bank
(SE1)

£20	La Lanterna	Italian	
	Tate Modern (Level 7)	International	𝔸
£15+	Konditor & Cook	British, Modern	★★
	Bankside	"	
	Butlers Wharf Chop-house	British, Traditional	(𝔸★)
	Cantina del Ponte	Italian	(𝔸)
	Baltic	Polish	(𝔸)
	Film Café	International	
	Horse	"	
	Pizzeria Castello	Pizza	𝔸★
	Ask! Pizza	"	𝔸
	Gourmet Pizza Co.	"	
	PizzaExpress	"	
	Konditor & Cook	Sandwiches, cakes, etc	★★
	Tas	Turkish	𝔸★
	Bengal Clipper	Indian	(★)
£10+	Meson don Felipe	Spanish	𝔸
	El Vergel	South American	★★

Battersea, Clapham, Wandsworth, Barnes, Putney, Brixton & Lewisham
(All postcodes south of the river except SE1)

£20	The Stepping Stone	British, Modern	(𝔸★★)
	Phoenix	"	(𝔸★)
	George II	"	★
	Willie Gunn	"	𝔸
	The Trafalgar Tavern	British, Traditional	𝔸
	Spread Eagle	French	(𝔸★)
	Giraffe	International	𝔸
	The White House	"	𝔸
	Popeseye	Steaks & grills	★
	Tsunami	Japanese	(★)
£15+	Tartuf	Alsatian	★
	Kennington Lane	British, Modern	(𝔸★★)
	Niksons	"	(𝔸★)
	The Castle	"	★
	The Sun & Doves	"	
	Chez Lindsay	French	(𝔸★)
	Gastro	"	(𝔸)
	Arancia	Italian	𝔸★
	Bibo	"	𝔸★
	Antipasto e Pasta	"	(★)
	Buona Sera	"	𝔸
	Zizzi	"	𝔸
	Antipasto & Pasta	"	
	Need The Dough!	"	
	Strada	"	

for updates visit www.hardens.com   *132*

SOUTH | **AREA OVERVIEWS**

	Café Portugal	*Portuguese*	𝔸
	don Fernando's	*Spanish*	𝔸
	Rebato's	"	𝔸
	La Rueda	"	(𝔸)
	Alma	*International*	𝔸
	Bread & Roses	"	𝔸
	Hudson's	"	𝔸
	White Cross	"	𝔸
	Chelsea Bun Diner	"	
	Cinnamon Cay	*East/West*	𝔸★
	Polygon Bar & Grill	*Steaks & grills*	(𝔸)
	Brady's	*Fish & chips*	★
	Pizza Metro	*Pizza*	𝔸★★
	Basilico	"	★★
	Eco	"	★
	Eco Brixton	"	★
	Ask! Pizza	"	𝔸
	Zero Degrees	"	𝔸
	PizzaExpress	"	
	So.uk	*North African*	𝔸
	Sarkhel's	*Indian*	★★
	Babur Brasserie	"	★
	Ma Goa	"	★
	Indian Ocean	"	
	Coromandel	*Indian, Southern*	★
	O'Zon	*Pan-Asian*	
	Thai Garden	*Thai*	
£10+	Ditto	*British, Modern*	(𝔸★)
	Cantinetta Venegazzú	*Italian*	(★)
	Fish in a Tie	*Mediterranean*	𝔸
	Gourmet Burger Kitchen	*Burgers, etc*	★
	Boiled Egg & Soldiers	*Sandwiches, cakes, etc*	
	Kastoori	*Indian*	★★
	Mirch Masala SW16	"	★★
	Sree Krishna	"	★★
	Fujiyama	*Japanese*	𝔸
	Talad Thai	*Thai*	★★
	Thai Corner Café	"	★
	The Pepper Tree	"	𝔸
£5+	Thailand	"	(★★)

sign up for the survey at www.hardens.com

AREA OVERVIEWS | EAST

EAST

Smithfield & Farringdon (EC1)

£20	Alba	Italian	(★)
	Hope & Sir Loin	Steaks & grills	
£15+	St John	British, Modern	(★)
	Smiths (Ground Floor)	British, Traditional	(𝔸★)
	Fox & Anchor	"	
	Carluccio's Caffè	Italian	
	Strada	"	
	The Eagle	Mediterranean	𝔸★
	Quiet Revolution	Organic	𝔸★
	Carnevale	Vegetarian	(★)
	Ask! Pizza	Pizza	𝔸
	PizzaExpress	"	
	Moro	Moroccan	(𝔸★★)
£10+	The Little Bay	Mediterranean	𝔸

The City & East End
(All E and EC postcodes, except EC1)

£20	The Wine Library	British, Traditional	𝔸
	Scuzi	Pizza	
	Royal China	Chinese	(★★)
£15+	LMNT	British, Modern	𝔸
	Cantaloupe	"	(𝔸)
	Frocks	"	(𝔸)
	Carluccio's Caffè	Italian	
	Faulkner's	Fish & chips	★★
	Bar Capitale	Pizza	★
	Gourmet Pizza Co.	"	
	PizzaExpress	"	
	Shanghai	Chinese	𝔸
	Rupee Room	Indian	
	K10	Japanese	★
	Noto	"	★
	Tokyo City	"	★
	Moshi Moshi	"	
	Wagamama	"	
	Touzai	Pan-Asian	
£10+	Simpson's Tavern	British, Traditional	𝔸
	Sweetings	Fish & seafood	(𝔸)
	Arkansas Café	Steaks & grills	★
	The Place Below	Vegetarian	𝔸★
	Lahore Kebab House	Indian	★★
	Café Indiya	"	★
	Fusion	Pan-Asian	
	Viet Hoa	Vietnamese	★
£5+	Futures	Vegetarian	★
	Soup Opera	Soup	★
£1+	Brick Lane Beigel Bake	Sandwiches, cakes, etc	★★

for updates visit www.hardens.com

MAPS

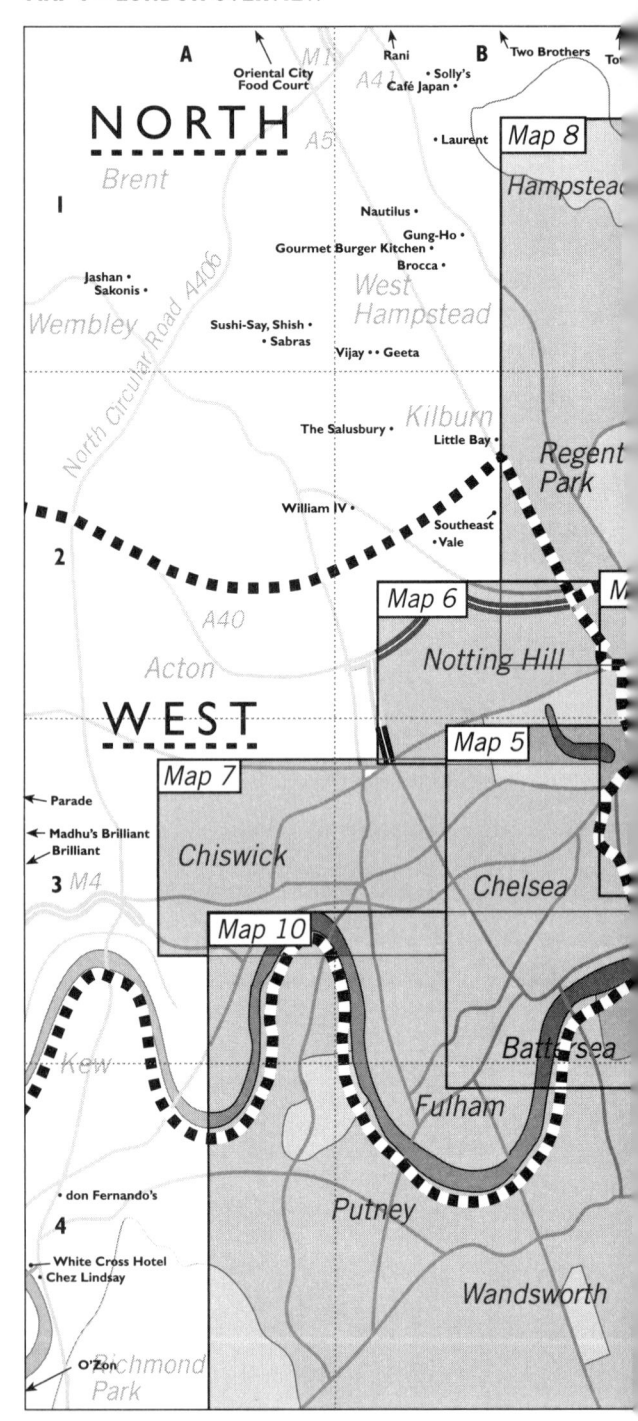

MAP 1 – LONDON OVERVIEW

NORTH
Brent
Wembley

WEST
Acton
Chiswick
Kew
Putney
Wandsworth
Richmond Park

Hampstead
West Hampstead
Kilburn
Regent Park
Notting Hill
Chelsea
Battersea
Fulham

North Circular Road A4406
M1
A41
A5
A40
M4

Map 5
Map 6
Map 7
Map 8
Map 10

- Oriental City Food Court
- Rani
- Solly's
- Café Japan
- Two Brothers
- Laurent
- Nautilus
- Gung-Ho
- Gourmet Burger Kitchen
- Brocca
- Jashan
- Sakonis
- Sushi-Say, Shish
- Sabras
- Vijay
- Geeta
- The Salusbury
- Little Bay
- William IV
- Southeast
- Vale
- Parade
- Madhu's Brilliant
- Brilliant
- don Fernando's
- White Cross Hotel
- Chez Lindsay
- O'Zon

MAP 1 – LONDON OVERVIEW

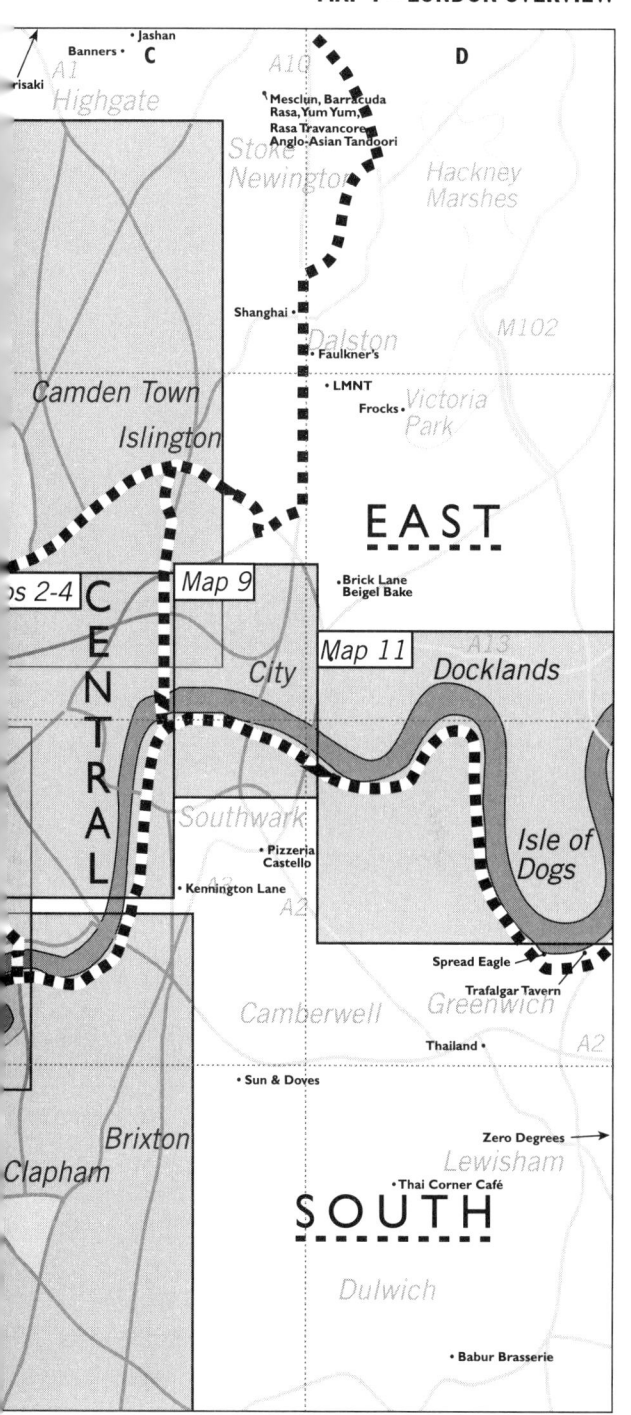

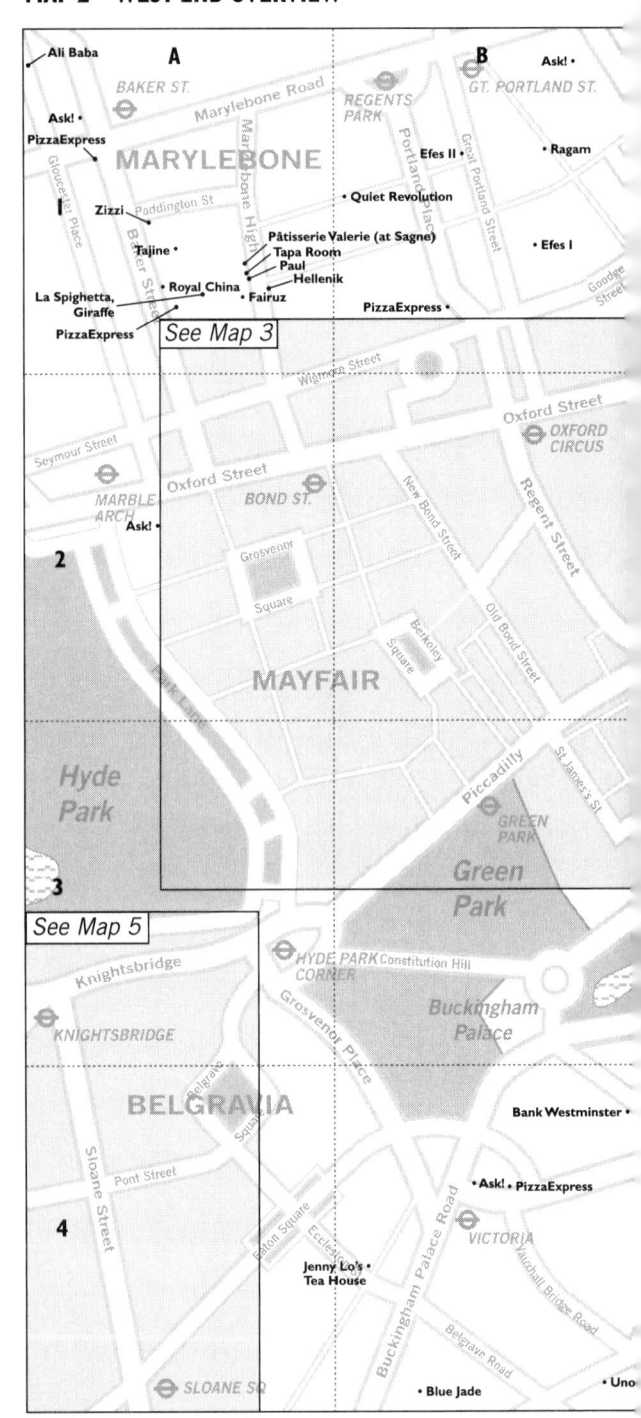

MAP 2 – WEST END OVERVIEW

A
- Ali Baba
- BAKER ST.
- Marylebone Road
- Ask!
- PizzaExpress
- MARYLEBONE
- Zizzi
- Paddington St
- Tajine
- Pâtisserie Valerie (at Sagne)
- Tapa Room
- Paul
- Hellenik
- La Spighetta, Giraffe
- Royal China
- Fairuz
- PizzaExpress

B
- Ask!
- GT. PORTLAND ST.
- REGENTS PARK
- Efes II
- Ragam
- Quiet Revolution
- Efes I
- PizzaExpress

See Map 3

- Wigmore Street
- Oxford Street
- OXFORD CIRCUS
- Seymour Street
- Oxford Street
- MARBLE ARCH
- BOND ST.
- Ask!
- Grosvenor Square
- New Bond Street
- Regent Street
- Berkeley Square
- Old Bond Street
- MAYFAIR
- Hyde Park
- Piccadilly
- St James's St.
- GREEN PARK
- Green Park

See Map 5

- Knightsbridge
- HYDE PARK CORNER
- Constitution Hill
- KNIGHTSBRIDGE
- Grosvenor Place
- Buckingham Palace
- BELGRAVIA
- Sloane Street
- Belgrave Square
- Pont Street
- Bank Westminster
- Ask!
- PizzaExpress
- VICTORIA
- Eaton Square
- Ecclestone
- Jenny Lo's Tea House
- Buckingham Palace Road
- Vauxhall Bridge Road
- Belgrave Road
- SLOANE SQ
- Blue Jade
- Uno

MAP 2 – WEST END OVERVIEW

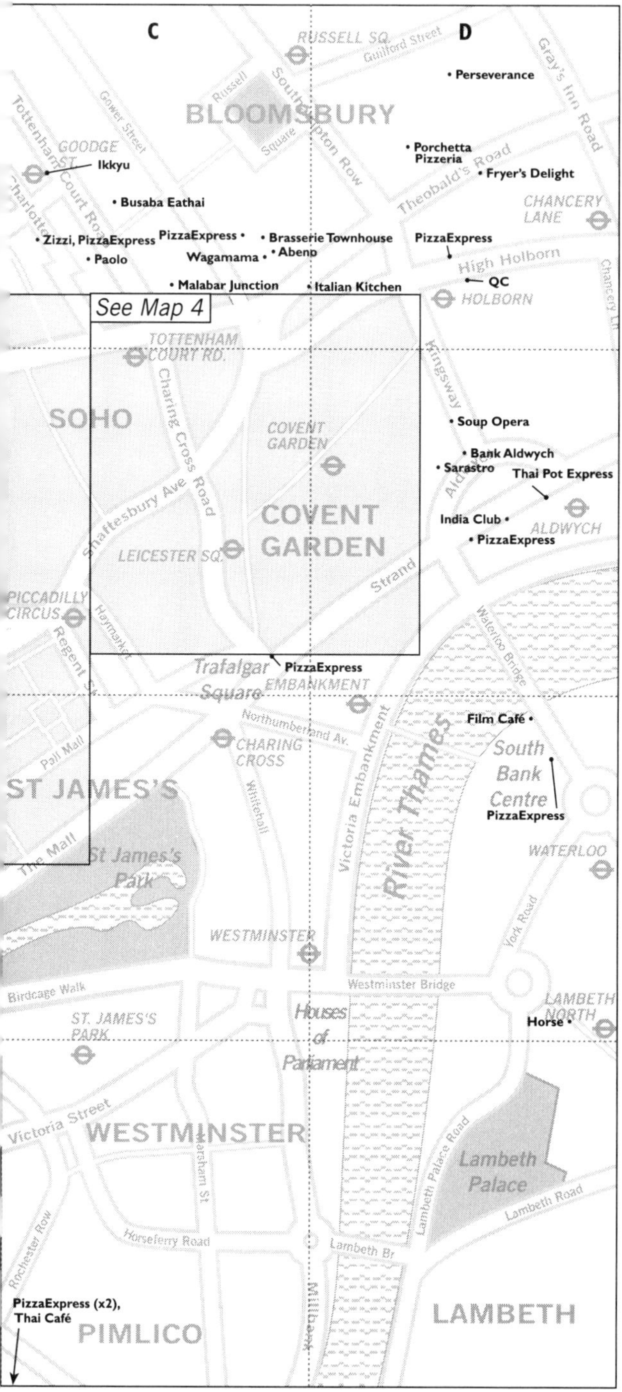

C RUSSELL SQ. **D**

BLOOMSBURY

GOODGE ST.
• Ikkyu
• Perseverance
• Porchetta Pizzeria
• Fryer's Delight
CHANCERY LANE
• Busaba Eathai
• Zizzi, PizzaExpress   PizzaExpress •   • Brasserie Townhouse   PizzaExpress
• Paolo   Wagamama • • Abeno   High Holborn
• Malabar Junction   • Italian Kitchen   ← QC
HOLBORN

See Map 4

TOTTENHAM COURT RD.

SOHO   COVENT GARDEN

• Soup Opera
• Bank Aldwych
• Sarastro   Thai Pot Express
COVENT GARDEN
India Club •
• PizzaExpress   ALDWYCH

LEICESTER SQ.

PICCADILLY CIRCUS

Trafalgar Square   **PizzaExpress**
EMBANKMENT

Film Café •
South Bank Centre
PizzaExpress
WATERLOO

ST JAMES'S
CHARING CROSS

St James's Park

WESTMINSTER

LAMBETH NORTH
Horse •

ST. JAMES'S PARK

Westminster Bridge

Houses of Parliament

WESTMINSTER

Lambeth Palace

Lambeth Br

PizzaExpress (x2),
Thai Café
PIMLICO   LAMBETH

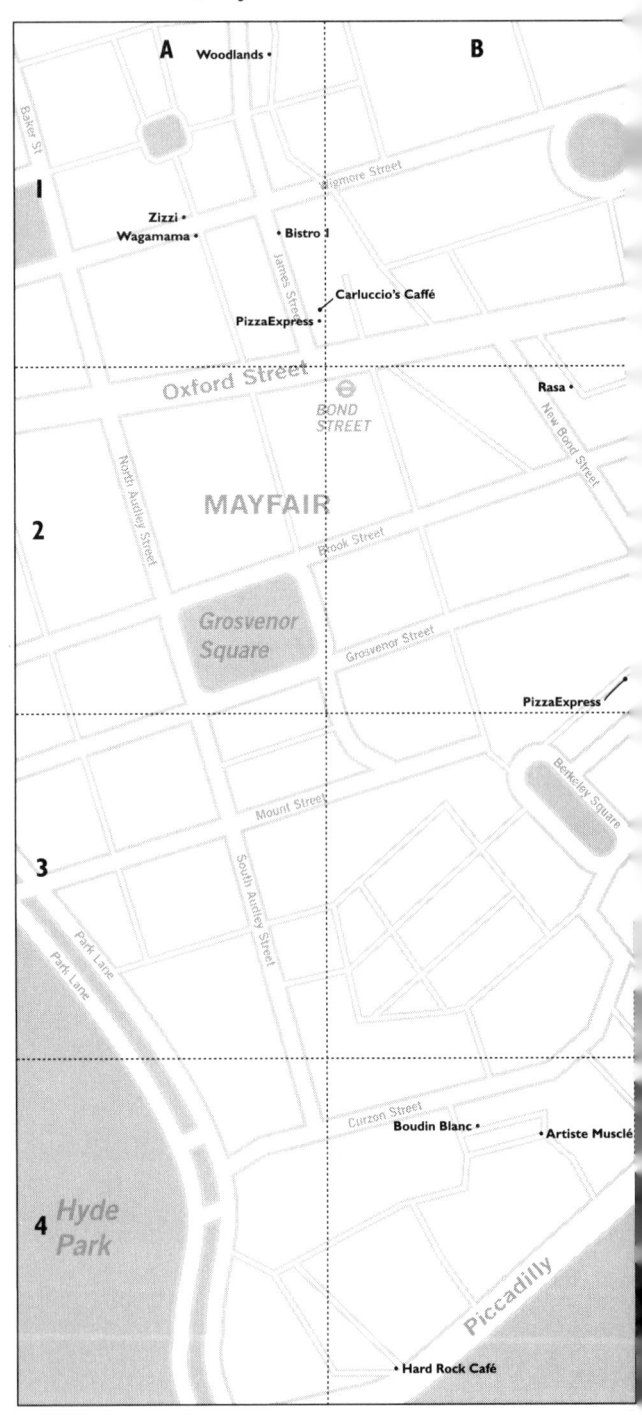

MAP 3 – MAYFAIR, ST JAMES'S & WEST SOHO

- Woodlands
- Zizzi
- Wagamama
- Bistro 1
- Carluccio's Caffè
- PizzaExpress
- Rasa
- MAYFAIR
- Grosvenor Square
- PizzaExpress
- Boudin Blanc
- Artiste Musclé
- Hyde Park
- Hard Rock Café

Baker St, Wigmore Street, Oxford Street, BOND STREET, New Bond Street, North Audley Street, James Street, Brook Street, Grosvenor Street, Berkeley Square, Mount Street, South Audley Street, Park Lane, Curzon Street, Piccadilly

MAP 3 – MAYFAIR, ST JAMES'S & WEST SOHO

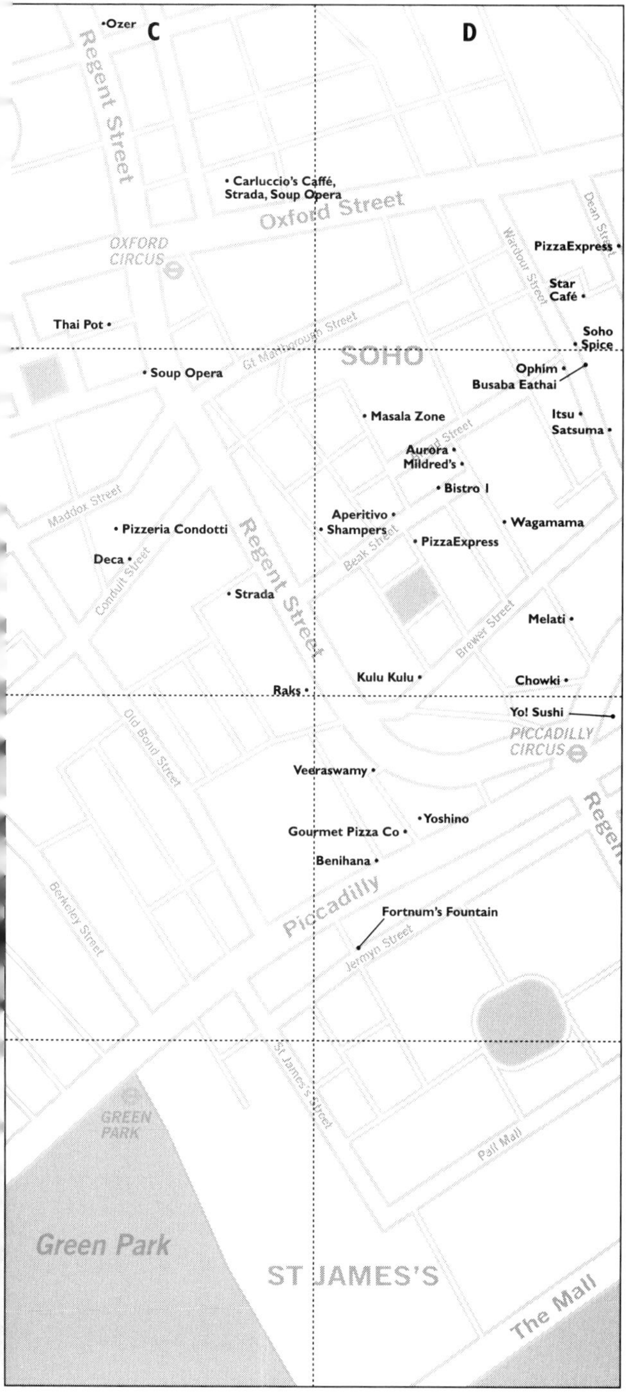

C / **D**

- Ozer
- Carluccio's Caffé, Strada, Soup Opera
- OXFORD CIRCUS
- PizzaExpress
- Star Café
- Thai Pot
- Soho Spice
- Soup Opera
- SOHO
- Ophim
- Busaba Eathai
- Masala Zone
- Itsu
- Satsuma
- Aurora
- Mildred's
- Bistro 1
- Pizzeria Condotti
- Aperitivo
- Shampers
- PizzaExpress
- Wagamama
- Deca
- Strada
- Melati
- Kulu Kulu
- Chowki
- Raks
- Yo! Sushi
- PICCADILLY CIRCUS
- Veeraswamy
- Yoshino
- Gourmet Pizza Co
- Benihana
- Piccadilly
- Fortnum's Fountain
- Jermyn Street
- GREEN PARK
- Green Park
- ST JAMES'S
- Pall Mall
- The Mall

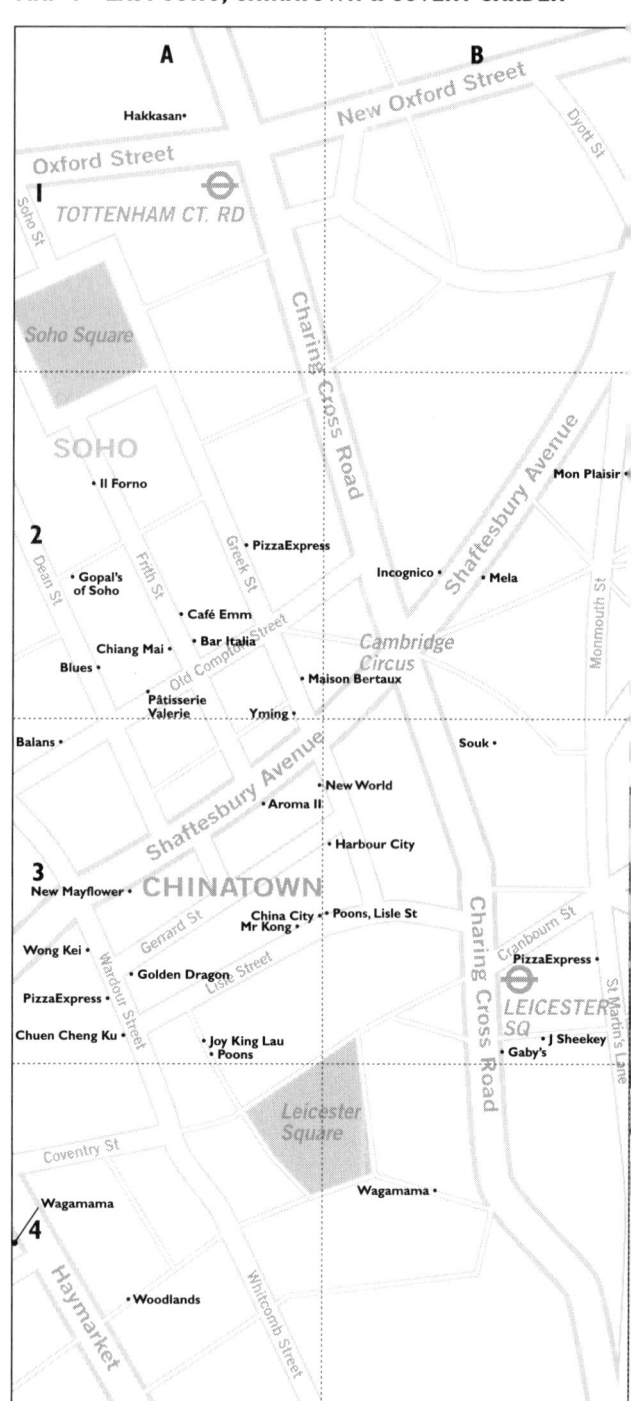

MAP 4 – EAST SOHO, CHINATOWN & COVENT GARDEN

MAP 4 – EAST SOHO, CHINATOWN & COVENT GARDEN

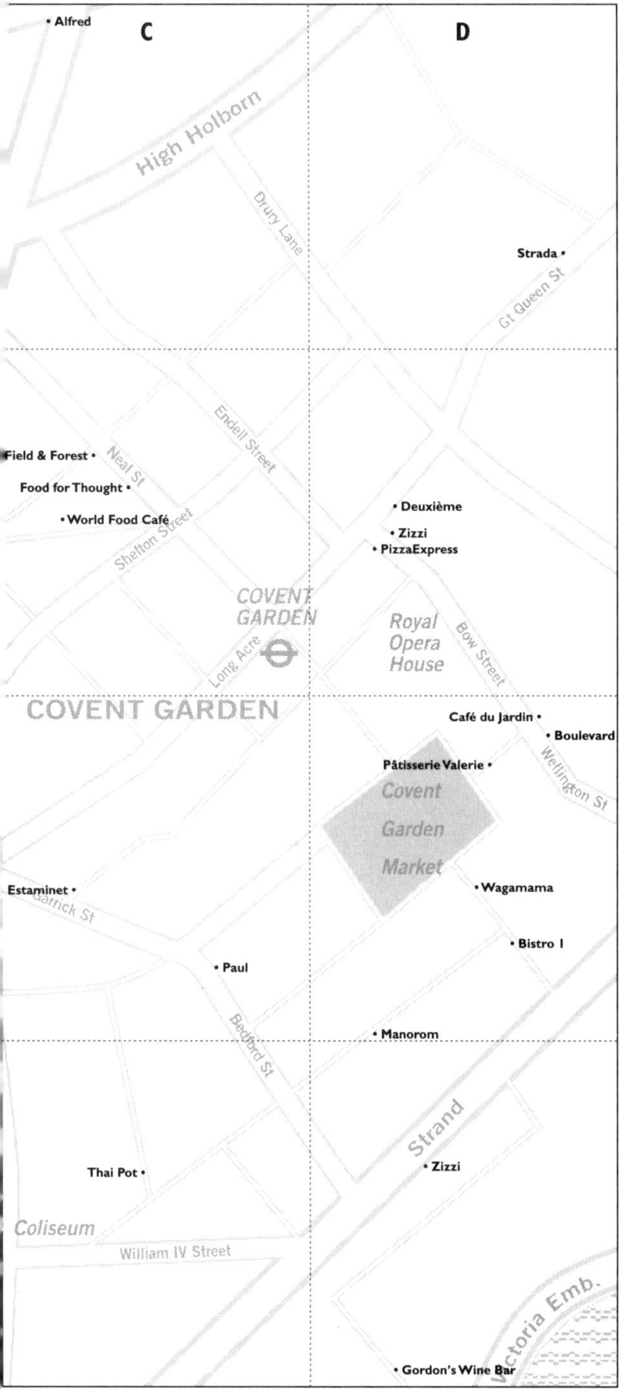

C

- Alfred

High Holborn

Drury Lane

- Field & Forest
- Food for Thought
- World Food Café

Neal St

Shelton Street

Endell Street

COVENT GARDEN

Long Acre

COVENT GARDEN

Estaminet •

Garrick St

• Paul

Bedford St

Thai Pot •

Coliseum

William IV Street

D

Strada •

Gt Queen St

- Deuxième
- Zizzi
- PizzaExpress

Royal Opera House

Bow Street

Café du Jardin •
• Boulevard

Pâtisserie Valerie •

Wellington St

Covent Garden Market

• Wagamama

• Bistro 1

• Manorom

Strand

• Zizzi

Victoria Emb.

• Gordon's Wine Bar

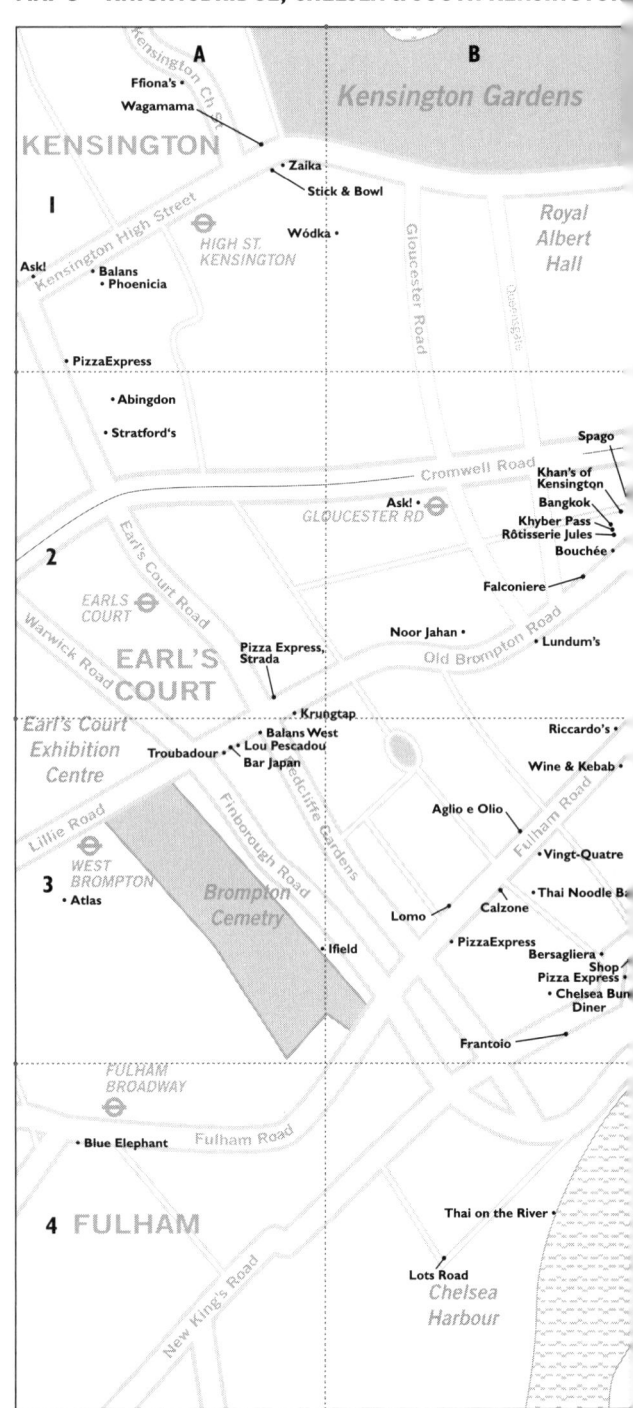

MAP 5 – KNIGHTSBRIDGE, CHELSEA & SOUTH KENSINGTON

KENSINGTON

- Ffiona's
- Wagamama
- Zaika
- Stick & Bowl
- Wódka
- Ask!
- Balans
- Phoenicia
- PizzaExpress
- Abingdon
- Stratford's

Kensington Gardens

Royal Albert Hall

HIGH ST. KENSINGTON

Kensington High Street
Kensington Ch...
Gloucester Road
Queen's Gate

EARL'S COURT

Cromwell Road

- Spago
- Khan's of Kensington
- Bangkok
- Khyber Pass
- Rôtisserie Jules
- Bouchée
- Ask!
- Falconiere
- Noor Jahan
- Lundum's
- Pizza Express, Strada
- Krungtap

GLOUCESTER RD

Earl's Court Road
Warwick Road
Old Brompton Road

WEST BROMPTON / EARL'S COURT

Earl's Court Exhibition Centre

- Troubadour
- Balans West
- Lou Pescadou
- Bar Japan
- Atlas
- Ifield
- Riccardo's
- Wine & Kebab
- Aglio e Olio
- Vingt-Quatre
- Thai Noodle Ba...
- Lomo
- Calzone
- PizzaExpress
- Bersagliera
- Shop
- Pizza Express
- Chelsea Bun Diner
- Frantoio

Brompton Cemetry

Lillie Road
Finborough Road
Redcliffe Gardens
Fulham Road

FULHAM

FULHAM BROADWAY

- Blue Elephant
- Thai on the River
- Lots Road

Fulham Road
New King's Road

Chelsea Harbour

MAP 5 – KNIGHTSBRIDGE, CHELSEA & SOUTH KENSINGTON

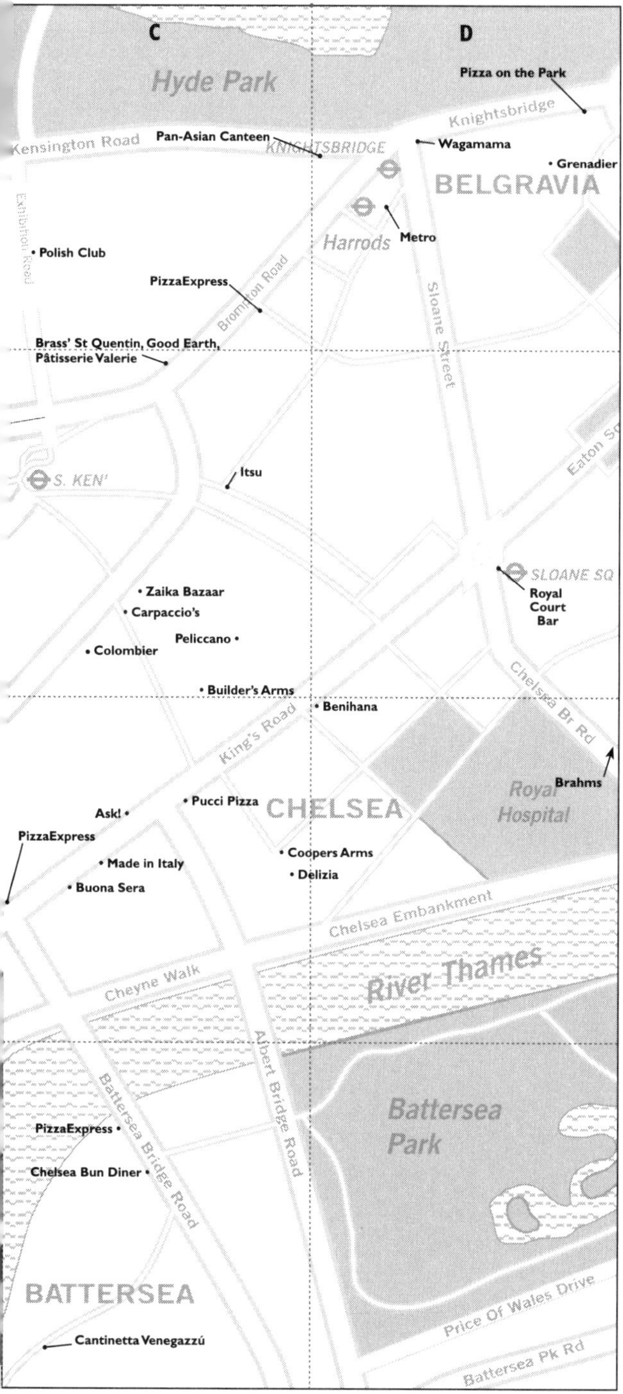

MAP 6 – NOTTING HILL & BAYSWATER

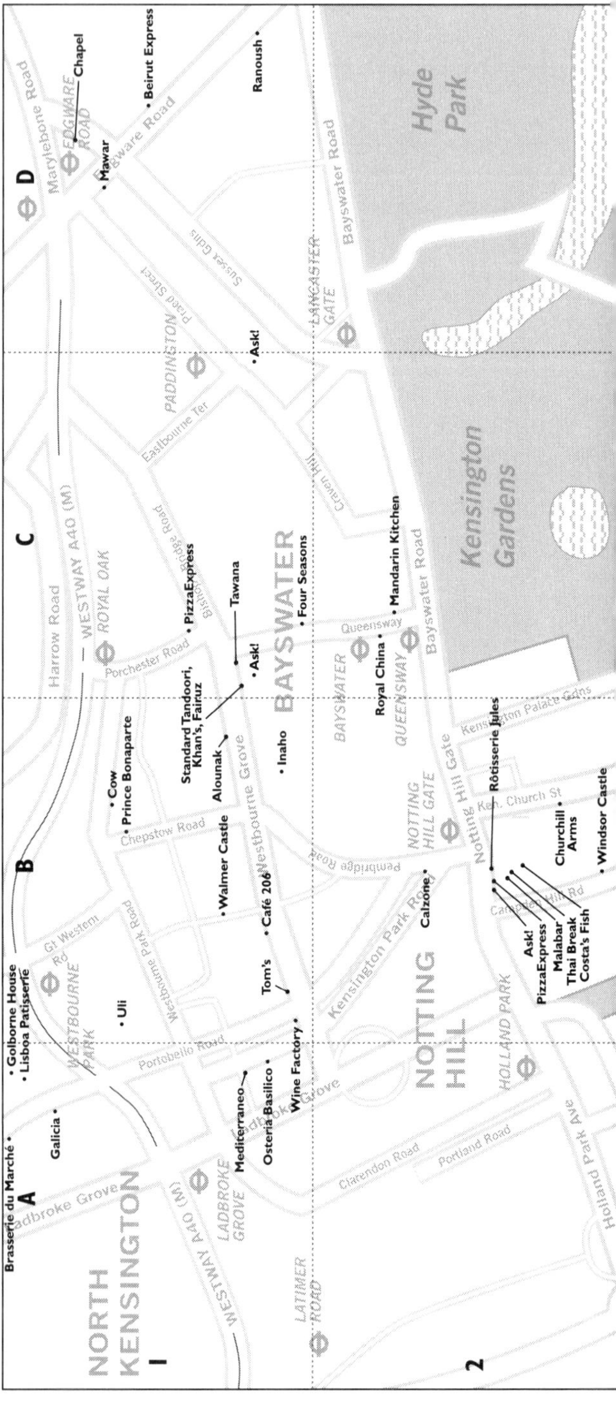

MAP 7 – HAMMERSMITH & CHISWICK

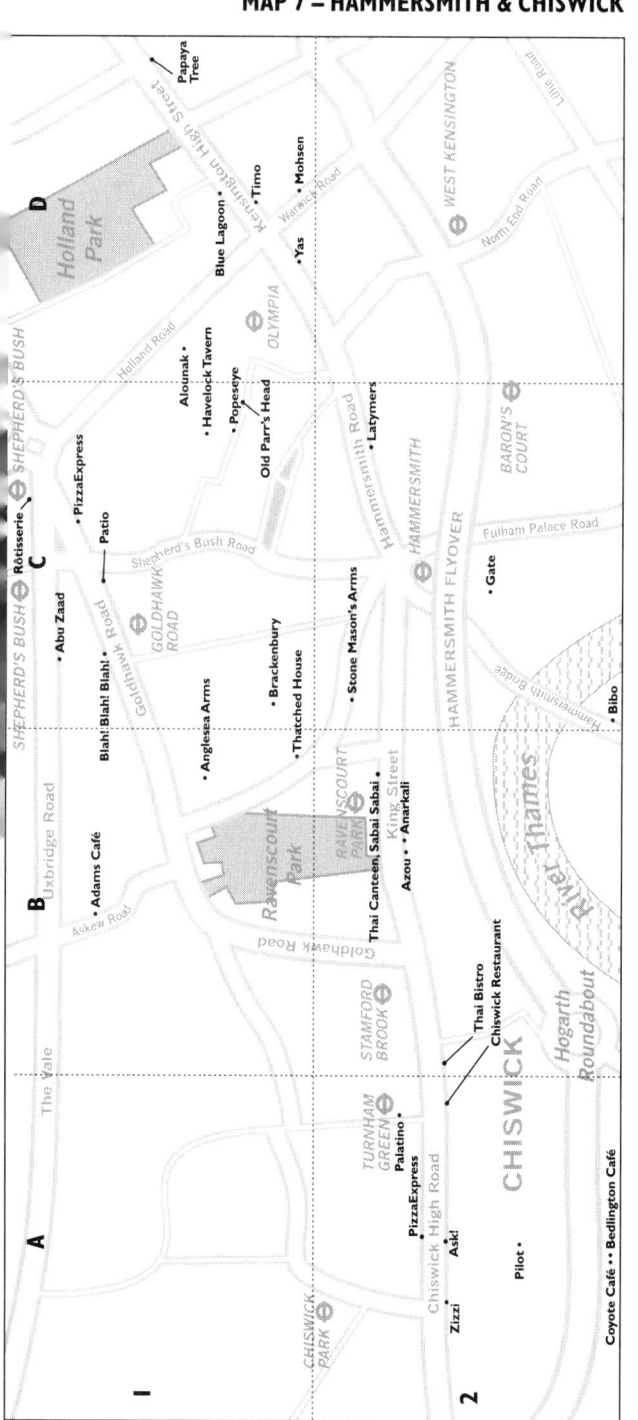

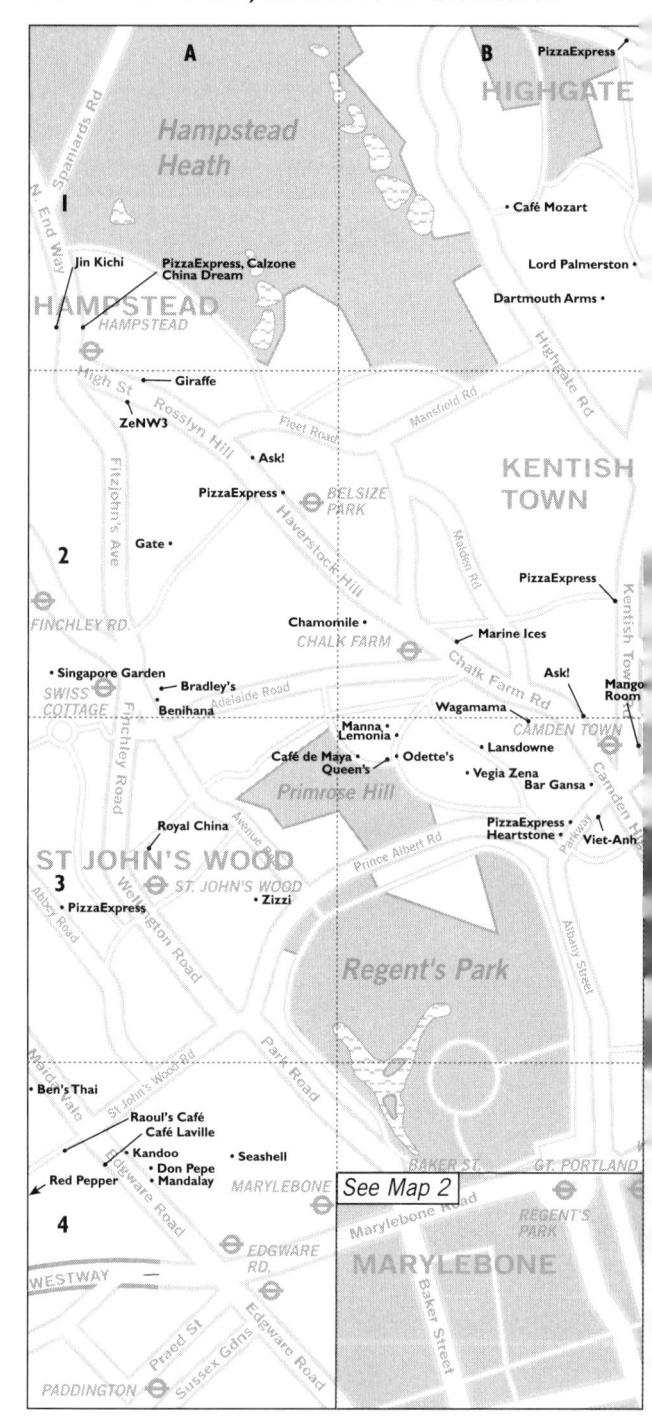

MAP 8 – HAMPSTEAD, CAMDEN TOWN & ISLINGTON

MAP 8 – HAMPSTEAD, CAMDEN TOWN & ISLINGTON

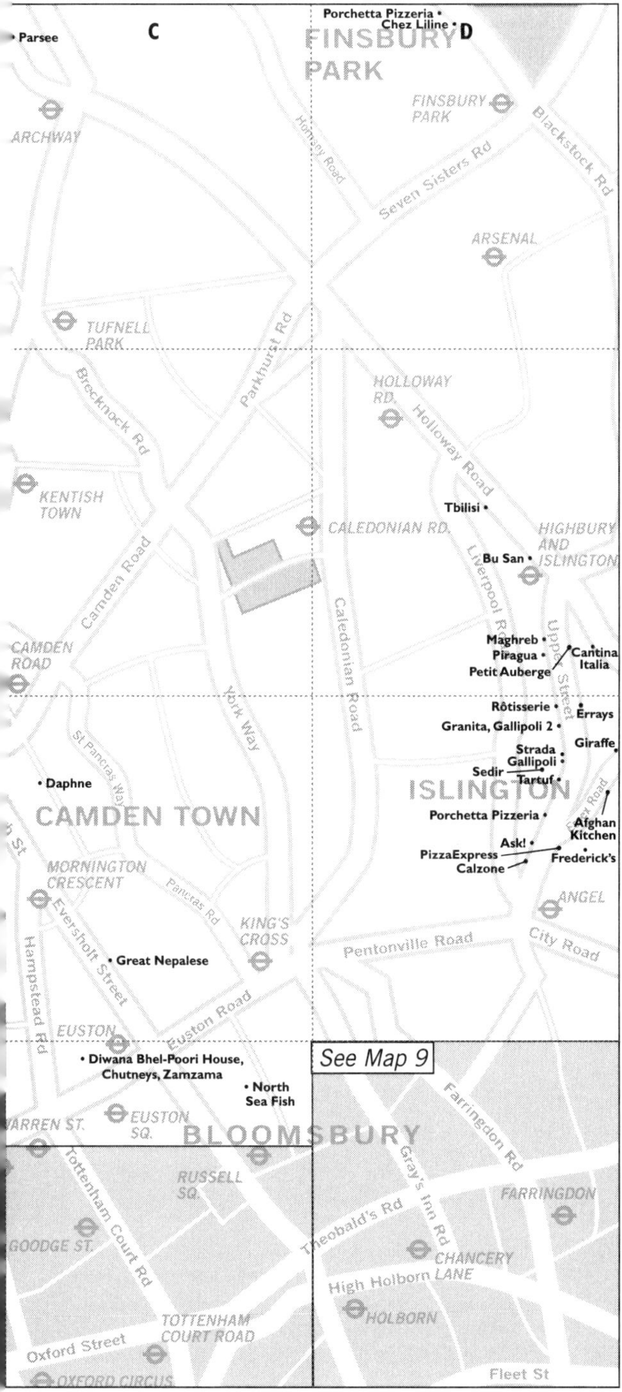

C

- Parsee

ARCHWAY

TUFNELL PARK

Harvey Road

D

Porchetta Pizzeria •
Chez Liline •
FINSBURY PARK

FINSBURY PARK

Seven Sisters Rd

Blackstock Rd

ARSENAL

HOLLOWAY RD.

Holloway Road

Brecknock Rd

Parkhurst Rd

KENTISH TOWN

CALEDONIAN RD.

Tbilisi •

Bu San •

HIGHBURY AND ISLINGTON

Liverpool Rd

Caledonian Road

CAMDEN ROAD

York Way

Camden Road

Upper Street

Maghreb •
Piragua •
Petit Auberge

Cantina Italia

Rôtisserie •
Granita, Gallipoli 2 •
Strada
Gallipoli •
Sedir •
Tartuf •

Errays
Giraffe

• Daphne

CAMDEN TOWN

St Pancras Way

MORNINGTON CRESCENT

Pancras Rd

KING'S CROSS

ISLINGTON

Porchetta Pizzeria •

Ask! •
PizzaExpress •
Calzone

Afghan Kitchen

Frederick's

ANGEL

Eversholt Street

• Great Nepalese

Hampstead Rd

EUSTON

Euston Road

Pentonville Road

City Road

• Diwana Bhel-Poori House,
Chutneys, Zamzama

• North Sea Fish

See Map 9

Farringdon Rd

WARREN ST.

EUSTON SQ.

BLOOMSBURY

Gray's Inn Rd

FARRINGDON

Tottenham Court Rd

RUSSELL SQ.

Theobald's Rd

CHANCERY LANE

GOODGE ST.

High Holborn

HOLBORN

Oxford Street

TOTTENHAM COURT ROAD

OXFORD CIRCUS

Fleet St

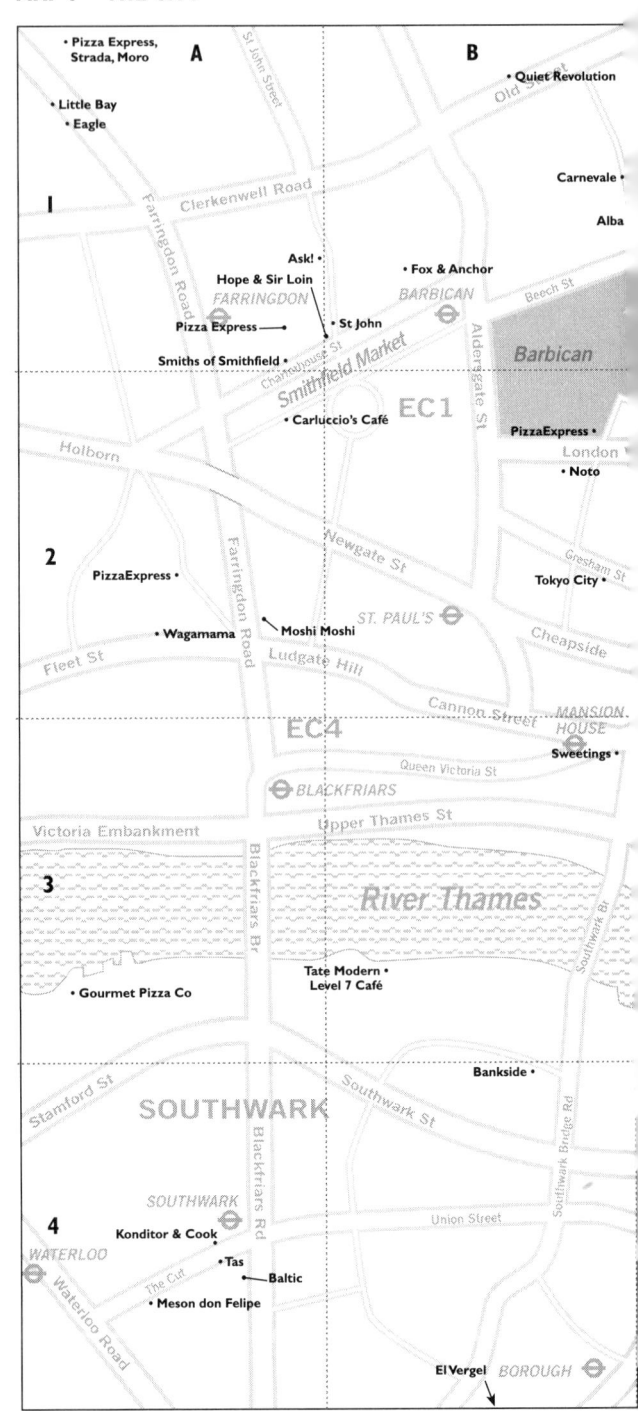

MAP 9 – THE CITY

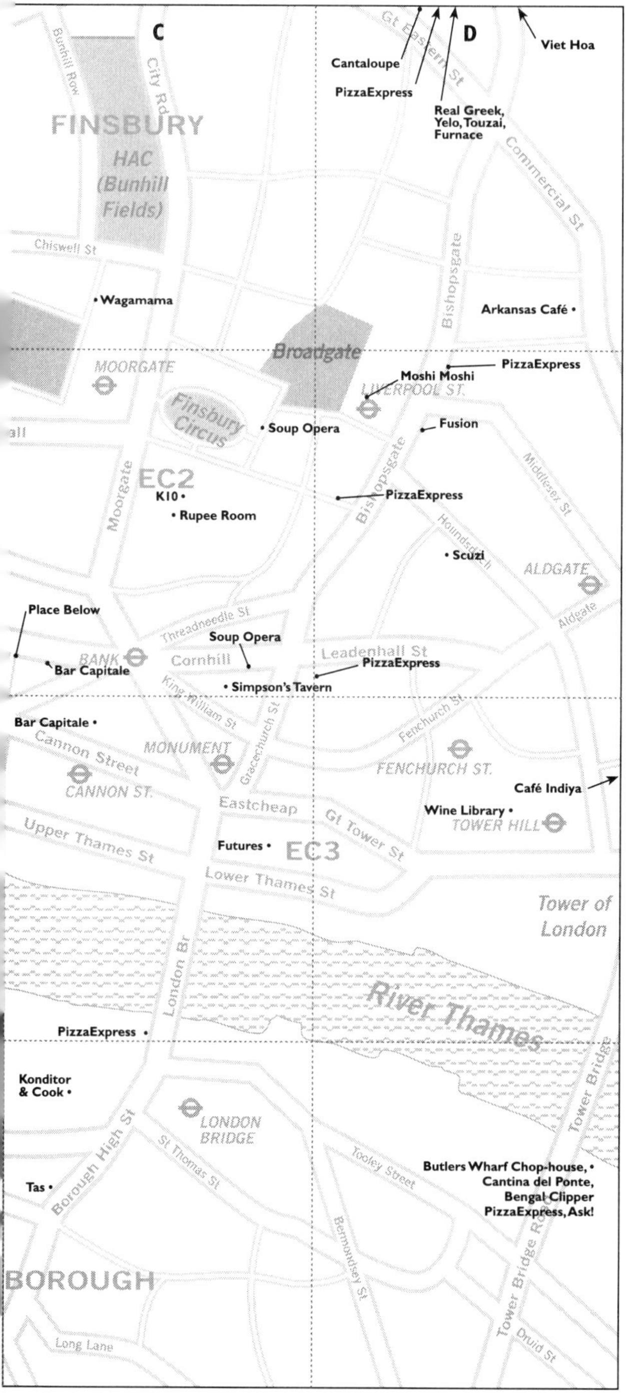

MAP 9 – THE CITY

C — **D**

- Viet Hoa
- Cantaloupe
- PizzaExpress
- Real Greek, Yelo, Touzai, Furnace

FINSBURY
HAC (Bunhill Fields)

Chiswell St

- Wagamama

MOORGATE

Broadgate

- Arkansas Café

Finsbury Circus

- PizzaExpress
- Moshi Moshi

LIVERPOOL ST.

- Soup Opera
- Fusion

EC2

- K10
- Rupee Room
- PizzaExpress
- Scuzi

ALDGATE

- Place Below
- Bar Capitale

BANK

Threadneedle St
Cornhill
- Soup Opera
- Simpson's Tavern
- PizzaExpress

Leadenhall St

- Bar Capitale

Cannon Street
MONUMENT
CANNON ST.
Eastcheap
Gt Tower St

FENCHURCH ST.

- Café Indiya
- Wine Library

TOWER HILL

Upper Thames St
- Futures
EC3
Lower Thames St

Tower of London

London Br

River Thames

- PizzaExpress

- Konditor & Cook

LONDON BRIDGE

St Thomas St
Tooley Street

Tower Bridge

- Tas

Borough High St

Bermondsey St

- Butlers Wharf Chop-house,
- Cantina del Ponte,
- Bengal Clipper
- PizzaExpress, Ask!

BOROUGH

Long Lane

Tower Bridge Rd
Druid St

MAP 10 – SOUTH LONDON (& FULHAM)

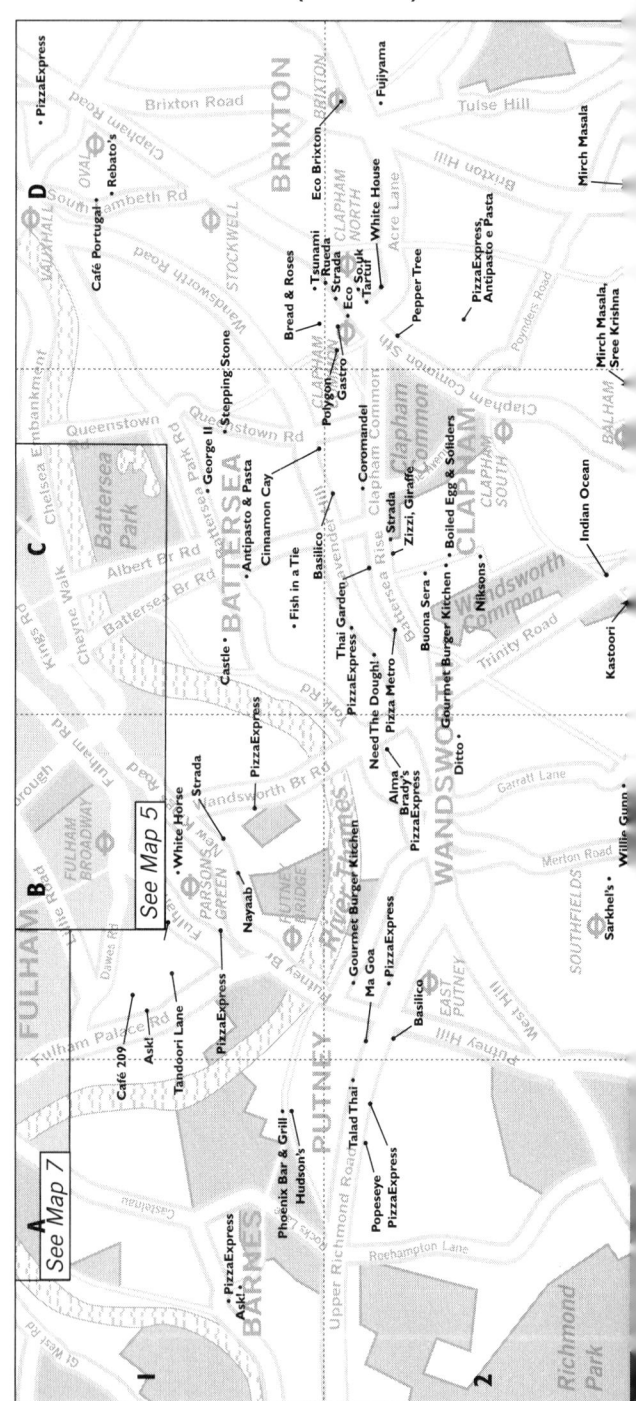

MAP 11 – EAST END & DOCKLANDS

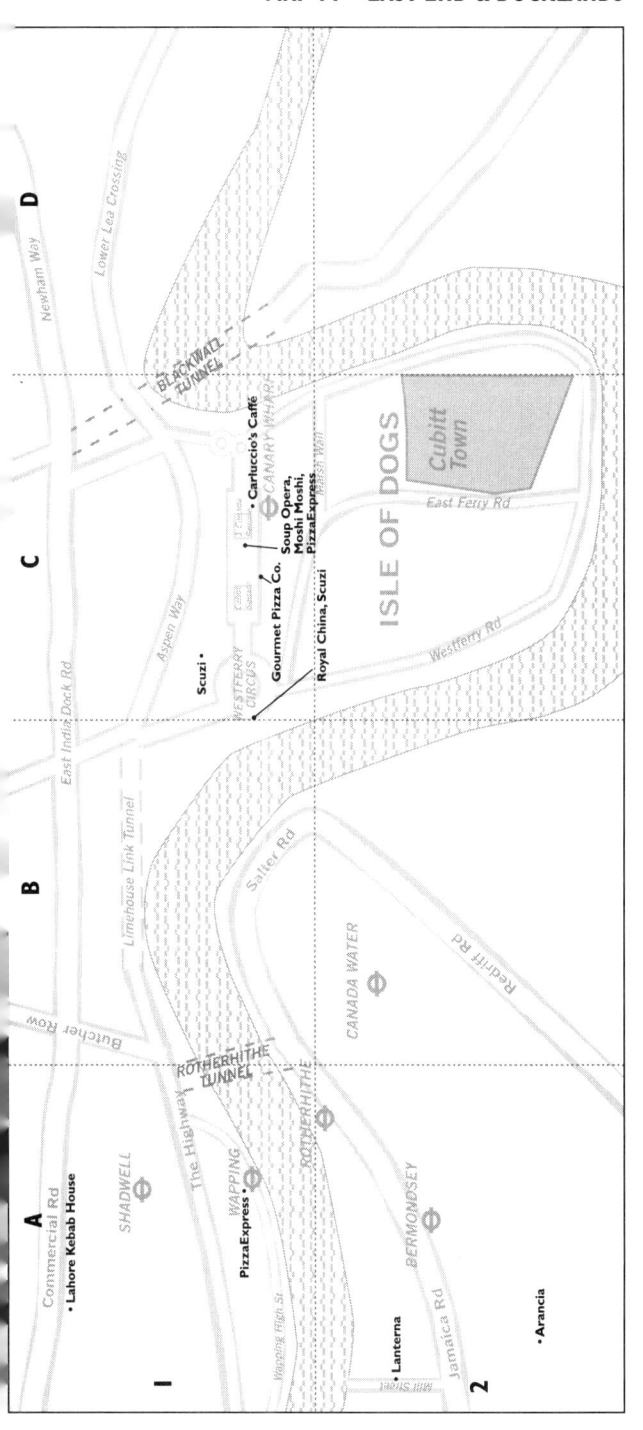

NOTES